SOUTH CENTRAL IS HOME

Stanford Studies in
COMPARATIVE RACE AND ETHNICITY

SOUTH CENTRAL IS HOME

Race and the Power of

Community Investment

in Los Angeles

Abigail Rosas

STANFORD UNIVERSITY PRESS
Stanford, California

STANFORD UNIVERSITY PRESS
Stanford, California

Printed in the United States of America on acid-free, archival-quality paper

Library of Congress Cataloging-in-Publication Data
Names: Rosas, Abigail, author.
Title: South Central is home : race and the power of community
    investment in Los Angeles / Abigail Rosas.
Description: Stanford, California : Stanford University Press, 2019. |
    Series: Stanford studies in comparative race and ethnicity | Includes
    bibliographical references and index.
Identifiers: LCCN 2018050364 (print) | LCCN 2018051206 (ebook) |
    ISBN 9780804799812 (cloth : alk. paper) | ISBN 9781503609556
    (pbk. : alk. paper) | ISBN 9781503609563 (ebook)
Subjects: LCSH: South Los Angeles (Los Angeles, Calif.)—
    Race relations—History. | South Los Angeles (Los Angeles, Calif.)—
    Social conditions. | Community development—California—
    Los Angeles—History. | Ethnic neighborhoods—California—
    Los Angeles—History. | Mexican Americans—California—
    Los Angeles—History. | African Americans—California—
    Los Angeles—History. | Working class—California—
    Los Angeles—History.
Classification: LCC F869.L86 (ebook) | LCC F869.L86 S687 2919 (print) |
    DDC 305.8009794/94—dc23
LC record available at https://lccn.loc.gov/2018050364

Cover design: Kevin Barrett Kane

Cover photograph: Bart Jaillet

Typeset by Kevin Barrett Kane in 10.5/15 Adobe Garamond Pro

*Para mis padres, Francisco y Dolores Rosas Medina,
con mucha gratitud, respecto, y cariño*

*For South Central neighbors, family, and friends, may this
history fuel your resolve to remain strong in the struggle for the
future of our community*

*Para mis vecinos, familia, y amigos del Sur Central, que esta
historia los anime a permanecer fuertes en la lucha por el futuro
de nuestra comunidad*

CONTENTS

ACKNOWLEDGMENTS

Investigating and writing South Central's history has been a heartening process and experience, during which I daily became indebted to the many people who have made completing this project possible. Revisiting South Central's history with my fabulously big-hearted and dynamic mother, Dolores Rosas, and godmothers, Leticia Nuno and (late) Maria Teresa Garza Rodriguez, most especially their recollections of how they invested themselves in thriving as *comadres*, workers, parents, and neighbors in South Central, has been a privilege and the best part of investigating and writing this book. Learning more about the enduring humanity and endless sacrifices of not only my parents but countless fellow Latina/o immigrant and African American South Central community residents has cemented my personal commitment to magnifying their impact on the diversity of this community's investments, contributions, and struggles. My having been born and raised in South Central has made me personally invested in the intellectual and social importance of interrogating the multigenerational, relational, and interracial dilemmas, opportunities, and relationships that have brought my working class, working poor, and poor neighbors, friends, and family relatives together. Our refusal to live, age, and grow as a devastated or divided interracial community has informed my resolve to write and publish this history as a challenge to the constant and recklessly inhumane public repression, representation, underappreciation, and treatment of migrants, immigrants, and communities of color. Thus, first and foremost, I am most thankful for my 'hood, as the geographical place that it is, as well as for the people and families that call South Central home.

Albert Camarillo was formative to my decision to undertake relational ethnic studies research. He provided the opportunity to pursue civically engaged
research. His sage advice and mentorship made it possible to value working
in our home communities with respect, humanity, and discipline. His role-
modeled optimism is what frames this history. He made Stanford University
an impactful community, one in which my appreciation and investment in the
future of my neighborhood have grown to incredible heights. His meticulous
comments, high expectations, and continued efforts in support of benefiting
from the wealth of opportunities Stanford had to offer scholars of color made
it possible to learn from him, Paula Moya, and Monica McDermott, and (late)
Margarita Ibarra. Their confidence and support have been decisive in my writing and publishing of this book.

George J. Sanchez has been a formidable mentor. He is unselfish in sharing his brilliance and hopes for the future of Los Angeles and first-generation
scholars of color in academia. His insistence on my writing with a relational
lens front and center, as well as his sharing his wisdom as I made the transition
into different stages of my intellectual career, inspires my deep-seated appreciation for his taking the time from his intense leadership and research agenda to
meet with me to provide advice that always has made a world of difference. At
every stage of my research and writing, I feel truly fortunate to have him as a
mentor, as I admire and gain so much whenever I read and teach his scholarship. He and his wife, Debra Sanchez, have been vital to my completion and
publication of this book.

I have learned from the amazing Robin D. G. Kelley. His insights on theorizing how everyday acts and on-the-ground realities of disenfranchised people
of color are influential to the future of ethnic studies research, especially when
theorizing relational racial agency, community, and placemaking, have been
formative to my investigation of South Central's complex inner workings and
struggles. I am deeply appreciative of Philip Ethington's generous production
and sharing of extraordinary maps on a moment's notice. His mapping talents
and expertise were critical to elucidating South Central's demographic change.
Sarah Banet-Weiser and Bill Deverell were also extremely helpful and supportive of my research and were critical to making USC a collegial, interdisciplinary community of researchers. USC also afforded me the ability to learn from
Ruth Wilson Gilmore, Roberto Lint-Sagarena, Jane Iwamura, Josh Kun, Shana

Redmond, Macarena Gomez Barris, and Pierrette Hondagneu-Sotelo. Our conversations and their comments on my work encouraged me to not give up on investigating and writing about South Central's multigenerational and interethnic diversity and power.

Luis Alvarez and Danny Widener's invitation to participate in the Comparative History Workshop on Chicana/o-African American Relations at the University of California, San Diego, led to an illuminating experience when conceptualizing this book. It made it possible to learn from George Lipsitz, Gaye Theresa Johnson, Catherine Ramirez, Jason Ferreira, and Lauren Araiza. Also, Vicki L. Ruiz, Gabriela Arredondo, Adrian Burgos Jr., Monica Perales, Anthony Macias, Stephen Pitti, Ernesto Chavez, Natalia Molina, Sonia Lee, Adrienne Petty, and Marc Rodriguez have similarly provided comments and feedback on different parts of this history, and on my pursuit of professional goals. Josh Kun, Laura Pulido, and Brian Benhken also have shared comments on select portions of my investigation of South Central's historical trajectory, as I had the privilege of publishing in their edited anthologies on Black and Latina/o relations. Their feedback enriched my analysis on the nuances of placemaking.

Financial support from the Social Science Research Council, Mellon Mays Fellowship, Institute for Recruitment Teachers, Ford Foundation Fellowships, and John Randolph Haynes and Dora Haynes Fellowships were critical to my traveling to conduct archival research throughout Southern California and the United States. Without the support and networks of these fellowships, I would not have been able to mine archives housed at the University of Southern California, Stanford University, and the Southern California Library for Social Studies and Research. A Smithsonian Institution Minority Visiting Fellowship at the National Museum of American History, under the mentorship of Steve Velasquez and Faith Davis Ruffins, was also invaluable to my progress. This fellowship made research accessible at the National Archives and Records Administration at College Park, Maryland, and at the Library of Congress. The Organization of American Historians' Nathan Huggins-Benjamin Quarles Award provided the financial support to conduct archival research and work with the generous archivists at the California State Archives, University of California, Los Angeles, and the Huntington Research Library. This rich combination of funding, resources, and collegiality has been indispensable to my pursuit and completion of the many stages comprised in the research, writing, and publication of this book. I hope that this book confirms the promise behind the investment in these fellowship programs and networks.

Undertaking a fellowship at the Institute of American Cultures at University of California, Los Angeles, and teaching a course on Black and Latina/o relations was instrumental in my approach to teaching and engaging with Chicana/o and Latina/o studies from a comparative and relational perspective. My writing of South Central's history, most especially my consideration of the resonance of Head Start programs beyond Los Angeles, was enriched by a fellowship in the Center for the Study of Women, Gender, and Sexuality at Rice University. Jose Aranda, Krista Comer, Rosemary Hennessy, Brian Riedel, and Angela Wall offered helpful comments on my research. These research and teaching experiences coupled with my experience as Assistant Professor and Co-Director of Ethnic Studies at California State University, Stanislaus (CSUS), familiarized me with the responsibilities that come with advocating for an interdisciplinary and interracial approach to research and teaching. At CSUS, I thank Sari Miller-Antonio and James Tuedio for your mentorship and leadership, and Ellen Bell, Steve Arounsack, Richard Wallace, Jeffrey Frost, Austin Avwunudiogba, Peggy Hauselt, Alison McNally, Virginia Montero, and Susan Helm-Lauber for our collective work in advising, teaching, and mentoring a diversity of students and experiences. Students such as Jocelyn Camarillo, Brenda Pedraza, Tamara Centeno, and Arion Herndon were a pleasure to work closely with, and forging friendships with Aletha Harven, Dana Nakano, Daniel Soodjinda, and Rashaan DeShay made Stanislaus the most rewarding of experiences.

Upon concluding my writing of this book, I have been afforded the opportunity to teach and research Chicana/o and Latina/o Studies at California State University, Long Beach. My colleagues Luis Arroyo, Antonia Garcia-Orozco, Jose Moreno, Anna Sandoval, Maythee Rojas, Rigoberto Rodriguez, Alfredo Carlos, Gen Ramirez, Kiki Shaver, Griselda Suarez, Michelle Seales, Sherry Span, Esa Syeed, and Steven Osuna and students Celeste Magana, Andrea Gonzalez, Carmen Gutierrez, Christian Castillo, Alexis Vega, Jazmin Maldonado, Nathan Carbajal, Leonardo Maldonado, Juan Barragan, Allen Alvarez, Neri Valdovinos, and Ana Canela have made this campus community an invigorating network of scholars, activists, and leaders. Our collective goal of being of support to our first-generation students has made my writing this history that much more of a priority. Working with our students closely has reaffirmed the resonance of providing our students with an interdisciplinary approach when learning about the experiences of the working poor and poor communities of color as a critical move toward an expansive approach to Chicana/o and Latina/o Studies, history, and social justice.

Stanford University Press and most especially the editorial eye and expertise of Kate Wahl, who from the beginning expressed interest in and support of my approach to ethnic studies, have been invaluable in the revision of my research. The generous comments of anonymous reviewers coupled with, respectively, the administrative, production, and copyediting talents of Leah Pennywark, Anne Fuzellier, and David Horne made publishing this book a productive process. I wholeheartedly appreciate the efforts of Paula Moya and Hazel Marcus, editors of Stanford University Press's Comparative Studies in Race and Ethnicity, in their support of my publication of this history.

Christel Miller, Hanna Garth, Michael Brown II, Anna Chen Arroyo, Alice Villatoro, and Saski Casanova have been extraordinary friends both before and during my research and writing of this book. In addition, Elda María Román, Amanda Branker-Ellis, Elizabeth Farfan Santos, Prisilla Lerza, Cynthia Gomez, and Karina Gookin are cherished friends, and I am thankful for our shared humor and intellect, forging of unconditional friendships, and their unwavering support. I have also had the great fortune to cross paths with and learn from Mario Obando Jr., Armando Garcia, Adrian Felix, Lorena Alvarado, Laura Gutierrez, Mark Padoongpatt, Chrisshonna Grant Nieva, Jimmy Patiño, David Villareal, Todd Honma, Lori Flores, Rosina Lozano, Gilbert Estrada, Julia Ornelas-Higdon, Celeste Menchaca, Genevieve Carpio, Margaret Salazar-Porzio, Laura Fujikawa, and Milo Alvarez. Their collegiality throughout the years has made it possible to enjoy the company of an enterprising network of scholars.

South Central has always been an empowering home, because of the friendship, love, and wisdom of Leticia and (late) Bernardo Nuno, Maria Concepcion and Magdaleno Ruiz, (late) Maria Teresa and Abel Garza Rodriguez, Catalina Ruiz and Antonio Ruiz, Ramona and Salvador Frias, Mario and Carmen Magallanes, Emma and Rogelio Solorzano, Erendira and Gabriel Hernandez, Yadira and Oscar Cervantez, Esther and Jazlyn Sanchez, and Ramon Rios. For years, their prayers, phone calls, food, celebrations, stories, and visits in support of whatever I may have needed inspired me not to lose sight of the personal relationships grounding and informing my commitment to publishing our community's history.

My parents, Dolores and Francisco Rosas, are my heroes and have made the publication of this book a reality. Without them and their decision to invest in South Central as our family's home and community, I am confident that my appreciation for this community would not have been possible. Throughout my life, they have always done everything within their reach to acknowledge the value of our family as critical to my education, career, and personal investment. They have offered me unending kindness and guidance, an amazing example of a goal-oriented and fearless work ethic, and an insistence on the lifetime value of striving to be a community member and family relative who acts with intellect and heart. This book is dedicated to them both. They are genuinely reflective of selfless investment in community and family.

Growing up in South Central was always about learning, because of my sister, Ana Elizabeth Rosas (Lizzie). She is a scholar in her own right, and there was never a moment in which we did not enjoy discussing the realities shaping our neighborhood community, and the need for humanity, compassion, and *corazón*. As sisters, best friends, and intellectual allies, it has been a blessing to share the fun journey of growing up together and the rigorous realities of publishing this book. Our sisterhood and conversations have become that much more meaningful, as they have served as the glue that keeps our growing family energized and connected. Ricardo Alvarez has been a charismatic and supportive brother-in-law. I can always count on his honest perspective and humor when confronted with the weight of the grievances shouldered by and facing our community.

Richard Bustamante has been an unconditional partner, a true best friend, and a champion of this book. He has gone the extra mile to ensure that we enjoy and build a beautiful future together. His editorial feedback has enriched this book, as it is born from his appreciation of and respect for not losing sight of the critical details and the power of South Central's history. He is a source of unending love, insight, and kindness, and for this, I am eternally grateful. Moreover, and integral to our thriving as a family together, are the love and support of Margaret and Ricardo Bustamante, the Rawls family, the Manning-Bustamante family, Luis Medina, Angelica Medina, Carmen Medina, Sandra

Medina, Olga Ramirez Medina, Moises Medina, Armando Medina, Sergio Medina, Maria Elena Medina, Gloria Medina, Miguel Rosas, Cesareo Rosas, Emmanuel Rosas, (late) Josefina Rosas Gomez, (late) Manuel Rosas, (late) Desiderio Medina, and (late) Francisca Medina Ramirez. Each in their own way has contributed to the feelings, priorities, and vision guiding my writing of this book. I hope that the publication of this book in some small way inspires everyone who has been a part of this undertaking to continue to invest in the worthwhile struggles for the community with history and heart.

SOUTH CENTRAL IS HOME

INTRODUCTION

UNCOVERING BLACK AND LATINA/O RELATIONS

IN FALL 1965, Ruth Smith and her husband boarded a train in Houston, Texas, and made the journey west to search for better housing and employment. They arrived in Los Angeles in the aftermath of the Watts uprising and settled into a community devastated by days of unrest. Shortly after their arrival, Ruth's husband found work in the rubber-tire industry, where he labored for many years until the plant's closure in 1980; he later became a janitor, an occupation he held until his death in 1989.[1] His job in the tire industry provided an income to purchase a home in South Central Los Angeles.[2] Ruth and her husband became proud owners of a modest home and chose the residential location because, as Ruth said, "I loved this street because there was a Baptist church at the corner."[3] Ruth spent her time and energy helping at the Baptist church, and throughout the years became publicly visible and accountable to her South Central neighbors and friends.

At the turn of the nineteenth century and into the mid-twentieth century, thousands of African American migrants boarded buses and headed west to leave the racial violence of the South in search of opportunity and survival in Los Angeles. Unlike the U.S. South, Los Angeles offered employment; political representation; and the ability to establish cultural, economic, and social centers. The promise of a better life in Los Angeles for Black migrants had its limits, as exclusionary policies in housing and leisure increasingly segregated

them into South Central. Black migrants transformed exclusion and segregation into spaces of investment and unity, and in doing so, developed a vibrant
African American community[4]—a community that Ruth would grow to call
home. The opportunities born out of segregation served to render South Central Los Angeles as space, place, and community marked as African American.

Eventually, however, South Central's racial character as largely African
American would collide with the increased settlement of Mexican immigrants
in the United States. Dolores Rosas's migration is one of myriad stories of
undocumented immigrants settling in South Central. In fall 1978, Dolores
boarded a bus in San Martin de Hidalgo, Jalisco, Mexico, to a train station in
Guadalajara, Jalisco. With her infant child in tow, like countless Mexican immigrants before her, she crossed the Mexican countryside by rail before arriving in Mexicali. Dolores relied on a *coyote* (smuggler) to bring them into the
United States, with her final destination being Los Angeles. Arriving in Los
Angeles, she and her daughter reunited with her husband, Francisco Rosas. He
had immigrated to Los Angeles before her to find an apartment and a job and
set up a home for Dolores and their young daughter.[5] Dolores's new home was
in the heart of Los Angeles's African American community—South Central
Los Angeles.

Dolores was shocked to learn that her new neighborhood was predominantly composed of African American children, women, and men. Francisco
had failed to mention that they were going to settle in a racially diverse community. Dolores recalls, "He told me, don't worry, there's all kinds of people.
Everything will be all right."[6] He had secured an apartment on 50th Street
and Main Street, a block away from where fellow Mexican rural hometown
friends had settled. However, their immediate neighbors were mostly African
Americans. At first, Dolores believed they would live in South Central only
temporarily, but as the years passed South Central became more and more their
world, their center, their home. Dolores and Francisco Rosas are my parents,
and my upbringing centered on learning more about South Central's history
with heart. They instilled in me the need to know our neighborhood's relational interracial history as a meaningful step toward discerning their personal
investment in raising me in South Central with humanity and optimism for
the future of this community. Such intellectual inheritance inspired my commitment to investigating and writing this history.

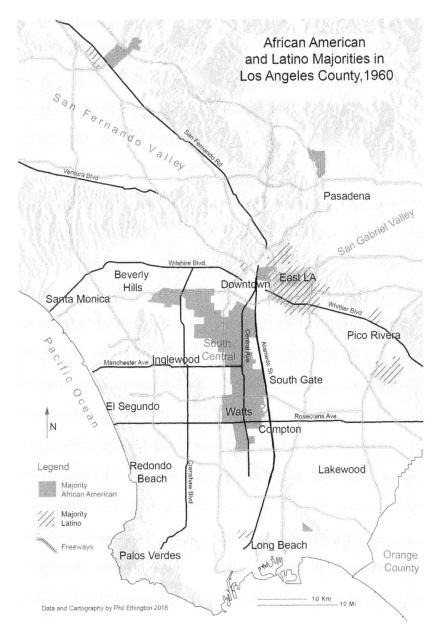

Map 1: African American and Latina/o Majorities in Los Angeles County, 1960
SOURCE: Data and cartography by Phil Ethington, 2018.

This personal connection to South Central and its history compelled me to consider how Ruth and Dolores navigated their way in South Central. Their movement, like that of other migrants and immigrants, was born out of necessity and the promise of improved prospects. They quickly learned, though, that they would settle into a community where they would experience the transformations of deindustrialization, joblessness, reindustrialization in the garment and service sectors, a drug epidemic and violence, and police aggression and surveillance.[7] In this changing political, social, and economic climate, thousands of Mexican immigrants settled throughout South Central's city streets.

By the mid-twentieth century, African American settlement had taken hold and became most prominent in South Central Los Angeles (Map 1). With the onset of the 1970s, the Latina/o population of South Central was approximately fifty thousand, or roughly 10 percent of South Central's total population. The Latina/o population had doubled to about 20 percent of the total South Central population by 1980 (Map 2).[8]

South Central was marked as an African American community because African Americans constituted 80 percent of the population, and businesses and social services catered to African American needs. Also, political representatives were almost exclusively African American, and in popular culture and the general public's mind, South Central was African American. Dolores's settlement was part of the wave of immigration that would change South Central in unforeseen ways, as by 1990, South Central was over 40 percent Latina/o, and by 2000 it was 64 percent Latina/o (Map 3).[9] This multiracial landscape was years in the making. Restaurants now serve both soul food and Mexican food, business signs are written in both English and Spanish, and murals showcasing both African American and Chicana/o pride are illustrative of how this community has changed.

The migration by both African Americans and Latina/os to South Central spanned different decades, but their long-term settlement within South Central illustrates that opportunities beyond the neighborhood were not easily gained or achieved. Tracing the impact of these demographic shifts in the mid-to-late part of the twentieth century demonstrates how Latina/o immigrant residents invested themselves in transforming the city's strong historical African American character into one that acknowledges a long history of African American

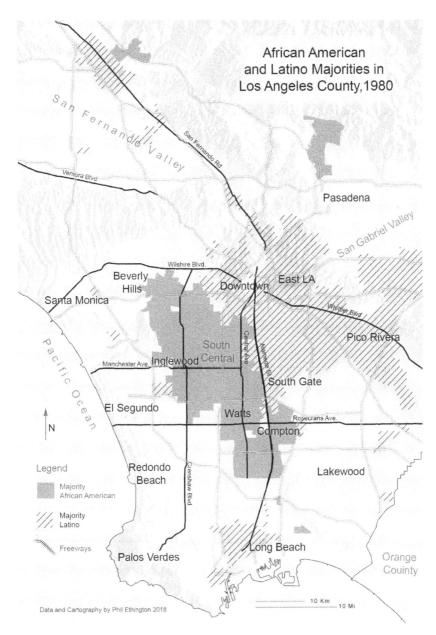

Map 2: African American and Latina/o Majorities in Los Angeles County, 1980
SOURCE: Data and cartography by Phil Ethington, 2018.

struggle but also is increasingly defined by its interracial relations between African American and Latina/o immigrants.

South Central Is Home illustrates that interracial interactions are muted, tense, and collaborative. Interactions between African Americans and Latina/os do not happen in a vacuum; structural changes such as deindustrialization, racial discrimination, increased law and immigration enforcement, and the decline in the welfare state shape these interactions. To demonstrate the weight of these structural realities, I examine how neighborly interactions, patronage of an African American–owned bank, and War on Poverty programs such as Head Start and community health clinics expose the daily elements of community activism, the dynamic nature of interracial relations, and the sense of belonging that made South Central home for African Americans and Latina/os. These interactions, relationships, and sites represent the ways in which Mexican immigrant South Central residents quickly learned that, like their African American neighbors, they faced a similar racialization by living in South Central together. Over time, such realization inspired a relational community identity between South Central residents that energized them to understand that they experienced and shared a vulnerability which required their individual and community investment in struggles against injustice, underrepresentation, and discrimination.

SEGREGATION LEADS TO SPATIAL RACIALIZATION

By World War II, South Central had become popularly known as the "heart of Black Southern California," and as such was seen as strictly a Black neighborhood.[10] This perception of South Central as Black was in large part attributable to the public depictions of its African American residents, but also to the ways in which African Americans constructed a Black identity tied to geography in the midst of bleak economic, political, and social realities.[11] The experiences of Mexican immigrant South Central residents are mostly those of individuals who migrated to the United States after 1965 and took residence in a predominantly African American community. To fully understand how this generation of Mexican immigrants became residents in this community entails uncovering how they had to quickly learn their new racial landscape and understand South Central's enduring Black character.

Race real estate covenants, bank lending practices, realtor behavior, and U.S. government support of white homeowner suburbanization facilitated the

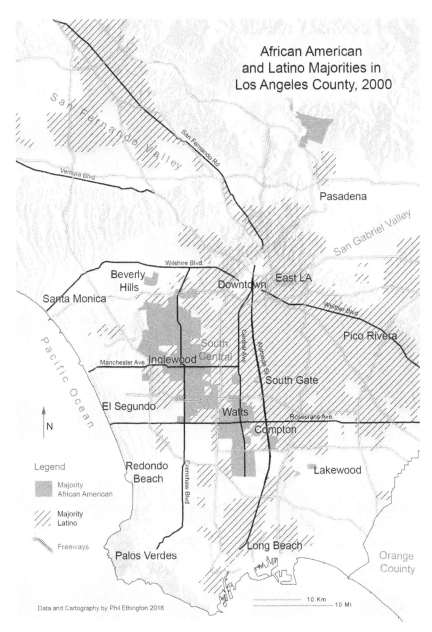

Within the map:

African American
and Latino Majorities in
Los Angeles County, 2000

San Fernando Valley

San Fernando Rd

Ventura Blvd

Pasadena

San Gabriel Valley

Wilshire Blvd

Beverly
Hills

Downtown

East LA

Santa Monica

Whittier Blvd

Pico Rivera

South
Central

Manchester Ave. Inglewood

Central Ave

Alameda St

Pacific Ocean

South Gate

El Segundo

Watts

Rosecrans Ave.

Compton

N

Redondo
Beach

Lakewood

Legend

Majority
African American

Crenshaw Blvd

Majority
Latino

Freeways

Long Beach

Orange
Couinty

Palos Verdes

10 Km
10 Mi

Data and Cartography by Phil Ethington 2018

Map 3: African American and Latina/o Majorities in Los Angeles County, 1960
SOURCE: Data and cartography by Phil Ethington, 2018.

racial segregation of residential communities throughout the United States.
George Lipsitz argues that the barring of African Americans from white neighborhoods has intricately bound race and geography. In the absence of easy access and mobility to suburban communities, the "battles for resources, rights,
and recognition not only have 'taken place' but also have required that Black
communities literally 'take places,'" and these spaces have come to be a part of
our nation.[12] The taking of places has had an impact on how we understand
the lived history of racialized space. Racial identity formation is the product of
social movements that are simultaneously place-based and race-based, and in
the case of South Central Black migrants led to the early efforts of placemaking community formation.

As Lipsitz expertly argues, the struggle for justice is much more than a fight
for inclusion in spaces previously denied. The pooling of resources, exchange
of services, and appropriation of private and public spaces for new purposes
"have been vital to the survival of Black people and Black communities, but
they also offer a model of democratic citizenship to everyone."[13] As a result
of the restrictions placed on where and how communities of color could live,
the African American community turned "segregation into congregation."
Gaye Johnson's framework of spatial entitlement, describing spatial arrange-
ments as everyday experiences in which communities of color utilize and claim
space in the most dehumanizing of situations, demonstrates the importance
of congregation for working-class communities of color.[14] Marginalized communities create "new collectivities based not just upon eviction and exclusion
from physical places, but also on new and imaginative uses of technology,
creativity, and space."[15]

Economic businesses such as banks, social spaces such as jazz clubs, and political representation bolstered the racialized image of South Central as a Black
space and community. By the 1960s and 1970s, the intensification of decades'
worth of disenfranchisement and racism had hampered the entrepreneurial
spirit of early twentieth-century Black migrants. Black residents increasingly
were unable to own the neighborhoods materially, and they developed innovative ways of augmenting the use and value of the spaces they inhabited for
the sake of securing political representation and mobilization.[16] Ultimately, the
relational community formation that emerged in the latter part of the twentieth
century operated within the context of South Central's racialization.

BLACK AND LATINA/O RELATIONS

The experiences of Latina/os and African Americans are increasingly influenced by life and work in multiracial and multiethnic contexts and are characterized by majority-minority demographics, "cities of color," in which race relations are among communities of color rather than with whites.[17] Undoubtedly, conversations regarding these "cities of color," and Black and Latina/o relations in particular, often center on moments of heightened anxiety and tension. In 2007, South Central was described as a war zone in which Black and Latina/o youth were depicted as participating in "ethnic cleansing" because of incidents in youth violence. Noreen McClendon, executive director of prominent organizations such as the Concerned Citizens of South Central Los Angeles and vice president of the Watts Gang Task Force, declared, "We need to go on the offensive to put an end to this idea of ethnic cleansing in L.A. . . . It is not happening."[18] There was violence occurring between both groups, but the levels were "blown so far out of proportion."[19] Newspaper headlines that focus on "tension" or on narratives similar to the example above of a "racial war" show only one dimension of what happens as a community comes to terms with change.[20] One thing that is obscured from such headlines is how school policies racially segregate African Americans and Latina/os within schools, thus foreclosing opportunities for collaboration or efforts for open dialogue of shared racialization and marginalization.[21] The physical barriers created by schools and school officials only facilitate tension and misunderstanding.

South Central Is Home does not aim to suggest that African Americans and Latina/os do not have tension-filled encounters, interactions, and experiences. Instead, it aims to discuss a diversity of experiences as well as highlight elements that newspaper headlines omit when they focus on narratives of tension and fail to account for the ways institutions frame these interactions. This is in line with the example of author Cid Martinez, who provides a nuanced approach toward understanding how institutions and neighbors throughout South Central respond to violence and tension among youth, gangs, and residents. In the absence of trusting law enforcement, alternative forms of governance and neighborhood-level street justice become commonplace ways to restore order.[22] South Central residents become agents in shaping their relationships and response to tension. However, these grounded realities of coping with violence are hardly ever reported in the headlines.

Scholars studying negative Black and Latina/o relations often cite resource competition as fueling tension.[23] Resources would prove scarce in South Central, as by the latter part of the twentieth century residents would experience the devastating effects of deindustrialization with manufacturing firms leaving South Central, escalation of the War on Drugs, and the growth of neoliberalism. In addition, decades after the 1965 uprising that illustrated the brutal reality that two-thirds of families living in Watts were on welfare and 40 percent of Watts's families lived below the poverty level, the needs of the community remained the same.[24] The anxieties South Central and Watts residents felt regarding their employment options only became heightened with the passage of the North American Free Trade Agreement (NAFTA) in 1994. This agreement resulted in encouraging the already-limited manufacturing sector to leave Los Angeles en masse.[25] Limited job opportunities, few employment placement and training programs, underfunded schools, embattled police relations, and the alarming rate of the feminization of poverty are the economic and social realities that make the enduring African American and Latina/o community relationships in South Central invaluable to understanding relational interracial community formation.[26]

These local economic changes shaping South Central are also critical in relation to understanding the impact of a national conversation between scholars and political officials regarding poverty in the United States. This conversation derived from scholars such as Daniel P. Moynihan and Oscar Lewis, who gave academic license to the theory that poverty was a result of a culture maintained by impoverished families' choices and values. Anthropologist Lewis in the late 1950s surveyed poverty in Mexico City and developed his "culture of poverty" thesis, which argued that poverty is transmitted generationally and becomes a way of life, a culture of the poor.[27] In 1965, The U.S. Department of Labor published Moynihan's *The Negro Family: The Case for National Action*, which tied Black poverty to the disintegration of the Black family. Moynihan argued that poverty in the Black community was "capable of perpetuating itself without assistance from the white world," and that the matriarchal structure of the Black family weakened Black men's ability to function as authority figures.[28] Both Moynihan and Lewis also offered structural explanations for economic inequality but were drowned out, as their work would be used by the U.S. government to expedite "antipoverty research and policy since the 1930s: from a focus on structural reform of the economy to a focus on managing and shaping the supposed 'pathological' behavior of individuals."[29]

The consequences of Moynihan's and Lewis's work would reinforce the poor view U.S. society holds of low-income families, and in particular how that society treats Black and Latina/o women and families. By the 1980s, news stories of African American families, most especially of women "abusing" the welfare system (despite the overwhelming lack of material evidence to support such claims), became commonplace and served to affirm Lewis's and Moynihan's arguments and to racialize poverty as a problem within the Black community.[30] South Central would then become synonymous not only with being a community of mostly Black residents, but also with poverty and disinvestment.

This culture of poverty arguments is magnified under our current neoliberal regime, in which racialized groups are perceived as "deserving" or "undeserving" under a market schema, with working class, working poor, and poor families of color often falling under the umbrella of "undeserving."[31] These views have fueled the vilification of South Central families relationally, as Black and Latina/o residents experience not only the debilitating effects of poverty but also a subsequent racialization as being poor and undeserving.

The convergence of capital flight and views of impoverished residents serve as the background for examining the impact of resource competition on Black and Latina/o relations in South Central. In particular, I investigate the infusion of War on Poverty funds in the South Central community from the mid-1960s onward. In 1964, President Lyndon B. Johnson declared an "unconditional war on poverty" and signed the Economic Opportunity Act (EOA). The Office of Economic Opportunity (OEO) would execute the EOA, with the goal of transforming the lives of impoverished people throughout the United States by forming the Community Action Program (CAP), which provided employment opportunities and community resources.[32] The program's experimental nature and its reach would mean that in many instances the dispersal of poverty funds in Los Angeles had its challenges and often caused tension between local advocates, beneficiaries, and politicians.

This tension emerged as a result of CAP's design, which divided the city into racially segregated, manageable poverty units. This division of resources at first glance seemed to favor impoverished Black residents overwhelmingly. Mexican Americans expressed their feeling that poverty funding was dispersed disproportionately to the African American community. This belief of "favor-itism" and the difficulty of acquiring funds in the first place caused friction, which led to a strain between both groups. It is essential to place this conflict within a context of how power structures mediate interracial relations.[33] De-spite these initial moments of competition, as the late 1960s and the 1970s unfolded, the political landscape opened up the possibility for cross-racial col-laboration between South Central African American and Latina/o residents—most especially in their struggle to secure poverty funds and embrace South Central as their home.[34]

Continuing past the initial years of the War on Poverty's implementation we can uncover a complex matrix of interracial relations that are not solely en-capsulated by experiences of tension. Long-standing institutions such as Head Start and health clinics illustrate the grounded efforts of placemaking as well as how maximizing on this social policy's promise required ingenuity and in-vestment by a multiracial cadre of residents that at every turn reinforced the notion that poor people are deserving of programming that is dignified and attentive to their needs. For impoverished, working poor, and working class communities of color, interracial relations are framed within the context of ever-diminishing resources. This supports theorizing the conditions for a "poli-tics of dignity," as argued by Luis Alvarez in his analysis of zoot suit culture, in which racialized communities develop "a profound connection between their efforts to reclaim dignity amidst difficult life conditions, including discrimi-nation and poverty."[35] In the case of South Central residents, this "politics of dignity" emerges from the coexistence of multiple racial groups. The labor and emotional work required by South Central residents to move past viewing each other as competition for resources and beyond the negative attributes associ-ated with impoverished families to develop a common ground are at the heart of this book and demonstrate that finding common ground is not easy or im-mediate, but decades in the making.

RELATIONAL COMMUNITY FORMATION

In the latter part of the twentieth century, the racial and ethnic character of the United States changed dramatically. Under President Lyndon B. Johnson, the Im-migration and Nationality Act of 1965 eliminated the use of racial quotas based on national origin set by the 1924 John-Reed Act, by using arguments that the

1924 Act did not align with U.S. democratic values. Instead, the immigration act of 1965 created a pathway for legal migration that favored family reunification and skill-based labor visas, though still involving restrictions, timetables, and hierarchies of preferred migration.[36] European immigration declined after the mid-1960s, and Latin American and Asian immigration increased, in part due to this policy's shift of providing, even if difficult, a pathway for legal migration. However, not all post-1965 migration utilized these legal channels, as economic, political, and social challenges, in many cases the result of U.S. intervention in home countries, produced conditions that encouraged immigrants from across the globe to take the risk of being undocumented.[37] The increased presence of Latin American and Asian immigrants would play a crucial role in Los Angeles's social, political, and economic outlook, and would provide an avenue toward relational community formation in South Central Los Angeles.

To understand the discursive impact increased immigration would have throughout the nation, and in Los Angeles in particular, it is useful to consider the work of Natalia Molina, who argues that race, immigration, and citizenship are relational, and are interconnected in the present and throughout time. Molina's framework of "racial scripts" offers a lens to understand how people of different racial groups are "acted upon by a range of principals, from institutional actors to ordinary citizens."[38] She points out that often groups fail to see race as relational, and therefore common connections between racialized groups are missed. Finally, Molina argues that racial scripts also offer a window of opportunity, as "racialized groups put forth their own scripts, counter scripts that provide alternatives or directly challenge dominant racial scripts."[39] Molina's theoretical intervention is useful when one is considering how immigrants and immigration policy have an impact on various racial groups.

In the case of my investigation of community activism, belonging, and relations in South Central, the interconnected racial scripts are race, poverty, and space. However, these connections are not readily apparent, and it takes labor and time to uncover them. Also, the relational aspect of community formation means that within communities of color, residents living together come to realize how they are similarly racialized and must create spaces of possibility in the wake of devastating forms of racialization, discrimination, and segregation. By placing Black and Latina/o subjectivities as relational to each other, we complicate how we analyze their politicization.

In line with scholars such as Luis Alvarez, John Marquez, and Gaye Theresa Johnson, an exploration of interracial relations requires investigating how communities of color enter, inhabit, and survive the racial landscape together.[40] John Marquez, in his investigation of Black and Latina/o relations in Houston, Texas, argues that the development of "foundational blackness," in which the routine nature of anti-Black violence produces the conditions to "experience the racial state of expendability," shapes how Latina/os understand their own racial and ethnic identity, experience, and expendability in the United States.[41] Low-income Mexican immigrants settling in South Central, unlike Latina/os in Houston, had to learn how to navigate the racial hierarchy that disadvantaged Black people, one that made their lives "expendable to the state," to develop an awareness that as South Central residents both groups faced similar racialization without an erasure of their difference. There is a particular way in which communities that live side by side—as neighbors—share a likeness of experience that shapes how similarly they are racialized, discriminated against, and, in the best of situations, energized to improve their conditions and terms together, and such is the fertile ground for understanding relational community formation and investment. Migration and settlement in this context proves a powerful development for the ways in which Mexican immigrants experience building community in Los Angeles. For a community whose racial discourse is based on *mestizaje*, the embrace of racial mixing between Spanish and indigenous, and where a discussion of Blackness is obscured, living in a Black neighborhood means quickly learning what a Black-white racial system entails for Mexican immigrants.[42] In particular, it does not mean that this wave of immigrants identified as Black; rather, that they similarly confronted living in a disinvested community.

The daily interactions that frame relational community formation became all the more complicated by the early 1990s, when Los Angeles's ability to "welcome" new immigrants had begun to serve as a source of celebration and would squarely place Los Angeles as a global city prepared to incorporate newly arrived migrants and immigrants. The incorporation of immigrants, unlike in previous iterations of assimilation, would rest on viewing difference as a source of strength, and therefore Los Angeles embarked on an era of cultural pluralism. Asian immigrants, in particular, were viewed as the "model" for immigrant incorporation, and they were described as resourceful and willing to invest their capital in the United States. The brand of multiculturalism being celebrated was one of welcoming global markets and investments throughout Los Angeles.[43] As city officials were beginning to celebrate immigrant incorporation during the 1980s, Mexican immigrant South Central residents faced anxieties over the presence of the Immigration and Naturalization Service (INS). Undocumented immigrants feared deportation at their worksites. The passage of the Immigration Reform and Control Act (IRCA) in 1986, the goal of which was to curb undocumented immigration by penalizing employers for hiring undocumented immigrants, provided amnesty to three million undocumented immigrants residing in the United States. IRCA made a difference for the millions of undocumented immigrants who qualified for the program. However, support for IRCA also ushered in a conversation on the need to secure our borders for national security and did not eliminate the racialization of Latina/os as undocumented and criminal.[44] What followed IRCA were statewide initiatives such as Propositions 187 (1994), 209 (1996), and 227 (1998), the goals of which were to bar undocumented families from social and government services; eliminate state government institutions from using ethnicity, race, and gender in hiring and school admissions; and bring an end to bilingual education, respectively.[45] On the federal level, legislation such as the Illegal Immigration Reform and Immigrant Responsibility Act (IIRIRA) of 1996, which furthered policies that criminalized the lives of undocumented families and individuals, limited prospects for legalization, and ensured the perception of immigrants, most especially from Mexico and Latin America, as perpetual foreigners and as undocumented.[46]

By the late 1980s and into the 1990s, the simultaneous narratives, of the threat that newly arrived poor Latin American immigrants would pose to the fabric of U.S. society and the entry of Asian immigrants with economic means to invest, had become the backbone of how Latina/o and African American residents and Asian immigrant merchants made sense of relating to each other throughout South Central. This complex matrix of immigrant discourse shaped the daily realities of interracial engagement throughout South Central, leading up to the 1992 uprising. South Central's racial transformation opened a space for strong emotional responses between Blacks and Latina/os. In many ways, understanding and acting on racial knowledge becomes a form of social capital that structures belonging, mobility, and subject formation.[47] These grounded understandings about race produce emotions that become all the more central when they are considered in an interracial scenario or relationship. African Americans and Latina/os come to terms with their racialized personhood through the affective responses of anger, anxiety, fear, and apprehension.

The uprising would demonstrate the limits of championing diversity without genuinely understanding its capitalist underpinnings. The uneven celebration of a global city resulted in African American and Latina/o South Central residents taking to the streets to demonstrate their anger and discontent toward police brutality and decades' worth of discrimination and disinvestment. The television coverage of the uprising provided visual affirmation that South Central was not only African American but also Latina/o, and its investors were a multiracial group of Asian and Latina/o immigrants and African Americans. This rebellion was the first multiracial rebellion in U.S. history; it illuminated the limits of multicultural boosterism and the complexity of interracial relations, racial nativism, and the power dynamics at the turn of the century.[48]

The uprising also showed that by the 1990s, the search for opportunities that drove early- to mid-twentieth-century Black migrants west had culminated with the realization that economic prospects in Los Angeles had dwindled with labor's flight from the community, residential segregation was followed by disinvestment, and police abuse had become much more commonplace. For Latina/os, immigration and settlement in the United States were driven by economic, political, and social turmoil in their home countries, and in some cases resulted in their employment throughout the U.S. service sector and their ability to purchase a home. Regardless of their generational presence in the United States, Latina/o immigrants grew to resent being understood nationally as solely in the United States to labor for poor wages as perpetually foreign and temporary people. These narratives of the limits of the U.S. promised land are not only the lived realities of South Central residents but also how they mutually invested in forging a relational community formation and in turn, a home.

It is important to note that I focus primarily on the massive wave of Mexican immigrant migration and settlement throughout South Central's city streets. However, Central American immigrants also settled into the area. The civil conflicts funded by the United States in Central America forced waves of Salvadorans and Guatemalans to seek asylum in the United States. Interactions and relations between Mexicans and Central Americans are fraught; one reason is connected to the hardships Central Americans faced while passing through Mexico. Central Americans also have a different relationship to immigration policy and immigrant discourse while in the United States.[49] Throughout the 1980s and 1990s, the initial settlement of Central American immigrants into South Central resulted in their racial identity being bound up with that of Mexican immigrants.[50] Often, African Americans called Salvadorans "Mexican" without much consideration for nationality or ethnic diversity and difference. The Central American immigrant presence is an important dimension in considering the changing landscape of South Central; however, this book centers on disentangling the complexity of Black and Latina/o relations with a focus on Mexican immigrants. *(not Central American)*

TWENTY-FIRST CENTURY "REAL ESTATE GOLD RUSH"

closed borders

In the aftermath of the September 11, 2001 tragedy, a renewed national investment in anti-immigrant sentiment stalled efforts to overhaul U.S. immigration policy that potentially could have granted over eleven million undocumented immigrants a pathway toward U.S. amnesty and legal residency. In 2006, half a million people participated in a series of immigrant marches in various U.S. cities in opposition to the oppressive immigration bill HR 4437—the Border Protection, Anti-Terrorism, and Illegal Immigration Control Act. Organizing marches of this magnitude required an organic effort by Latina/os and allies, as well as public engagement by radio personalities who understood the disastrous effects HR 4437 could have had for undocumented immigrant people, as it would have further criminalized their existence in the United States, separated mixed-status families, and continued to allow racial profiling.[51] HR 4437 failed in Congress; however, individual states passed measures that mirrored many of HR 4437's provisions.

Protest marches

In fall 2008, the election of Barack Obama as the first African American U.S. president ushered in dreams of hope and change, most especially for African American South Central residents. For Latina/o residents, even if they were at first skeptical, a national African American politician mirrored the local political representation they had grown accustomed to in South Central.[52] However, shortly into his presidency, Obama was faced with a devastating financial and housing crisis that led to an unprecedented housing market decline and a wave of foreclosures, which affected South Central residents painfully.[53]

In addition, immigration advocates had expected that under the Obama administration they would have energetic allies for the passing of comprehensive immigration reform. However, this failed to materialize, and instead the administration continued to fund the mechanisms for increased immigration enforcement through Immigration and Customs Enforcement (ICE), leading ultimately to the deportation of millions of undocumented people across the United States.[54]

The celebration of racial progress in the United States in the form of having our first African American president in office came crashing down in 2013 with the acquittal of George Zimmerman for his fatal shooting of the young Trayvon Martin. The social-media hashtag #Blacklivesmatter emerged, representing the demand for recognition of the humanity and dignity of Black people in the United States. It opened up a national discussion of the racist attitudes and physical violence faced by African Americans throughout this country. The hashtag grew into a movement that called for the end of the premature death of Black people at the hands of the state and white supremacy.[55] The development of the Black Lives Matter movement also emboldened a critique of the limits of the beyond-race-and-colorblind discourse that the two-term Obama presidency represented.

The devastating effects of anti-immigrant and anti-refugee rhetoric and neoliberalism further increased the bifurcation between the rich and poor in the United States. Coupled with such discourse, limited employment options that offered very little in the way of mobility and livable wages would be felt in the lack of affordable housing throughout South Central. Hence, South Central currently faces a new set of challenges and realities, most strikingly, middle-class families of different racial backgrounds buying homes in South Central because of alarmingly high home prices in "desirable" neighborhoods throughout Los Angeles. The relative affordability of homes in South Central has caused real estate agents to boast, "There is cheap housing in L.A. . . . The American dream is still affordable in Watts, Compton, South L.A., and all the forgotten ghettos."[56] Calling South Central a "forgotten ghetto" signals the article's audience, as South Central residents would attest that to outsiders South Central may be forgotten, but not by them. Selling South Central's desirability is only possible because affordability is in tandem with gentrification and investment in the form of a public transportation system that connects South Central to downtown Los Angeles, shopping and sports stadiums, L.A. International Airport, and the revitalized Baldwin Hills Crenshaw Plaza.

Some South Central residents welcome this development, as it will elevate property values; nevertheless, town hall meetings throughout South Central overwhelmingly capture residents' fear that these economic changes will displace long-term residents and aggravate the homeless problem.[57] South Central residents in the past made calls for investment in the community in the form of jobs, education, public health centers, and economic investment by and for community residents, out of their interest in forging community and a sense of home for themselves. The current "promise" of urban areas such as South Central rests on outside private development to continue expansion, even as this growth threatens residential relationships that have taken decades to foster. In an unanticipated manner, South Central could cease to be affordable and the community and home it has grown to be for long-time African American and Latina/o residents. South Central residents are most fearful that after decades of neglect and poverty, this new "real estate gold rush"[58] will threaten the alliances, friendships, and interracial character of South Central. Herein lies the urgency of uncovering interracial dynamics in South Central over the course of the late twentieth century; I argue that at every turn, South Central's African American and Latina/o residents advocated for investment and care for the community, but an investment that would not leave them behind. Investigating the lived realities of South Central residents offers the hard lessons of inclusion as a result of demographic change. Over the course of this book, I argue that both African American and Mexican immigrants have similarly struggled to pursue the crafting of a community formation that is relational, and seminal to the creation of multiracial spaces of shared grievance and belonging that can lead to generative and collective possibilities.

South Central Is Home focuses on how working class and working poor interracial relationships are mediated within U.S. government and institutional forces. It describes a relational community formation in which the collective efforts of African Americans and Latina/os—even if such efforts are small, everyday acts of community investment and solidarity—have power because they go against the grain of expectations of people living in interracial spaces and communities. New local investments in South Central are likely to have an economic impact on African American and Mexican immigrant relations, most especially their struggle against the growing reach of homelessness, underemployment, and deportation.

THE UNFOLDING OF THIS HISTORY

By utilizing archival research, newspapers, government documents and reports, and oral life histories, *South Central Is Home* focuses on the power of Black and Latina/o residents' community investment when they confront demographic change and development in South Central together. Chapter 1 centers on early- to mid-twentieth-century African American migration from U.S. Southern states to Los Angeles, when this generation of migrants established important economic, political, and social spaces such as Broadway Federal Bank. This generation's enterprising inroads would influence South Central's identity as intimately tied to the entrepreneurial spirit of the African American community. This chapter also chronicles how the onset of post–World War II deindustrialization stalled job opportunities for African Americans and paved the way for the introduction of War on Poverty funds into South Central. The succession of these events clearly illustrates the city's growing economic and racial inequalities and the appeal of residents becoming empowered via their community investment in forging a sense of belonging and home.

The availability of War on Poverty funding was crucial to the development of Head Start and comprehensive health centers in South Central throughout the late 1960s and the 1970s. Through an analysis of Head Start in Chapter 2, I demonstrate that the racial diversity of the West meant that the benefit to impoverished families from War on Poverty funds went beyond Black families, and that instead Mexican American children were often understood and publicized as being key beneficiaries of the program. I also discuss how fervently South Central residents and advocates fought to secure community control of Head Start, making its origins a window into this community's investment and creativity. In Chapter 3, I argue how public health became a central axis for combating poverty, as South Central residents desired access to dignified, quality, and easily accessible health care options. The health care centers that emerged from South Central residents' investment in this realm of public services were government-sponsored or privately financed clinics, and ultimately resulted in the successful opening of a hospital in the community.

From the 1970s onward, Latina/o immigration to South Central would change the community's sense of belonging and opportunity. Chapter 4 centers on the ways in which Mexican immigrant residents came to terms with viewing South Central as their neighborhood and community—their home. It shows the labor involved in becoming "bona fide residents" of South Central, where the development of relational community formation made Mexican Americans and Mexican immigrant residents of this community aware of how similarly racialized they were to Black residents by virtue of living in South Central.

By returning to Head Start in the 1980s, Chapter 5 reveals that Head Start's long-term presence and resonance in South Central were shaped by the transformative power of Head Start classrooms for not only children but also parents in the community. The multigenerational reach of Head Start ensured that as it shifted to embrace a multicultural curriculum, it became representative of how increased immigration had a greater reach beyond neighborly interactions. — *it had pol. power to bend est programs toward its needs*

A celebration of diversity would play a role in Los Angeles Mayor Tom Bradley's vision during his two decades in office (1973–1993). In Chapter 6, I argue that although Bradley's championing and celebration of diversity was an attempt to be inclusive of the increased presence of immigrants in the greater Los Angeles area, bleak economic realities for South Central's African American and Mexican immigrant residents would make them painfully aware that while they experienced some benefits from diversity, this did not fully encapsulate their on-the-ground realities. Finally, in Chapter 7, I analyze how leaders and residents view and react to the fact that by the start of the twenty-first century South Central was over 60 percent Latina/o. By investigating Broadway Federal Bank in the latter part of the twentieth century and into the twenty-first, I unearth how difficult it can be to let go of a race- and place-based politics of leadership and shift to a broader community-based politics that understands South Central as a multiracial community and home.

Finally, I conclude by arguing how decades of disinvestment, along with the changes mentioned above, have weighed heavily on the shoulders of Black and Latina/o South Central residents. It has not, however, deterred their fierce determination, most especially in the form of interracial collaborations urging for a renewed proactive investment in the community life of South Central. Impoverished and working poor conditions characterized South Central, where the lack of investment in the welfare state not only exacerbates but frames the interracial lived realities of Latina/os and African Americans. The fight for community preservation is pressing because South Central has for a long time been a place, community, and neighborhood that has been painfully ignored, yet many residents continue to imagine and work toward the creation of a desirable future in and for South Central.

This spirited undertaking is at the heart of this book, as despite U.S. society's consistent disregard and lack of care for this urban community, South Central residents have fought and expressed pride of investment in it. Such was the case when, adjacent to Manual Arts High School in South Central, graffiti artists Akut, Case, and Hera in 2011 spray-painted an image of two young African American girls playing and painting two pigeons, with a caption that read, "Anything can be beautiful when you look at it with love." This graffiti art urges the viewer to consider that—despite the violence, police aggression, and poverty—this community is beautiful and worth fighting for, caring for, and preserving. It is this spirit that energizes this consideration of how South Central emerges and continues to be valued as a home by both African American and Latina/o residents.

CHAPTER I

PLACEMAKING IN OUR COMMUNITY

Race Enterprise and the War on Poverty

IN 1923, thirty-two-year-old M. Earl Grant, originally from Parksburg, West Virginia, migrated to Southern California after spending ten years as a railroad worker in Chicago. Sometime after settling in Pasadena, he noticed that garbage collection did not exist for residents outside of the downtown city limits.[1] He began a garbage disposal business on his own, walking door to door through Pasadena, Altadena, and Flintridge soliciting customers. Over the course of thirty years, Grant had successful garbage disposal and hog businesses. With his business earnings, he decided to follow his father's advice to buy land, "so I would go and buy little pieces of property here and there."[2] In the late 1940s, Grant desired to purchase a home near an African Methodist Episcopal Church on Vernon Avenue in South Central Los Angeles. On the day of the open house, he could not personally attend and asked his wife to go to the bank and ask for details regarding the property. She went and was told that they "couldn't sell it [to Grant] because it wouldn't be fair to the white people on that side of the street." This experience made him "pretty sore," because as he saw it, there was a "Negro church and the parsonage and the negroes that lived on the other side of the street."[3] The bank's reasoning did not appear honest or logical to Grant. The next morning, he was going to go down to the bank and "draw my money out and put it in another bank. They weren't going to treat me like that and me take it laying down." Yet upon further reflection, he "decided it was the same soup warmed over," that what he really needed to do was start a bank—a banking system—that would not systematically deter future investments spearheaded by African Americans.[4] He knew then that he needed to collaborate with other African Americans in the Los Angeles area to create a bank of their own.

To best understand the complexity of Black and Latina/o relations in the latter part of the twentieth century, one must first understand events in the early to mid-twentieth century as key in the development of community building and placemaking efforts transforming South Central into an African American community. Early twentieth-century Black migrants spearheaded a host of different causes and businesses throughout Los Angeles. Grant, along with other successful African American businessmen and women, realized that one of the most significant impediments to homeownership and business entrepreneurship was that major lending institutions relied on racist ideas that described African Americans as character and financial risks. Grant and others agreed that a lending institution was necessary to build a thriving community, which led to the establishment of Broadway Federal Savings and Loan and other banks. By uncovering and focusing on the efforts of early Black migrants, this chapter highlights how African American residents staked a claim, organized community, and established a sense of ownership in South Central Los Angeles. Black migrants' entrepreneurial and community spirit inspired their embracing South Central as a place of their own. This sense of South Central as their community extended beyond business and homeownership practices: it was their community because many memories of settlement into Los Angeles were also bound to leisure activities found along Central Avenue, spaces they carved out in the face of racism and discrimination.

However, by the 1960s, a new generation of African American residents called Los Angeles home, one that "compared their opportunities not to what African American people in other cities had . . . but rather to the opportunities enjoyed by their white peers in Los Angeles."[5] In the years that followed, spatial segregation, systemic deindustrialization, and poor schooling options made African Americans painfully aware of their second-class status throughout the city. The origins of the urban crisis that catalyzed the Watts uprising in

1965 and the outmigration of middle-class Black residents ensured that South Central became increasingly marked as working class, working poor, and impoverished. This dimension is understated when one considers that well before Latina/o immigration into South Central began in earnest, there was community anxiety over how to grapple with and understand the changing terrain of the community's class dynamics. The Watts uprising and its residents' reflections on its causes serve as an indicator of economic, political, and social limits to Black opportunity. South Central's African American residents did not enjoy the middle-class status achieved by early twentieth-century Black migrants, but residents remained steadfast in their commitment to understanding South Central and Watts as their community even in the midst of neglect and isolation.

The introduction of War on Poverty funds in the mid-1960s would open the possibility of creating programming in and for the community that aimed to fix these economic inequities. From the beginning, War on Poverty efforts in Los Angeles had many obstacles, ranging from the desire of the mayor's office to control funds, difficulty in gaining community representation in the poverty board and programs, and the need to build effective collaboration between African Americans and Mexican Americans on War on Poverty programs. Interracial tensions emerged between Mexican Americans and African Americans, and these offer a window to understanding how interracial coalitions are fragile when framed in relationship with power structures and limited economic resources.

This chapter captures the multiple changes South Central would undergo prior to Mexican immigrant and Mexican American settlement in the latter part of the 1960s and in the 1970s. Black migrants in the early twentieth century arrived in Los Angeles with the drive to build a strong and flourishing community. They purchased homes, and opened the first African American bank, local chapters of the Urban League and the National Association for the Advancement of Colored People (NAACP), and jazz clubs along Central Avenue.[6] They transformed segregation into a space of empowerment. Their efforts created a sense of ownership for South Central, and placemaking that would prove enduring. Long-term African American residents came to terms with the many ways in which their community would undergo changes by the mid-twentieth century. The economic transition of South Central into a working class and working poor community understandably was met with anxiety and tension. Chronicling this shift is key for understanding how African American residents responded to Mexican immigrants settling and using War on Poverty programming throughout South Central and how relational community formation emerged in the latter part of the twentieth century.

THE DEVELOPMENT OF
THE LAND OF MILK AND HONEY

African Americans ventured west to escape the racial violence inflicted on them throughout the U.S. southern states. Explaining how the first wave of African Americans made the trek west in search of better life chances, historian Douglas Flamming argues that these migrants "were bound for freedom because most of them were leaving a dangerously unequal south for a potentially equal west. Black Angelenos thus fought a double battle, laboring to attain those rights they did not yet enjoy while seeking to protect the rights they already had."[7] With this goal in mind, the first generation of Black migrants arrived in Los Angeles in the 1880s. The period between 1890 and 1915 is characterized as migration by educated, ambitious, and affluent African Americans.[8] Their middle-class identity was based on "aspirations, lifestyle, and values" rather than in material wealth, and most were part of the blue-collar workforce; if white collar, they understood how tangible that label could be.[9] The level of education and economic ability made this wave of migrants critical to the establishment of Black Los Angeles. As historian Scott Kurashige astutely documents, African American industrialism, entrepreneurial spirit, and creativity were vital in the establishment of essential race enterprises, businesses, and employment options, as well as significant outlets, spaces, and venues for popular culture and recreation at sites such as the Dunbar Hotel.[10]

In 1913, W. E. B. Dubois's visit to Los Angeles led him to believe that the city was a racial paradise—"California is the greatest state for the Negro."[11] Augustus Hawkins, an African American migrant who would serve as a U.S. congressman from 1963 to 1991, said, "[W]hen people from Texas or Louisiana came out and wrote back South, it made people in the South believe that it was heaven . . . it was a land of golden opportunities—orange groves and beautiful beaches—and life was all a matter of milk and honey."[12] California was indeed viewed as the land of milk and honey: after it became a free state in 1850, it repealed testimony restrictions in 1863 and outlawed de jure racial segregation in California schools and passed anti-discrimination laws in 1893.[13] This drew attention to California in the imagination of African American southerners, as a venture worth pursuing.

Upon arrival, men worked as Pullman porters, janitors, and waiters, and in other service occupations, yet the 1920s and 1930s experienced a growth in the professional sphere as migrants from the professional class were arriving: dentists, lawyers, physicians, and ministers.[14] Between 1900 and 1920, roughly 70 percent of wage-earning African American women gained employment as domestics in private families and hotels. The opportunities for Black women broadened when they also became teachers. In 1900, Black female teachers were not part of the workforce; however, by 1920 there were twenty-five African American women teachers throughout Los Angeles.[15] In cities such as Atlanta, New Orleans, and San Antonio, Black women made up half of the labor force, yet in Los Angeles they were one-third of the workforce; "these figures reflect the middle-class nature of Black migration to Los Angeles, as well as the higher wages that Black husbands could earn out west."[16]

African Americans in Los Angeles managed to achieve a higher rate of homeownership than those in other U.S. cities. By 1916, roughly 36 percent of African Americans owned their homes in Los Angeles County. This rate of homeownership, compared to 2 percent in New York City or 11 percent in New Orleans, served to bolster the argument of how Los Angeles was the land of opportunity. In fact, no other large city in America had such a high rate of homeownership among African Americans.[17] In pre–World War I Los Angeles, outstanding homeownership rates throughout the city conveyed an image of inclusivity, as the segregation of African Americans was not solely into one geographic space and instead the sprawl of the growing city provided an illusion of tolerance. However, during and after the war, race restrictive real estate covenants began to have an impact on the homeownership op-portunities of Black migrants.[18] These covenants held property owners and real estate agents to a contractual agreement that they refuse to rent or sell housing options to African Americans and other groups in majority white neighborhoods. These covenants were "the most effective tool for corralling the massive influx of Blacks."[19]

Race restrictive covenants ensured that upwardly mobile African Americans as a collective group did not have housing options beyond the scope of areas

middle class Blacks in S. Central

adjacent to Central Avenue.[20] Despite countless efforts to challenge these covenants, African Americans increasingly were forced to live in South Central.[21] The 1948 U.S. Supreme Court *Shelley v. Kraemer* decision made restrictive real estate covenants legally unenforceable. Despite this ruling, not much changed for incoming Black migrants, as realtors continued to deter them from renting and purchasing homes in all-white neighborhoods, and instead "unleashed whites' fury and a panoply of new techniques to keep Blacks in their place."[22] The sources of intimidation went beyond personal harassment and acts of violence and included gerrymandering school districts to "protect" public schools from being integrated, barring African Americans from patronizing white businesses, creating and utilizing redlining policies to deny home loans to African Americans, and planning and developing public housing in locations outside of white neighborhoods.[23]

African American migrants, however, built opportunity out of segregation. By the mid-1910s, Central Avenue had become the economic and social center of the community.[24] The *California Eagle* was one of the most prolific African American–owned newspapers of the time. John James Neimore created it around 1879, under the name *The California Owl*.[25] The goal of the paper was to help recent African American migrants adjust to their life in the west. Charlotta A. Bass took over the *Owl* in 1912 and renamed it *The California Eagle*. The *Eagle* had its headquarters along the avenue, and it focused on political and social issues affecting the African American community, most especially the discrimination and segregation African Americans experienced in labor, public spaces, law enforcement, and residential spaces. The *Eagle* was the largest African American newspaper in California, and it sustained publication until 1964.[26] The creation of race enterprises like the *Eagle* that were owned and operated by African Americans began to render Central Avenue as a racially identified space.

place making w. this newspaper

In addition to the *Eagle*, Central Avenue became the center of nightclubs and jazz. The growth in leisure activities grew such that by the 1920s and 1930s the Somerville Hotel (later the Dunbar Hotel) served performers and patrons alike. The Dunbar was the finest in the community, and this alongside the Apex Club ensured a dynamic nightlife.[27] Central Avenue's active and lively nightclub scene made it a famous destination and as such one of Los Angeles's multiracial spaces. Whites, Asian Americans, African Americans,

it was unique in what it offered so drew a multicultural patrons

and Mexican Americans lived and worked in the area, and participated in the avenue's leisure activities.

The multiracial and multiethnic landscape that once defined downtown and Central Avenue in the 1920s, however, increasingly became more segregated during the Great Depression, with the deportation of over one-third of the Mexican and Mexican American population. In the wake of the Pearl Harbor attacks, the forced internment of Japanese Americans caused the decline in their presence in Bronzeville and Central Avenue, and what were once communities defined by their multiracial character again became predominantly African American during the 1940s and 1950s.[28] In addition, the coming together of communities of color in these spaces of popular culture and dance heightened anxieties of racial intermixing. Law enforcement and urban whites who disfavored such interactions would violently break up these dances and shows as well as impose harsh rules and laws against racial commingling.[29] Los Angeles police intensified violence against African Americans and Mexican Americans and began an "intimidation campaign in the Central Avenue jazz clubs, prompting the more affluent white and Black club goers to stop coming." The jazz scene at the Dunbar declined, and as jazz musician Marshall Royal said, "It just faded away. Nothing was happening. It just went kaput."[30] Thus South Central's diverse landscape in terms of its residents, business owners, and leisure culture participants became predominantly African American by the mid-twentieth century.

George Lipsitz argues that spaces have layered meanings and identities attached to community demographics, history of segregation, and a sense of ownership.[31] In the case of South Central, the community is geographically racialized and marked. The forced separation of communities of color meant that they had to "take places" and make something of their own. Businesses along Central Avenue were clear indicators of this taking and making of space, even though many of them were open in properties that their proprietors did not own. This inability to open or own businesses throughout Los Angeles ensured that businesspeople had to create community in segregated spaces.[32] In the early twentieth century, Central Avenue was one of the few spaces that allowed African American entrepreneurship. As such, it has a legacy of ownership, proprietorship, and community resources that for a long time rendered Central Avenue, and by extension, South Central, an African American community.

ESTABLISHING A BANK IN
SOUTH CENTRAL LOS ANGELES

In the late 1920s and the 1930s, Liberty Savings and Loan, Golden State Mutual Life, Morris Plan Loan Company, and Unity Finance Company opened
storefronts throughout Los Angeles to serve the increasing numbers of African
American migrants. The most successful of these organizations was Golden
State, providing insurance policies to a growing middle-class African American
community. It provided the model and impetus behind the support for opening "race enterprises" that would "take care of their own."[33]

Growing employment opportunities characterizing placemaking along Central Avenue had spurred the largest wave of African American migration into
the community in the 1940s and 1950s. Like previous migrants, they originated mostly from Texas (24 percent) and Louisiana (18 percent).[34] By 1950,
more than 85 percent of the most recent African American migrants had come
from a metropolitan area, and the population grew from 1 to 8 percent. From
1940 to 1970, the African American community in Los Angeles grew faster
than in any other metropolitan city in the country, as it increased from 63,744
to almost 763,000.[35] Labor shortages in defense and aerospace meant that the
postwar period offered a window of opportunity for African American men
and women. African Americans organized to be included in unions for higher
wages. The proportion of African American men working in white-collar jobs
rose from 16 percent in 1950 to 28 percent in 1970, but more impressive was
the percentage of African American women employed in white-collar occupations, which rose from 17 percent to 50 percent during the same years.[36]

With their incomes growing, African Americans were able to buy homes
in South Central. The success of Golden State Mutual encouraged professional
and prominent African American men and women living in South Central Los
Angeles, such as M. Earl Grant, H. J. Howard (real estate broker), H. Claude
Hudson (dentist and president of the Los Angeles NAACP branch), Paul Williams (architect), Thomas Griffith Jr. (city judge), Helen Douglas, and Ellen
Taylor to collectively pursue and secure funding to begin the first federal bank
in South Central.[37] They started a federal savings and loan association, with
the goal of assuring investors "that this thing was not going to be a failure, so
that you couldn't take nobody else's money." They solicited support from the
community and made impassioned and pragmatic arguments to the Federal

Home Loan Bank Board and its sponsors that both discrimination at white-owned institutions and Golden Mutual's limited funds for personal and home loans placed African Americans at an unfair disadvantage.[38] The group quickly realized that the task of having people see the need for a bank was not as difficult as expected. The bank loan board expected to fundraise one hundred fifty thousand dollars; however, they successfully raised "two hundred and some thousand dollars," well beyond the board's demand. They fundraised heavily within African American churches. Thus, in 1946, the team was able to secure a federal charter for Broadway Federal Savings and Loan and the acquisition of property on 4325 South Broadway Street in South Central Los Angeles (hence the name of the establishment).[39] Finally, on January 11, 1947, the originators' dreams of a bank became a reality: Broadway Federal Savings and Loan opened its doors and welcomed the general public with a grand inaugural celebration that celebrated the "foresight and initiative taken by the Negro organizers of Broadway Federal."[40]

African American advocates and supporters of the bank envisioned and committed themselves to Broadway Federal's fulfillment of African American South Central residents' banking needs. As H. J. Howard, chairman of Broadway Federal, explained days before the opening,

> We recognize that numerous persons, principally Negroes, have been long sufferers from rank discriminatory policies employed by many home loan establishments. This has served only to place these people at the mercy of clever loan "sharks" and similar fly-by-night setups. Our organization has declared war on these unfair policies and seeks instead to inject into the picture fair treatment and lower rates of interest to our customers.[41]

Broadway Federal was the first Black-owned financial institution in Los Angeles, and the second in the nation, that was secured and supervised by the federal government. It had the financial capital and resources to cater to the growing African American community. This bank's founders considered Broadway Federal the core financial institution by and for the African American community. Their struggle and commitment to make banking a fair and accessible process for African Americans framed their mission in the late 1940s and had a direct bearing on the continued purpose of the bank. Broadway Federal's management continually reassured the African American community that they were

[handwritten margin note at top: as are all black-owned businesses and institutions]

different from other banks in the region because they, in fact, were much more than a financial institution—the bank was a cultural enterprise designed to serve African Americans' particular needs.

H. J. Howard served as Broadway Federal's inaugural chairman, yet shortly after that, the board voted for H. Claude Hudson. Hudson's tenure as chairman of Broadway Federal was from 1949 to 1973. Hudson's relationship to the African American community was shaped by his civil rights activism within the NAACP, his commitment to Black progress and education, and his leadership in Broadway Federal Bank. He was born on April 9, 1886, in Alexandria, Louisiana, and experienced segregation and discrimination firsthand in the South.[42] In 1913, he completed his dentistry degree at Howard University and returned to Louisiana to begin his practice. By 1923, he could not bear the thought of having his children grow up in the throes of the Jim Crow South, and like many other African American migrants from the South, he looked west for the possibility of raising his children under different circumstances and options. In Los Angeles he established his dental practice in a building designed by Paul Williams (one of the initial group of men and women who started Broadway Federal) across the street from notable African American locations such as the Dunbar Hotel and Golden State Mutual Life Insurance Company in the heart of Central Avenue.[43] He had been active in his local NAACP branch in Louisiana, and his migration west did not change his unwavering commitment to the organization. His presence at the heart of the commercial and cultural district in African American Los Angeles and his work in the NAACP catapulted him, and his family, to the center of African American life in the city.

In the late 1920s, he was instrumental in reviving the NAACP's branch in Los Angeles, an endeavor for which Walter White, as assistant secretary to the national NAACP office, celebrated Hudson's management of L.A. as "one of the branches of which we are most proud."[44] In 1927, he was integral to promoting the NAACP's involvement in the "beach wars" for African Americans to gain access to the Los Angeles recreational coastline.[45] During this period the Los Angeles chapter of the NAACP was also engaged in organizing a Budweiser boycott, protesting, "No job, no Bud!" to discourage African Americans from buying beer from a company that failed to employ them. They also encouraged participation in campaigns against the Los Angeles Fire Department's discriminatory practices.[46] In addition, they were extremely active in organizing

[handwritten margin note, left side: nature also segregated not just built environment]

[handwritten note at bottom: Claude Hudson – bank chairman and NAACP leader]

desegregation cases in schooling, housing, and employment.[47] Hudson's participation in the bank's founding and subsequent leadership and management of Broadway Federal comes as no surprise.

As chairman, Hudson laid the groundwork for Broadway Federal to be an economic necessity for the African American community of South Central. His activism within the NAACP did not waver as he worked arduously to further the bank's significance in the city. Part of his initiative within the bank was to actively recruit and train African American bank employees. He considered this part of a broader political project to educate and train future African American professionals. In an oral history, Hudson stated that when the board discussed the workforce behind the bank, they agreed that it had to be representative of the community. In 1947, one would rarely find African American men and women working as employees in commercial banks anywhere in the region, but in the first few years of the bank, Broadway Federal was committed to reconceptualizing the workforce to include young and trained African American men and women.[48]

By the late 1950s, Hudson had accomplished his mission of hiring and training the next generation of African American accountants and tellers. Joan Penn Lockett, a bank employee, stated that Broadway Federal was "just like a big, happy family" and said, "[T]he community as a whole should be proud of Broadway Federal because it is modern in every way and completely equipped in handling customers' business efficiently."[49] Alfred L. Walker Jr., a home loan accountant, mentioned that over a period of six months Broadway Federal had facilitated the dreams of over one thousand African American families wanting to buy houses. Thus, "not only does it stress efficiency in serving their customers, but the friendly atmosphere here is noticeable to both our patrons and employees. It is a fine progressive organization."[50] Courtney R. A. Bain, head accountant of Broadway Federal, echoed Walker's statements: "I think Broadway Federal is an inspiration to me daily and I think it would be the same to many others if they came in and opened savings accounts and arranged for home buying through our association."[51] Similarly, Ruby Jones, a telephone operator, explained, "I am prouder of this position than any I've ever had. My employers are wonderful people. And just one visit to Broadway will convince you that Broadway is tops in its field."[52] Hudson imagined Los Angeles as being at the forefront of the economic modernization of the African American community,

and he stated that L.A. led in "the establishment of Negro institutions, financial institutions, we took a much more liberal policy and grew more rapidly
until Broadway is the largest financial institution in control by Negroes in the
country, with the capital around something over 50 million dollars, with assets
something over 50 million dollars."[53]

The positive appraisals of pride, honor, and a family-like employment environment depicted Broadway Federal as not only a financial entity tied to the
local community but also one intimately linked to the politics and economic
growth of the African American community. The *Los Angeles Sentinel*, the largest
and longest-running African American newspaper in Los Angeles, ran a series of
articles promoting Broadway Federal as a vital force helping African American
families to realize their homeownership dreams and to open savings accounts,
as well as employing the best-educated and brightest African Americans in the
community.[54] The *Sentinel*'s coverage and photos of Broadway Federal showcased African American employees serving African American patrons. These
photos inspired community patronage and enabled African Americans to see
themselves as part of the success of the bank. The effect of the images, which
now adorn the walls of various Broadway Federal branches, is to place the bank
squarely in the history of Black Los Angeles. Notably, the bank's history is en-
capsulated through visual images of three generations of Hudson leadership and
African American bank employees serving the African American community.
Through their rhetoric and visual representation, local newspaper articles affirm that the bank is a "race enterprise." The Hudson legacy did not end when
Hudson retired: he passed down the project of African American economic
advancement to his son, Elbert, and grandson Paul.[55]

In the late 1960s and early 1970s, it became locally urgent to get local corporations to invest in minority banks in Los Angeles and across the nation.
Legal precedents that desegregated schools, employment, housing, and public
facilities opened up new opportunities for African Americans, especially those
of the middle class, throughout the United States and in Los Angeles in particular. The federal government put into place laws that offered greater support
for Black-owned business through Small Business Administration programs.[56]
These changes in legislation and the growth of minority-owned banks throughout the United States prompted Augustus Hawkins and Edward Roybal, representatives of Los Angeles, to encourage major corporations and community

organizations throughout the city to invest in minority banks. They both believed that "minority banks have the potential to play a vital role in the economic development of their respective communities," and felt that "promoting economic development for minorities from within the system by increasing deposits in minority banks is an important part of this nation's quest for economic opportunity for all citizens."[57]

Hawkins's letters urged corporations to invest not in Broadway Federal but rather in Bank of Finance or Family Savings and Loan because by the 1970s those banks had larger portfolios than Broadway Federal (in part because a more significant percentage of their stock owners were white businessmen). By the 1970s, Broadway Federal was branded a community bank rather than a commercial bank, marking its economic scope as local rather than national; thus Hawkins did not see fit to recommend Broadway Federal as a minority bank in which to invest. Despite the failure of Hawkins to promote Broadway Federal for investment, corporations such as Litton Industries and Avery Products Corporation had been investing since the late 1960s in minority banks in the region, which included Broadway Federal.[58] It is unclear to what extent Hawkins continued to urge local businessmen to invest in minority owned banks; however, what is clear is his firm belief in "maintaining deposits in minority banks as a sound business approach to dealing with some of the problems facing our country."[59] Hudson and the board of directors similarly believed that investment in minority-owned banks would help the African American community. The African American community could assert its independence from the white economic and political world by supporting minority-owned banks and therefore engage in modernity under its own terms. The formation and growth of this bank demonstrate the commitment of African American patrons to sustaining a "race enterprise," which itself helped craft a sense of ownership and success in South Central.

The African American community's committed patronage of Broadway Federal Bank explains the bank's longevity. African American migrants, in their "search for a better life, often found urban America to be uneven terrain, bitterly reminiscent of the old south one moment, brilliantly bursting with opportunity the next."[60] This reality of South Central as simultaneously the land of opportunity and the place reproducing the experience of the U.S. South characterizes the experience of early twentieth-century migrants to the area.

These early migrants had a middle-class ethos and used their mobility out west to originate businesses and establish a community. The founding of an African American–owned bank is one example of this wave's entrepreneurial spirit and its understanding of the needs of a growing population. The bank started as a resource for African Americans wanting to secure home and business loans; it serves as an example of how a "race enterprise" was able to thrive in an increasingly working class and racialized space. Thus the bank was part of the African American community's placemaking process of creating opportunities in an otherwise hostile environment.

THE SHIFTING CLASS DYNAMICS
IN THE COMMUNITY

The postwar entrepreneurial gains of homeownership and employment stalled in the mid-1960s, as such opportunities were not offered to all African Americans. The origins of inner cities are not accidental but rather a reflection of white homeowners, real estate agents, policymakers, and public officials working in collaboration to create communities that are racially separated. By the mid-1960s, South Central and Watts were overwhelmingly African American, two-thirds of families were on welfare, three-fourths of adult males were unemployed, and 40 percent of Watts's families lived below the poverty level.[61] Between 1959 and 1965, the purchasing power of South Central families fell, with housing options becoming characterized as "dilapidated" and "deteriorated."[62] As early as 1963, manufacturing firms started leaving South Central and the Alameda industrial corridor for other areas in Los Angeles. Aircraft, aerospace, and electronics were the first industries to desert the urban core, followed by manufacturers of electrical machinery, apparel, metals, and food and petroleum products.[63]

These economic changes were among the many underlying reasons for the 1965 Watts uprising. The catalyst for the unrest came on August 11, 1965, after Marquette Frye, who had been drinking, was driving home accompanied by his brother, Ronald. Two blocks from his destination, he was pulled over by police officers. Ronald walked to their nearby home and returned with their mother; as she approached the scene, she saw her son Marquette being beaten by police officers and attempted to subdue the officers. Police arrested all three Frye family members.[64] During this incident, hundreds of residents arrived at the scene, and a six-day uprising ensued. The bulk of the destruction took place on Watts's commercial corridor. One thousand people were injured, thirty-four died, more than eleven thousand people were arrested, and there was roughly $35 million in property damage.[65] Watts's residents were responding to police aggression, but also to the accretion of struggles against police violence and the labor, housing, and public inequities facing African Americans in Los Angeles.

The Watts rebellion demonstrated that the best efforts of enterprising African American community residents were not enough to solve virulent racism and discrimination. City officials argued that the Watts uprising caused the employment sector in Watts and South Central to relocate; however, the industry had already begun the process of leaving the urban core. The frustration manifested during the Watts uprising indicated that a segment of the community felt left behind. *Los Angeles Times* reporter Charisse Jones interviewed African American residents to discuss whether, if they had the option, they would leave South Central. Catherine Williams, migrant to South Central in 1943 and homeowner in South Central since the 1950s, vividly recounted her experience living in the community as being nostalgic for the legacy of efforts by previous Black migrants. In South Central, she went to her first nightclub, where she saw Nat King Cole perform, but also wondered how long she would call South Central her home.[66] Her contemporary Beverly Blake recalled the old-fashioned soda fountain in the community; the shop was a place where she and her girlfriends could chat as they ate burgers and fries. Fifty-five-year-old Major Cobb stated, "If I had money I wouldn't be here. If I had the money, I'd be up there in Baldwin Hills or somewhere where they have those swimming pools and everything."[67] African Americans who could relocated to affluent neighborhoods such as Baldwin Hills and Ladera Heights.[68] "For Sale" and "Cash for Your House" signs were placed across lawns in South Central, reminding residents that if they wanted, they could leave and someone could take their place. Beverly Blake added, "When we move, we lose. The more we move out, the less political clout we have. If we don't live together geographically, how do we empower each other?" Blake was indicating how on-the-ground political and community power could be lost with Black residents' continued outmigration.[69]

Catherine Williams moved out of the neighborhood for a brief period in the mid-1960s when she became a widow and, in her estimation, the community's economic change—specifically, the new prevalence of liquor stores—started to make South Central unattractive. Williams returned to South Central and told Jones, "Honey, it didn't make me no difference whatsoever because . . . this is mine. It may not look like anything to anybody else, but my husband's blood, sweat, and tears went into this house. This is mine and I'll fight like hell to keep it."[70] African Americans may feel that in some ways South Central did not live up to its promise, yet some still deemed it a community worth fighting for.

COMMUNITY CONTROL:
REBELLION AND POVERTY FUNDING

The Watts rebellion illustrated that the community built by Black migrants in the early twentieth century had undergone meaningful internal changes that required residents to adapt and shift their understanding, in that now they were part of a working class, working poor, and increasingly impoverished community. President Lyndon B. Johnson in his state of the union address in 1964 declared an "unconditional war on poverty," promising "not only to relieve the symptoms of poverty but to cure it and, above all, to prevent it." Johnson's declaration was spurred by what some academics called a rediscovery of poverty in the early 1960s, when politicians and policymakers alike aimed to assist those who had not shared in postwar economic progress.[71] The War on Poverty initiatives included Medicare, Medicaid, federal subsidies for education, new urban renewal initiatives, the expansion of Social Security, and the creation of federal arts and humanities endowments.[72]

The War on Poverty was executed through the Economic Opportunity Act (EOA), with the Office of Economic Opportunity (OEO) administering the EOA's provisions and programming. The EOA required that as cities applied for War on Poverty funds, they needed to establish delegate agencies that would work with the mayor's office and have maximum participation by the poor to create and operate poverty programs. A political battle of how to distribute funds into communities most in need was waged among then Mayor Samuel Yorty, Representatives Augustus Hawkins and Edward Roybal, and South Central residents. Mayor Yorty, elected as a populist, was the first mayor to hire a female deputy and a racially integrated staff. However, this did not assuage African American residents' distrust of Yorty because they still faced high levels of unemployment and housing discrimination across the city.[73] Also, a battle began over the level of community control these programs would have, as Yorty believed that monitored and minimal community control was necessary for the successful implementation of the program, and he thwarted efforts to distribute War on Poverty funds to the South Central Los Angeles and Watts regions.[74]

In 1962, Yorty established the Youth Opportunity Board of Greater Los Angeles (YOB) to tackle juvenile delinquency and unemployment among out-of-school youth. The YOB board was composed mostly of city and county officials from the California Department of Employment, the Los Angeles Unified School District, and the Los Angeles Junior College District. Yorty wanted to allocate War on Poverty funds to the YOB; however, dissatisfied with the lack of community input in the YOB, a group of middle-class professionals in Watts formed their own private organization, called the Economic Opportunity Federation (EOF). Opal Jones, an African American social worker and member of the Welfare Planning Council and the Los Angeles Area Federation of Settlement and Neighborhood Centers, supported the EOF. The EOF's mission and belief were that the War on Poverty initiatives needed to work with the neighborhood and establish "family-centered resources, volunteer training, and job programs." Supporters of the organization were Congressmen Augustus Hawkins, Edward Roybal, James Roosevelt, and George E. Brown.[75] Congressman Hawkins was an outspoken advocate for community participation and control, mainly by African Americans in Watts and South Central Los Angeles and Mexican Americans on the northeast side of his district. Hawkins asked, "Why shouldn't Compton, Willowbrook, Watts area, Enterprise, or the Avalon community have some say about their own conditions?"[76] He argued for the involvement of the poor at every stage of activity, meaning the administrative and operational levels, as it was not enough to "merely put community leaders on an advisory committee, or a few minorities on the staff, or to consider a few proposals from independent groups." That is not the genuine involvement of the poor. Hawkins stated, "[T]hey are involved only if they are also included at the policy level where the actual decisions are made and in the actual over-all planning of programs." Key to his argument was that "folks needed to be from the poverty areas," in this case from the African American and Mexican American community, to successfully draft a program that would serve the poor.

Congressman Hawkins urged local groups such as the EOF to end the war with Mayor Yorty to receive the benefits of antipoverty programs. Mayor Yorty believed the formation of the EOF was a "personal and political affront," and his opposition to the organization was "as much selfish as principled."[77] Efforts to merge the YOB and the EOF came to a head when Yorty wrote to President Johnson about the conflict in Los Angeles regarding War on Poverty funds. Sargent Shriver, head of the OEO, responded that an effective War on Poverty program required low-income representatives on the board and delegate agencies and that the EOF and the YOB needed to merge and include more low-income representatives on the board. This would mean that the board would consist of twenty-two members, of which ten were public agency representatives, six were from private agencies, and six were community representatives. Yorty had little option but to accept the merger, and Hawkins believed it was necessary in order to receive federal money for community projects. The merger produced the Economic and Youth Opportunities Agency of Greater Los Angeles (EYOA).[78] Despite what appeared to be a political truce, Yorty continued to seek political power and control over the program while Hawkins and Roybal continued to fight for and ensure that the representation of the poor was at the heart of the War on Poverty agencies and organizations. The origins of the War on Poverty in South Central Los Angeles were fraught with residents, political officials, and community delegate agencies trying to make sense of the federal antipoverty program.

Another of the underlying causes of the Watts rebellion was the failure of City Hall to address the issues plaguing the community and to expedite funding of War on Poverty programs in the area. Mayor Yorty did not take seriously accusations of police misconduct leveled by African American and Mexican Americans residents. Congressman Hawkins was the most vocal about the impact that the delay of War on Poverty funds had in Watts. To identify the causes of the uprising, Governor Pat Brown established the McCone Commission, headed by John A. McCone. Hawkins testified that "had politics not been played with anti-poverty funds, more youths would have been in meaningful activities this past summer, more indigenous leaders would have been in neighborhood programs, and more job-creating activities would have been in operation the early part of this year."[79] OEO director Sargent Shriver agreed with the assertion by Hawkins and Watts residents that the lack of poverty agencies in the area contributed to the revolt. For Shriver, the antipoverty programs were "not an anti-riot program, but the more chances you give people to get out of

poverty, the less chance there is of revolt."[80] The McCone Commission recommended that the OEO increase its funds for employment and job-training
programs and preschool education, which included more youth opportunity
centers, legal aid services, and the full implementation of Head Start.[81]

THE WATTS UPRISING:
FRUSTRATION AND ANGER

The President's Task Force for the Los Angeles Riots was assembled in addition
to Governor Brown's commission to uncover the root causes of the 1965 Watts
uprising. The task force was composed of Ramsey Clark (deputy attorney general), Andrew Brimmer (assistant secretary of commerce), and Jack Conway
(deputy director of the War on Poverty), and aimed to enhance the findings
of the McCone Commission, with the ultimate goal of this report being to
provide a blueprint for what the federal government could do to eradicate the
threat of such an event occurring once more. This report showcased feelings of
community frustration and anger, a community in transition and reckoning
with its increased poverty, and the need for community control in programs
aimed at the poor.

The report reached out to community residents and activists to solicit their
sentiments about police and neighborhood dynamics. The first recommendation
was for the federal government to secure more funding for self-help programs.[82]
Residents voiced distrust toward power structures: "The white power structure
wants us to stay in our place, to be kept in poverty, in ghettos, uneducated on
relief." Similarly, feelings of isolation and being forgotten were expressed: "Everything in the slums is absentee: We have absentee teachers, absentee business,
absentee landlords, absentee politicians, and we even have absentee preach-
ers." This critique from residents highlighted the power dynamics at play, that
within the context of the United States a community or neighborhood is an
appendage of ownership: "This is colonialism in America; the Negro ghetto is
just a colony."[83] This assertion of how Black inner city residents feel within the
United States signals the level of alienation and frustration that fuels anger and
discontent and can lead to events like the 1965 uprising.

The people of Watts compiled a list of complaints that would act as a guide
to the issues that were pressing the community. The complaints ranged from education to homeownership to poverty. Residents made the following statements:

"We can't borrow money, buy homes, obtain insurance."

"Ghetto education is a sham. Our kids learn nothing. The teachers are afraid and don't try to get help. Our children are promoted to get rid of them whether they've learned anything or not."

"They don't teach our kids the things they need to know to get jobs. They don't do enough for kids from bad homes to make up for what they don't get in the home, like an interest in books."

Finally, Watts was characterized as "Los Angeles' dumping ground": "We carry the burden of poverty, crime, vice, and disadvantage for the entire city."[84]

The belief that inner city residents seize the opportunity to collect government assistance was commonplace during this period, yet respondents in this report argued against that assertion. Many expressed bitterness toward public assistance: "We resent crooked, twisted laws. Relief has hurt many people." "We don't want relief. We want independence that only good jobs can give."[85] They demanded jobs that would provide opportunity, challenging the notion that all African American and Mexican American poor residents crave government assistance over employment opportunities. Countless complaints demonstrated that residents wanted jobs, and that investment in public assistance was the government's attempt to avoid dealing with the fundamental problem of unemployment.

The Watts uprising signaled a sense of disillusionment because Black migrants who moved out west to California "for a better life" had "hoped for more and expected more. They were funneled into the slums as they arrived and there is no way out." Black migrants "weren't treated as humans. They still call us boy. A boy lives in the jungle with Tarzan. We've got names." This lack of respect angered Black residents; they demanded respect and dignity, as the lack thereof bred "widespread fear and distrust."[86] The struggle for dignity and humanity seemed impossible. Watts residents declared, "[T]here is so little humanness in our lives—how can we have self-respect?" Part of this effort for respect meant that the residents demanded beautification—"[W]e want beauty in our lives: good shopping centers, good housing, clean homes, and streets." And there was a cadre of dedicated, hardworking people in Watts who strived and continuously worked toward a better life, yet that was not sufficient without further economic support. As one resident stated,

The prevalent attitude in the white community is to condemn the lawlessness, the impatience, and the destruction. There is a widespread feeling that
the Negro community lacks gratitude for recent economic and civil rights
advances and that this demands will grow. Many feel that relief and welfare
should be reduced and police control tightened. Many see a close connection between peaceful demonstration for civil rights and rioting. They fear a
breakdown in respect for the law. And many in the white community have
expressed a determination not to yield to demands related to violence and feel
the assistance to the riot areas rewards lawlessness.[87]

The findings highlighted the degree to which Watts residents—poor, working
poor, and working class people—desired to be active in shaping their future. It
also shows the enduring legacy of residential placemaking ushered in by previous
migrants, that even as Black people increasingly owned less in the community
(in terms of homes, business, and employment opportunities), they still felt a
connection and responsibility to the community. The urgency to safeguard the
neighborhood proved all the more crucial in a period of increased social isolation
and division. White people had little sympathy for the Black people's struggle and
experience. Black residents wanted to participate in the decision-making process,
to shape their own lives, declaring that if "people in the depressed areas can participate in the planning and execution of welfare and poverty programs, they will
be doing better." Residents repeatedly stated that employment opportunities were
what they desired most: "We need employment, give us jobs and everything else
will take care of itself. Jobs first!" Another said, "We don't want any make-work
or relief work. We want real work that gives self-respect."[88]

    The Watts rebellion was a manifestation of Black people's rage over limited
and stalled opportunity and the culmination of decades of struggles against
police violence, labor, housing, and public injustice. A survey of Watts residents
"corroborated the frequency and routine occurrence of police abuse: half of the
respondents reported that they had been lined up on the sidewalk, frisked for
no apparent reason, and slapped, kicked, etc."[89] The report shed light on how
Watts residents had grown tired of initiatives aimed at identifying the needs
of their community without making much difference to their everyday existence: "[W]hite people always survey us and experiment on us. They get the
grants. Let us experiment on ourselves." Another resident said, "We must help
the people to help themselves. Watts should be planned out, improved by the

Jobs?
Self determination
Wanted
What's

people of Watts." In the end, the report gathered the emotive landscape of South Central and Watts residents in the aftermath of the rebellion, capturing their frustration and anger, and the accountability they were asking of the city and government for employment, education, and community growth. Demands to build such programs of and for themselves dovetailed with a critical tenet of the War on Poverty: funding through the provision of maximum feasible participation of the poor. *How did it work out?*

RACIAL TENSIONS IN THE WAR ON POVERTY

In addition to grappling with the underlying causes of the Watts uprising and ways to gain community control of poverty programming, African American South Central residents and politicians needed to consider how the War on Poverty in greater Los Angeles had to establish programs that could benefit a diverse population. The McCone Commission recommended that the African American problems in Los Angeles "apply with equal force to the Mexican Americans . . . whose circumstances are similarly disadvantageous and demand equally urgent treatment." However, both African Americans and Mexican Americans hesitated to craft alliances with each other concerning War on Poverty funds. In 1965 (a few months before the Watts uprising) the County Human Relations Commission reported a high degree of tension between African Americans and Mexican Americans in the city. The study found that only 16 percent of Mexican Americans surveyed supported any type of Black-Chicano coalition.[90]

Chicano youth were wary of aligning with African American civil rights organizations to create interracial antipoverty organizations. According to Rudy Acuña, the War on Poverty encouraged competition between African Americans and Mexican Americans, "each wanting control of their portion of the windfall funds that suddenly came to the communities."[91] The War on Poverty programs were also important sources for community organizing and the "training grounds" for many students to become participants in local community politics. As Mexican American youth became part of the War on Poverty programs, they felt they were "low on the war on poverty agenda."[92]

Congressman Edward Roybal was most vocal about securing War on Poverty funds for East Los Angeles residents. In October 1965, Roybal told OEO that his constituents felt they were not getting "a square deal" from OEO and that the administration had a policy of "Negroes first." He went on to state

that perhaps the Mexican Americans should "riot to get attention." Roybal told
OEO officials that racial conflicts could develop and escalate between African
Americans and Mexican Americans "unless something is done to indicate that
the Mexican American group is getting a good deal." OEO director Sargent
Shriver agreed: "We should be doing much more with Mexican-Americans."[93]
Roybal pointed out that of the thirteen Neighborhood Adult Participation
Project (NAPP) programs in the county, only two served Mexican American
neighborhoods. The purpose of NAPP was to link antipoverty programs to the
grassroots level so that people in poor communities could have a voice in the
War on Poverty rollout. Phillip Montez, a board member of Neighborhood
Centers, whose responsibility was to delegate NAPP posts, argued that Mexican Americans were the "largest minority in the county and the community
[had] not been adequately served."[94] Genuine fears abounded among residents,
who are reported to have said, "We don't want a Watts." Rudy Ramos, the lead
attorney of the GI Forum, complained to the White House that the predominantly Mexican American community of East Los Angeles had lower incomes
than found in the Watts area, yet it had received little War on Poverty funding. In September, the Mexican American Political Association, the League of
United Latino American Citizens, the GI Forum, and the Community Service
Organization wired Sargent Shriver, urging him to investigate the distribution
of programs in Los Angeles. They wanted "to instill in the Mexican-American
community the belief that the Office of Economic Opportunity is really interested in their plight and will correct those inequities" and "bring a halt to the
rising bitter feelings of the Mexican-American in the streets that antipoverty
funds and job opportunities are going principally to Negroes."[95]

The OEO was in large part to blame for the unequal distribution of funds. It
was responsible for breaking the city down into manageable poverty units. The
focus on remedying African American poverty obscured how they envisioned
helping Mexican Americans. In places outside of Los Angeles, the OEO served
the needs of Mexican Americans, but when confronted with a multiracial landscape such as Los Angeles, it was not prepared to divide the city to offer assistance
equally to both groups. The OEO did attempt to create opportunities for Mexican
Americans, but on a much smaller scale than to African Americans.

In the fall of 1966, tensions between African Americans and Mexican Americans over the War on Poverty reached new heights: Opal Jones, the founder of

EOF and director of NAPP, fired Gabriel Yanez, the Mexican American director of a NAPP field office in East Los Angeles. Jones defended her choice to fire him, as she believed that Yanez was contributing to the split between Mexican Americans and African Americans, both within NAPP and in Los Angeles at large. Mexican Americans organized and picketed NAPP offices and criticized both NAPP and EYOA for showing favoritism toward African Americans. Jones eventually offered to divide NAPP programs equally between the two groups. This statement angered many African American NAPP members, who believed that the programs should stay in the community. The pressure to rehire Yanez mounted, and despite his reinstatement, the political damage had been done. Irene Tovar, NAPP director of an outpost in Pacoima (and one of two Mexican American directors), resigned in protest over Yanez's firing and believed "what's good for Watts and the civil rights movement is not necessarily good for the Mexican-American community."[96]

In the wake of the accusations directed at Opal Jones and NAPP about their unwillingness to work with different communities of color, Jones issued the report, "How to Work with People of All Ethnic Groups." In the report, she stated that there has to be a desire to want to work with all ethnic groups first and foremost and proposed a multipoint program to achieve such collaboration.[97] The strategies suggested that "you have to take the time to listen to the people of ethnic groups and hear what they have to say," as listening facilitated the knowledge of the history, facts, and cultural understandings that were considered critical to dismantling stereotypes.[98] One of the key elements of Jones's platform was that one has to "accept the fact that you may be uncomfortable, you may be ill at ease—at times and you may be defensive and wonder why they say negative things and react in a hostile way."[99] Part of the plan highlighted the idea that all ethnic and racial groups will not always agree with suggestions and proposals, and that "people of all ethnic groups have learned about the creative use of conflict. They have learned the pain is a step toward growth and social and institutional change." Jones's report makes an argument that interracial community formation requires work, and that conflict is productive. The initial moments of disagreement and the effort it takes to work through these disagreements are necessary, as the conflict experience offers a "meaningful way to help you foster your growth and increase your understanding towards maturity." The suggestions presented by Jones demonstrate that one cannot take disagreements personally because critiques and discussions are "attack[s] against racism, neglect, exploitation, discrimination, prejudice and hostility." Jones's ten-point plan for working with people of different racial groups is applicable not only to African Americans working with Latina/os but also to communities of color working with white allies, with the plan touching upon alliance creation more generally.

The initial years of the War on Poverty and OEO presence in Los Angeles were characterized by a majority of Mexican American residents living in East Los Angeles and African American residents in South Central Los Angeles. Mexican Americans were not against African Americans creating programs that aimed to alleviate the problems in their communities but were adamant about the equal distribution of funds. What bolstered these racial divisions was the inability of OEO officials to understand fully how Mexican Americans fit into their Black/white paradigm of poverty. In their minds, the impoverished were predominantly African American, but in Los Angeles, this was not the case. The leadership role of African American activists in War on Poverty programming was in large part due to the OEO's receptiveness and expectation that African Americans were the majority of recipients. Beyond the OEO's tenure (1964–1981), the geographical racial divisions quickly diminished between these two groups. Mexican Americans settled in communities outside of East Los Angeles and into South Central. Community organizations that once served the needs of African Americans had to develop a more inclusive notion of community, an issue further discussed in the chapters that follow.

Gordon Mantler's history of the development and rise of the national poverty rights movement discusses the ways that many activist efforts overlapped. He astutely points out that this convergence of activism and poverty meant that for some activists of color the question became how class—poverty—fit into their framing of activism and the struggle for justice and civil rights. Mantler's analysis of inclusive approaches to understanding and pursuing social justice revealed that as activists worked toward a collective notion of justice, they approached a model of activism that accounted for the intersectionality of eradicating racial and class injustice. For example, Reies Tijerina, active in the Chicano movement, noted that "the Black man has his cause and we have ours" but wondered whether "it is the same cause—justice."[100] Tijerina's line of questioning offered an opportunity to ask what "justice" really meant. Justice could become the source for building and developing a multiracial alliance.

In the end, the development of the War on Poverty in Los Angeles broadly, and South Central in particular, required an acknowledgment that both Mexican Americans and African Americans were in dire need of programming to combat poverty. It required that both communities in South Central contend with how economic disinvestment and neglect would have a compounding effect. In addition, it would expect African Americans and, with time, Mexican Americans and Mexican immigrants, to view their experiences as intimately tied to their shared racialization.

It also required them to grapple with the complexity of the ways in which the placemaking and community building born out of racial struggle and pride by early to mid-twentieth-century Black migrants would take on new meanings by the mid-to-late 1960s. The shift in the economic realities of South Central would open the doors to a broader community-based politics that encompasses the needs of the working class, working poor, and poor interracial South Central residents. In the public imaginary, South Central would continue to be seen as a Black enclave; however, as the forthcoming chapters will highlight, African American and Mexican American residents of South Central came to understand the similarity of their working class and working poor realities to create community relationships relationally for a community-based politics that would sustain cross-racial collaboration.

most jargon here, but pretty good at explaining

CHAPTER 2

"LET'S GET THEM OFF
TO A HEADSTART!"
Community Investment in Head Start

IN 1967, Head Start administrators produced a short documentary film titled *Pancho* to demonstrate how Head Start could have a positive impact on the lives of working class children of color.[1] The documentary chronicled the life of five-year-old Mexican American Frank "Pancho" Mansera in the agricultural community of Nipomo, California. It opens with Mercedes and Simon Mansera at the dinner table with their four children, Esperanza, Martha, Agustin, and Pancho. Mercedes describes all her children as independent, yet when discussing Pancho, she talks about him as "different" and says, "[T]here was a time where he wasn't like he was now. He was slow; now he's so active. Won't be still for a minute."[2] As she describes, Pancho was developing much slower than his two-years-younger brother. His younger brother had grown as big as him, as Pancho "was always sick, sick, sick all the time." On a fortuitous day, Mrs. Burt knocked on Mercedes's door. She was a welfare nurse, who urged Mercedes to enroll Pancho in a new summer school program, Head Start. Burt told Mercedes that Pancho "didn't look quite right but [she] couldn't say what it was."[3] Mercedes could not afford private medical attention, but as she learned, part of the Head Start program was a complete physical examination for each child.

The next sequence of the film illustrates Pancho's impoverished home and community. As Mrs. Burt describes, "Children in isolated areas live a dreary life because they live miles away from town" and "They sit out there in the middle of nothing, and nobody cares—[like] many other children that are in desperate need of help, children who have been confined to the rural areas and have been constrained to play with dirt."[4] Images of children, Mexican children, lingering and playing with dirt drive the point home. She goes on to say that the houses are dilapidated and not large enough for the family size, children are sleeping four to a bed and thus not sleeping well, and they are performing poorly in school. "They are the dropouts. They are the ones that end up on the welfare rolls. And they need to be same as the other kids. They deserve to be the same."[5]

Pancho was part of the initial cohort of children enrolled in the program in 1965. In a transitional scene, he and fellow neighbors board a bus on their way to their local Head Start center. Pancho is then shown going through a routine health physical examination with Dr. Tibbs. Shirtless and sitting in the doctor's office like a seasoned pro, Pancho is asked whether he had cleaned his ears and his teeth; he answers in the affirmative. Dr. Tibbs touches Pancho's stomach, at which Pancho breaks into laughter. Dr. Tibbs shares that Pancho had undergone considerable improvement: when they first met, Pancho could not be interested in anything near him. He was also physically bloated in the face and stomach, which Dr. Tibbs diagnosed as a thyroid problem. After treatment, over the course of eighteen months, Pancho went from toddler age to school age. According to Dr. Tibbs, Pancho not only improved because of the medication to treat his condition but also by "continued engagement in a stimulating experience that allowed him to further develop." Achieving stimulation was due to daily participation in Head Start; thus Pancho is then shown playing in the Head Start classroom.

The first visual markers of Head Start's promise in Los Angeles had a similar public depiction of a young Mexican American child gaining confidence from participating in the program.[6] The first day of Head Start classes throughout Los Angeles was July 6, 1965. Jack Jones, *The Los Angeles Times* staff correspondent for the area of South Central, wrote a cover story about the promise of Head Start at Pacific Oaks College in Pasadena. The majority of Pasadena's Head Start students were white, with substantial numbers of African American and Mexican American children.[7] Similar to the *Pancho* documentary, Jones featured a Mexican American child, four-year-old Blanca Castillo, in the story.

He discussed Blanca's initial days at Head Start as marked by her apprehension of mingling with other kids in the playground. For three weeks, she silently participated in Head Start activities and playtime. Many of the teachers attributed her apprehension to the fact that she did not speak English. However, Jones writes, the universal language of laughter with her fellow playmates opened a space for her and her "fellow Spanish-language friends" to come out of their shells and engage in classroom and playground activities. Teachers at the Pasadena Head Start discussed the level of language development going on in the center, with activities centered on play and trust to help non-English speakers such as Blanca engage in class.[8] In many instances, Mexican American children were not as behind as was expected, as they were able to describe objects (for example, if shown a picture of a cow, children would yell *vaca*, the Spanish term for the animal). Unlike other children who were not able to describe the animal, Mexican American children were fully aware of its name and purpose—however, their responses came in the "wrong" language, a "deficiency" that Head Start aimed to correct.[9] It was in instructing Mexican American children to learn English and lose their apprehension about engaging with children who did not speak Spanish that Head Start boasted its most significant and most immediate success (Figure 1).

Figure 1: The *Los Angeles Times*'s coverage of the launching of Head Start in Southern California highlighted the program participation of Mexican American children.
SOURCE: Staff photographer, *Los Angeles Times*, July 25, 1965, copyright 1965. Used with permission.

Blanca's story, like Pancho's, posits a complex narrative of Head Start's origins in the West Coast and Los Angeles. Jones's selection of the Pasadena Pacific Oaks Head Start was strategic in that it showcased the public vision of Head Start's educational promise through the lens of one of the most successfully established centers in Los Angeles. In doing so, he obscured the political battles waged in South Central between Los Angeles Mayor Sam Yorty, U.S. Congressman Augustus Hawkins, and community residents over acquiring funds to establish Head Start centers. Only fifteen miles separate South Central and Pasadena, but such geographic division makes a world of difference in our understanding of the social, political, and economic opportunities in these two communities. On the one hand, Pasadena in the 1960s was a majority-white neighborhood with a small number of African American and Mexican American families. On the other, South Central was overwhelmingly African American working poor and working class. Jones's discussion of Pasadena strategically served to gain support for the program and offered an exciting entry into understanding Head Start's history in Los Angeles. His choice of Blanca's story, "her success," documented how Los Angeles's multiracial landscape opened a space to illustrate the ways in which War on Poverty initiatives served the needs not only of African Americans but also of Mexican Americans.

Jones in the years that followed documented South Central's struggle to implement the program because of lack of classroom space, initial poor class attendance, and political clashes over the distribution of funds—mainly because of the lack of infrastructure. The War on Poverty meant to do "something specific for the children of the poor." Gender, racial, and class discourse about poverty demonized mothers and fathers for "lacking the motivation to get out of poverty," and thus the "cruel legacy of poverty [was seen to be] passed from parents to children."[10] The War on Poverty, and Head Start in particular, utilized reductionist and racially loaded cultural arguments to justify funding—these ideas underlay the logic of the documentary *Pancho*. The cultural arguments for poverty obscured and evaded the real, structural reasons for poverty, and this is the War on Poverty's biggest shortcoming, in that it reduced poverty to personal-familial characteristics that could be changed rather than a real overhaul of structural inequities.

This chapter centers on how the government intervened in the lives of African American and Mexican American children and families through a school-readiness program. The scholarly literature on Head Start has primarily focused on the national political battles for funding, contemporary studies that focus on the success rate of the program, and differences between white and African American children who participated in the program. As discussed in Chapter 1, there were many challenges in setting up War on Poverty programming such as Head Start for low-income families throughout Los Angeles, such as the dispersal of funds by the mayor's office to Mexican Americans and African Americans. The diverse landscape of Los Angeles offers an opportunity to uncover and interrogate how a program such as Head Start managed to transform the lives of children of color. Nationally, the program's readiness mission meant getting children to learn their colors, alphabet, and numbers. However, concerning South Central, Head Start readiness meant much more. It entailed the hard work of getting past the political battles in the mayor's office, getting the actual spaces (classrooms) ready to teach children these necessary skills, and seeing inner city children as children who must not be forgotten. Readiness thus meant a multitude of things and required the vision, execution, and commitment of a multiracial cadre of residents, families, and community activists. Head Start also offers an entry point to uncovering relational community formation and placemaking in South Central, in that it was an institution that outwardly appeared to serve only the needs of African American children and families, whereas in reality, the racial makeup of the community was much more diverse. Exploring the origins of this racial diversity within Head Start and placing it in relation to the creativity needed to build resident commitment for the government-sponsored program allows for a nuanced analysis of how racial misunderstandings and collaboration became part of the implementation of the War on Poverty in Los Angeles. Also, it uncovers how Mexican immigrants and African Americans worked together to create spaces for empowerment and visionary responses to education.

CHILDCARE PROGRAMMING IN THE WAR ON POVERTY

After President Johnson signed the Economic Opportunity Act of 1964 (EOA), it would go on to revolutionize the availability of educational programs for young children. Before its passage, early childhood education was mentioned only briefly during deliberations. Neither Sargent Shriver nor congressional Democrats stressed preschools as a critical component to eradicating poverty.

Maris Vinovskis's *The Birth of Head Start* argues that the key figures in developing Head Start were House Republicans who pressured for early childhood education as part of the poverty discussion.[11] They invited Urie Bronfenbrenner, social psychologist and early childhood education expert, to testify at the House hearings on the EOA. Bronfenbrenner criticized the administration's proposal for targeting assistance to those aged sixteen to twenty-two while ignoring early childhood education. Bronfenbrenner's role meant that Republicans critiqued the Democrats for their initial failure to embrace and acknowledge the need for preschool education.[12]

Educational debates over the costs and benefits of nursery schools were contentious; however, by the mid-twentieth century the promise of what early education could offer made it an acceptable component of education. Kindergarten, then, gradually became incorporated into the public school system.[13] Departing from previous studies about childhood intelligence, scholars such as J. McVicker Hunt and Benjamin S. Bloom argued that a child's intelligence was not fixed at birth or determined by parental intelligence; instead, improving a child's environment could have a significant impact on learning opportunities.[14] Head Start therefore found itself in the middle of debates over the biological versus environmental impact on children's ability to learn.[15] Psychologist Edward Zigler recalls that educators, foundations, and think tanks conducted studies on childhood education on "slum kids" in New York City's Harlem, children in Baltimore, and children in the South.[16] Researchers at the Institute of Developmental Studies of New York Medical College believed that the reason educational efforts failed was because "we start much too late, after the damage is already done . . . [the] environment in which lower-class Negro and white children grow up does not provide the intellectual and sensory stimulus they so desperately need."[17] Researchers were beginning to see the importance of, as well as the financial support for, pilot educational programs targeting preschool-age children. The majority of these programs catered to African American and poor white children. The type of curriculum developed was intended to eliminate the incremental learning inequalities that were the common fate of children who started school so far behind in knowledge and skills that it was difficult for them to catch up without some intervention.

These studies concluded that "overcoming the cultural deprivations of economically disadvantaged children is achieved by developing effective preschool programs."[18] Bronfenbrenner indicated the importance of healthy early childhood thus: "[W]e now have research evidence indicating that the environment of poverty has its most debilitating effect on the very young children in the first few years of life . . . growing up in poverty often means growing up in a situation in which stimulation is at a minimum. What is more, the effect is cumulative, the longer he remains in school, the further he goes."[19] Government officials believed that "children from economically deprived areas traditionally represent the bulk of behavioral and teaching problems in the school system" and the "first five years of life [are] the most critical in the development of personality."[20] To them, the effects of poverty were evident in children's first day of class at Head Start. Teachers reported that many children "hadn't seen common kinds of food, such as pineapples and bananas." Poor children had "never used cut-out scissors, looked at a picture book, or scribbled a crayon, been told a fairy story, painted, and played with a tricycle and toy kitchens."[21] Overall, Bronfenbrenner has held prejudiced beliefs about poor children, yet his views bolstered support for the ways in which early childhood education is vital to developing poor children's opportunities. Bronfenbrenner was not the only one who understood poverty through the lens of cultural deprivation. Daniel Moynihan's and Oscar Lewis's framing of poverty through the lens of cultural and familial pathology had an impact on how theories of cultural deprivation "became the backbone of a series of research projects on poverty and community-based programs" that became seminal to the War on Poverty.[22] Unfortunately, War on Poverty advocates could not work beyond these cultural trappings to understand poverty, and in many ways only reaffirmed the negative perspective of impoverished communities rather than changing how we understood and viewed them. These understandings of poverty obscured how structural and economic inequality contributed to a lack of opportunities and placed the burden of poverty on individuals and families. Low-income families had to find strategic ways to find empowerment in the midst of these racialized ideas of poverty.

As a result of these studies and the enactment of the War on Poverty program, in 1965 Congress passed the Elementary and Secondary Education Act (ESEA), which allocated federal funds for compensatory education programs because "federal policymakers claimed that early childhood education would reduce juvenile delinquency and help lift children out of poverty."[23] Under the ESEA, OEO placed Head Start under the purview of Community Action

Programs (CAPs) delivered by Community Action Agencies (CAAs).[24] Head Start and preschool education programs would have a structured curriculum. Sargent Shriver stressed that Head Start programs needed to provide comprehensive health, social, and educational services. The initial iteration of the program was an educational summer session in which four- to five-year-old children attended Head Start classes the summer before they entered kindergarten. The first two summer-session cycles were "experimental." In 1966, despite reports that questioned the advantages of Head Start, the administration moved from funding the summer program to footing the bill for a full-year program.[25]

It is important to note that in the midst of Head Start's creation, there had been an effort under way by working mothers to establish childcare centers that would help them take care of their children while they sought or were at work. The Lanham Act supported working mothers by providing childcare.[26] Working mothers felt that this was a "greater good to society" and countered conservative resistance to women in the workplace by arguing that childcare allowed mothers to remain self-sufficient and stay off welfare. Cultural arguments about poverty used to support War on Poverty funding fractured what could have been a natural alliance between working mothers, childcare advocates, and Head Start administrators. To make the gulf bigger, Los Angeles Assemblyman Jesse M. Unruh introduced the Unruh Preschool Act to establish a preschool program that was more in line with the constituency that would be served by Head Start. The proposal drew a negative reaction from working mother childcare advocates, as under this act, only children whose parents were on welfare would be eligible. In response to this bill, local legislators, the governor, and other state leaders received countless letters stating that they needed to work toward preserving "'our present wonderful child care program.'"[27] As a Long Beach mother informed Congressman Mervyn Dymally, restricting the program to the Department of Welfare would fundamentally change the centers; she explained that she was "self-supporting and [had] a limited income . . . I would rather pay my weekly fee to the child care center for the type of service I have been receiving for the past year and a half, than pay higher taxes for an inferior service which would have the added stigma of 'welfare' or 'charity' attached to it."[28] She was not alone; in April 1966 Grace J. Angstman wrote a letter to Assemblyman Corley Porter (D-Compton), the South Los Angeles County legislator who had been a vocal supporter of childcare since the late 1940s. Angstman stated that the "unsettling events around here . . . local and national race riots, War on Poverty programs perceived to be prioritizing services for African Americans, and increasingly violent clashes between antiwar demonstrators, the police, and National Guard," angered her as she wondered where "a white, low-income working mother's child care needs fit in this racialized political context." Angstman asked Assemblyman Porter, "Must we desperate parents move to Watts, create a riot, loot, and be directly or indirectly responsible for deaths (and be colored), in order to even be heard, let alone receive any consideration? To date, it appears, unless one breaks the law, gets arrested, causes untold expenses (the National Guard), yet, claims emotional strain—perhaps shoplifts—and makes headlines, he or she cannot be heard . . . if one creates anarchy, the Governor is nothing but sympathetic with 'the plight of the poor people' and the world is their oyster."[29] Although Angstman had benefited from a state-sponsored social program of subsidized childcare, she drew clear distinctions between herself and African Americans who benefited from War on Poverty programs and other forms of government aid. She represented the reaction of many working class white women had who expressed discontent with what War on Poverty funds and programming would mean for their childcare programs.

The discourse on who the War on Poverty beneficiaries were led many childcare practitioners and working mothers to grow hesitant about what this infusion of poverty money would mean for their centers. They worried that working mothers' need for childcare could be eclipsed. Their childhood centers, they feared, would be seen as being utilized by welfare mothers and not working mothers. Working mothers did not want the association of being in desperate need of government assistance. Most working mothers "did not see themselves as fundamentally different from those on welfare (many, in fact, had been forced onto welfare for short periods of time themselves), but they desperately did not want their child care program to be viewed as a welfare service."[30] Laura Briggs astutely argues that even though people of color have never been the majority of welfare recipients, welfare in the latter part of the twentieth century became synonymous with Black women and families.[31] In the letters mentioned above, this sentiment had been visible since the late 1960s and meant that a possible alliance between white working mothers and Head Start advocates did not materialize, the result of a growing stigmatized and racist perception of welfare recipients of being of color and undeserving.

LOS ANGELES HEAD START: OFF TO A GOOD START?

Head Start's establishment in South Central proved extremely difficult and almost impossible. *Los Angeles Times* writer Jack Jones returned to profile Head
Start's promise by showcasing its move from a summer program to a year-round
school-readiness program. This time he spotlighted African American children
in South Central Los Angeles. On September 22, 1966, four-year-old Sammy
Burks began his first day at Head Start at Sacred Heart Catholic Church, one
among many religious institutions that housed Head Start programs in Los Angeles.[32] Like others in the class, Sammy put his paintbrush to paper. He smiled
at his finished purple-and-red work of art. Sammy's teacher, Mrs. Maryanne
Levine (a new Head Start teacher who was also African American), said that
this move from summer to year-round Head Start classes was "going to make
quite a difference. Someone like Sammy will be able to learn to play and go
on to other things rather than being cut off after two months as in the summer programs." She observed that along with the need to be exposed to basic
skills, children needed "more than that, they need the feeling of success . . . to
get over the feeling of failure."[33] In Mrs. Levine's class, "veteran" Head Start
children, children who had been enrolled in the program over the summer but
were not old enough to enter kindergarten, were making her job easier because
they "had taken over the class." Mrs. Levine was counting on the "veterans" to
help with other children "who have never seen crayons or paste before or who
shrank shyly from the overwhelming sight of strange adults and play equipment."[34] The socialization of children into the rigors of becoming good and
ready students as well as the remedying of their "language deficiencies" became
one of Head Start's early achievements.

In the wake of the national passage of the ESEA, Head Start funding was dispersed to delegate agencies under the umbrella of CAPs. CAP officials entrusted
the fate of impoverished children like Sammy to delegate agencies such as the
Los Angeles Chapter of the Urban League, the Los Angeles Alumnae Chapter of
the Delta Sigma Theta Sorority, the Los Angeles Area Federation of Settlements
and Neighborhood Centers, the Parents' Improvement Council, and African
American churches to expose them to essential life tools.[35] A memo between
CAP officials stated that they had to make the tough choice between funding
"only those communities which had an adequate quality of resources (staff and
facilities) and funding communities who displayed intense motivation even

though they might be deficient in quality resources."[36] This readiness mission would prove Head Start's greatest challenge. Head Start decided to offer programs in communities where resources were deficient. During its first summer in 1965, Head Start operated in more than two-thirds of the poorest counties across the nation and received 38 percent of all Community Action Program funding.[37] Priority funding for impoverished communities encouraged African American South Central and Watts residents to form their own delegate agencies to receive federal government antipoverty funds.

Establishing Head Start centers in Los Angeles differed from other communities in the United States, posing its own set of challenges to the school-readiness mission. Poverty in Los Angeles County was not contained to one geographic community or one housing project or one racial group. The communities with the greatest need for War on Poverty programming were in Watts, South Central Los Angeles, and East Los Angeles, areas boasting large working class and working poor African American and Mexican American communities. An issue facing Head Start centers in Los Angeles was how to use similar approaches and curriculum but also adapt them to the community being served. In Los Angeles's Eastside, thousands of children did not speak English when they entered public school or Head Start, a problem that educators felt harmed them socially and psychologically. In South Central, children were living in houses where families had limited literacy due to limited educational opportunities. The geographic sprawl and racial-ethnic diversity of Los Angeles dictated that a flexible curriculum was needed, but at the heart of these different curricula was the need to formulate "appropriate inter-personal experiences" in which "positive feelings must constantly be engendered and reinforced."[38]

Head Start's scheduled classroom operations were from 8:30 a.m. until 12:00 p.m., Monday through Friday. The daily classroom activities and pattern can be seen in Table 1. This classroom schedule was an effort by early childhood educators experimenting with a classroom routine that would offer children the openness to experiment and play but also learn the future demands of being part of a classroom setting.

Establishing delegate agencies to operate Head Start was no easy feat. As previously mentioned, the Pasadena Pacific Oaks College Head Start, one of the best-organized Head Start programs and agencies in Los Angeles, began

8:30–9:00 A.M.	Setting up materials and serving nutrition to each child individually upon arrival
9:00–9:50 A.M.	Pledge of allegiance, singing, roll call, free play, games, painting, cut-and-pasting, science
9:50–10:00 A.M.	Toileting and washing up
10:00–10:15 A.M.	Storytime
10:15–10:50 A.M.	Outdoor activities such as supervised play, group games, watercolor painting, tricycle riding
10:50–11:00 A.M.	Toileting and washing up
11:00–11:30 A.M.	Snack time, discussion emphasizing verbal skills
11:30–11:50 A.M.	Rest time, music
11:50 A.M.–12:00 P.M.	Brief question and answer period for parents, dismissal

Table 1. Head Start Daily Activities Schedule, 1965
SOURCE: "Head Start Report, Spring/Summer 1966," Box 1, Los Angeles Area Federation of Settlement and Neighborhood Centers, Special Collections, University of Southern California, Los Angeles.

reporting progress at a much higher rate than other centers in Los Angeles. Pasadena's Head Start students were African American, Mexican American, and white children.[39] Quarrels and strategic negotiations between Mayor Yorty, Congressman Hawkins, and African American and Mexican American poverty advocates hindered speedy progress in establishing delegate agencies. As these arguments subsided, ten delegate agencies administered 270 Head Start centers throughout Los Angeles and 131 centers in South Central. Every year, these agencies needed to apply for federal and state funds to keep their centers operating. In fall 1965, federal grants approved several antipoverty projects in Los Angeles for $8.2 million. In early 1966, following the suggestions of the McCone Commission and Hawkins's lobbying, the OEO office announced that $4 million in federal monies were approved solely to carry out the most comprehensive Head Start program in Los Angeles. Thus, by 1966, the Head Start centers throughout Los Angeles was serving 8,800 kids, with about sixty community organizations sponsoring Head Start programs. Each Head Start classroom accommodated fifteen children.[40] The level of financial support, number of delegate agencies, and quantity of affiliated centers made Los Angeles the city with the largest Head Start program in the country.[41]

In the first summer of the program's operation, the Urban League served 665 youngsters in twenty-one centers, with a staff of thirty-six teachers, thirty-six teacher aides, thirty-six Neighborhood Youth Corps, and forty-two community volunteers.[42] Most of their initial classes began in housing projects or local churches, with nursery courses involving dancing, games, music, and art. They firmly believed that an "involved, sincere, dedicated classroom" offered a "rare opportunity for concerned people to make a direct, meaningful contribution to youngsters who will face a better life through education."[43]

The Urban League's success in garnering support was an achievement in the midst of incredible odds. They opened centers throughout South Central; however, the location of these Head Start centers raised many concerns. Head Start delegate agencies in South Central did not have the infrastructure to begin instruction in the summer of 1965, nor in the years that followed.[44] Readiness for South Central Head Start's delegate agencies meant finding open, available spaces to set up classrooms for the initial cohort of children enrolled in the program. This feat required ingenuity and creativity. In the initial years of the program, Head Start often operated in church classrooms or makeshift warehouses. The mayor's office often threatened to close these centers because they were not compliant with proper building codes.[45] South Central Head Start advocates never wavered in their commitment to the program, and thus found creative ways to keep Head Start operating despite the less-than-ideal classroom space.

In an oral history, Compton-born and -raised resident Phillipa Johnson warmly remembered her first summer working with Head Start. She was a teacher's aide in 1965 and worked at the center on 120th Street and Main Street. She described the classroom as a big warehouse, with limited windows, lighting, and ventilation—not a building or space readily associated with childhood education. Two "classrooms" were created by using a cardboard partition to divide the big warehouse space. Teachers creatively built bookcases from empty milk cartons and tables from wood lying around the neighborhood. The toys that the children played with were objects found throughout the neighborhood, such as rubber tires.[46] Despite the shortcomings, Phillipa recalls this summer with a particular fondness—it was a transformative moment in her life journey because she felt she was helping build a program from the ground up. The physical, creative, and emotional stress that came from such an unprecedented undertaking was worth it: she saw her young students respond positively to the program.

In response to these shortcomings, the following year's proposal for Head Start centers throughout South Central featured the need for safe play equipment such as jungle gyms, treehouses, balls, beanbags, jump ropes, musical instruments, and dolls. Along with equipment, the coordinators asked for funding to support field trips that included going to the local bakery, a supermarket, a shopping center, a department store, the police and fire departments, parks, a museum, the zoo, the beach, a library, and at least an opportunity to go to Disneyland.[47] Head Start teachers and coordinators believed that exposure to such toys, instruments, and field trips was essential to the creative development of the children. Successfully carrying out the mission of Head Start meant "broadening children's horizons and increas[ing] their understanding of the world in which they live." By exposing children to professionals and taking them on field trips to local museums, the program was providing them "the chance to succeed, develop a climate of confidence, increase the ability to get along with others in [their families], plan activities which allow groups from varying social, ethnic, and economic levels to join together with those of limited income in the solving of community problems."[48]

ENROLLMENT AND DIVERSITY IN HEAD START

Along with makeshift classrooms and tools, Head Start centers needed to convince South Central residents to enroll their children in the program—again, a challenge delegate agencies did not account for in their planning and implementation of the program. The general distrust of communities of color for government programs and assistance was commonplace; thus, the delegate agencies administering the program, along with residential community activists, had to "sell" the promise of what this program could bring to their children and families. These delegate agencies drafted flyers, mailers, and advertisements in the African American–run newspaper—*The Los Angeles Sentinel*—in hopes of getting South Central residents interested and inquiring about Head Start. Newspaper headlines that declared, "Let's Get Them Off to a Headstart!" were followed by statements that discussed how "admission to the program was not based on race, religion, national origin or color . . . it was designed for families with incomes of less than $4,000 annually, with the goal of the program to help both the child and his family to gain greater confidence, self-respect, and dignity."[49] Articles featured in the *Los Angeles Sentinel* and *Los Angeles Times* served not only to bolster financial support for the program but also to convince residents of the program's promise and rid it of the social stigma attached to government-supported programs.

Residents in South Central rallied for the need to establish a Head Start center in many of the housing projects throughout the community. Many local Head Start reports suggested that for real success, they needed to "enlist the enthusiasm and interest for the program" from parents and residents and also "encourage and develop the leadership of these groups in order that they may become self-sustaining." Ernestine Fitzhugh, director of the Parents' Improvement Council, worked closely with a core group of African American residents of Watts and South Central to launch a Head Start center in the Jordan Downs Housing Projects. The Parents' Improvement Council was located in the heart of Watts and served the needs of Watts, South Central, Bell, and Huntington Park residents. In and of themselves, these communities would undergo a tremendous racial and ethnic change in the wake of the Watts uprising.

Community residents such as Fitzhugh used the newspaper articles as a starting point to populate the Head Start center at Jordan Downs. She supplemented such advertising by actively canvassing the community through door-to-door efforts to locate the children most in need of Head Start and to promote the program.[50] Fitzhugh wrote to Congressman Hawkins to tell him about her recruitment concerns and express that those who joined Head Start during the first summer were "brave little children." She was proud of high enrollment because at the beginning of the summer the Head Start center she operated had been only half full (with about six children), but by the end of the summer, more and more parents had enrolled their children in the program.[51] As the summer wore on, parents who initially claimed they did not have any four-year-old children when teachers went knocking on their doors suddenly appeared to register their children. Word of mouth that started with families participating in the program made other community residents reconsider. Many initially believed that Head Start was a free babysitting service, but "they saw the progress their children were making in the program, thus, they took a second look." As one resident, Ethel Taylor, said, "[I]t has been inspiring, adventurous and educational for my little girl, Sabrina Taylor."[52] Building a program that showed children's progress in a few short weeks was no easy feat. The level of commitment by Fitzhugh, and other community activists like her, speaks to the emotive landscape of support Head Start had in the community from the beginning. Fitzhugh's uphill battle would disprove the myth that poor residents are ready prime users for social services, and showed that building support for an institution like Head Start would take work and vision and add to the labor of resident placemaking in the community.

By September 1965, the Parents' Improvement Council was serving two thousand children across Los Angeles. Table 2 illustrates the racial demographics of its five Head Start centers in Watts and South Central.

CENTER	NEGROES	SPANISH AMERICAN	CAUCASIAN	ORIENTAL	TOTAL
117th Street Center	35	8	2	0	45
Palm Lane Center	60	0	0	0	60
120 Avalon	109	11	0	0	120
West Adams	26	30	4	0	60
Jordan Downs	110	20	0	5	135
Total	340	69	6	5	420

Table 2: Parents' Improvement Council Head Start Centers, 1965
SOURCE: "Head Start Reports," n.d., Box 94, Collection 1642, Augustus F. Hawkins Papers, 1935–1990, Department of Special Collections, Young Research Library, University of California, Los Angeles.

The West Adams location served more Mexican American children and families than any other Head Start center. This was mainly because of its location, as residential address determined attendance and participation. The West Adams location was further northeast than the center of South Central Los Angeles. West Adams also emerged as an affluent white suburb in the early twentieth century, but as Los Angeles expanded further west, white flight transformed West Adams. From the 1920s onward, middle-class and affluent African Americans moved into the West Adams community, and these demographics came to define it. That the Parents' Improvement Council in West Adams served a slight majority of Mexican American families illustrates that while the West Adams region was a majority–African American community, the residents who needed Head Start services were most prominently Mexican

Americans. This might be attributable to the financial guidelines set by Head Start centers: the majority of the children served had to come from impoverished backgrounds, thus foreclosing the possibility for more substantial participation among middle-class African Americans in the area. In addition, the West Adams location was adjacent to the area in South Central that was closest to downtown Los Angeles, a region of South Central that in 1965 boasted a sizable Mexican population of 17 percent.[53]

In the 1960s, the diverse racial character of the Jordan Downs Head Start program reflected the character of public housing writ large. Public housing provided working class families with desirable housing options, as they often featured beautiful personal gardens and front lawns. These well-built and racially integrated housing units offered children safe space to "encounter one another" in an "often convivial atmosphere."[54] From its inception, public housing was clean, comfortable, safe, and racially integrated. These were temporary housing options for people trying to pursue private homeownership. According to historian Josh Sides, by the late 1940s and early 1950s, as veterans, whites, and Asians moved out, "more poor Black families moved in and stayed for longer terms" because they were "unable to afford private housing" due to limited economic options.[55] Many African American families found public housing to be their only alternative. In 1947, African Americans represented less than 30 percent of public housing tenants, but by 1959 they accounted for 65 percent. The proportion of Mexican Americans also rose, though not as dramatically as African Americans, from 15 to 19 percent.[56]

Jordan Downs in Watts was converted to public housing between 1953 and 1955 and quickly became seen as a "self-contained ghetto in which the worst effects of segregation life—including racial isolation, overcrowding, crime, and frustration—were highly concentrated."[57] By the time Head Start opened in Jordan Downs, the complex was racialized as "solidly Black."[58] The Parents' Improvement Council served a majority–African American population; however, as indicated in Table 2, it still had to consider and tailor its instruction to Mexican Americans and Asian Americans who were not the majority, but were still part of the program. Head Start centers demonstrated that in the years leading up to the massive influx of Mexican immigrants across Los Angeles, such social services had to be savvy about how to train their teachers, organizers, and administration on how to work with diverse communities—an issue that would prove all the more crucial by the 1980s and which is discussed in Chapter 5.

While offering an opportunity for cross-racial collaboration, the diversity in Los Angeles also opens the possibility for racial tensions and misunderstandings. Alexander Yeh, an Asian American Los Angeles resident, moved his way up within the Parents' Improvement Council's Head Start organization. He developed the dual role of Head Start teacher and accountant for the centers. In the summer of 1967, Alexander became the Parents' Improvement Council project director, replacing Ernestine Fitzhugh. In that summer, he was very active in organizing a benefit show at the Memorial Sports Arena in South Central, from which all the proceeds went to supply the Improvement Council's Head Start centers with furniture, school supplies, and toys for the children.[59] His participation also opened the door for a transnational relationship between Los Angeles and China. This partnership, while short-lived, showed how racial diversity within these programs served as a precursor to the celebratory narrative of inclusion that would later shape the greater Southern California area. Yeh's efforts made him both locally and nationally recognized as an asset to the Parents' Improvement Council, and the organization received recognition from the OEO in DC for its tremendous growth and development.

Head Start parents revered Yeh's efforts; however, in the summer of 1969, there was some outrage over Yeh's decision to close a class in South Central and open one in Chinatown. Yeh defended his choice to close down one of the two classes operating at the Head Start center on 114th Street and Wilmington Avenue on the grounds of poor attendance.[60] Teachers, staff, and parents across South Central in turn defended Yeh, pointing out that he had been "selfless and had dedicated himself to a cause he believed in." One South Central resident and mother added, "Mr. Yeh has worked for several months without pay to make this program go and these few people who want to attack him should be ashamed of themselves because this man has made a definite contribution to the community." Augustus Hawkins also expressed his support for Yeh's efforts throughout Head Start in Los Angeles. One observer of the critique against Yeh said, "[I]t seems a shame that three teachers and three parents could raise this hell."[61]

The attack on Yeh and the Parents' Improvement Council appeared to be racially motivated. As director of the council, Yeh had been working within the community without problems for over four years. It was when he decided to open a Head Start program in Chinatown, well within the council's boundaries, that allegations of racial favoritism and racism emerged. Yeh's racial identity had been overlooked by many residents until then. Some residents seemed to view Yeh's choice as a racial preference rather than a strategic choice of where he could maximize limited resources and reach the greatest number of children and families. This is the reality of interracial interactions; they occur within the context of diminished resources and opportunities.

The Parents' Improvement Council was open to hiring a non–African American director for its program at a time during which most directors for delegate agencies in South Central and Watts were African American. It was especially groundbreaking to have an Asian American leader within a predominantly African American, and increasingly Mexican immigrant, service area. Shortly after the allegations, Yeh left his post as director of the Parents' Improvement Council. His story and involvement with Head Start in South Central and Watts and what transpired illustrate the power that community residents and parents have within Head Start and demonstrate that the leadership of Head Start delegate agencies and centers needs to be attentive to the needs, demands, and concerns of their constituencies and the perception of choices in the context of scarce resources.

Yeh's leadership of the council also serves to remind us that while South Central's community was majority Black, there were children and families of Latina/o, Asian, and white descent in the community as well as in Head Start classrooms. People of different racial backgrounds were neighbors and used the same social services as early as the mid-1960s. The trials of developing a program from the ground up, when resident and parent involvement is key, demonstrate the ways in which relational community formation is dynamic and can lead to racial tension.

"THERE ARE CHILDREN HERE"

For Head Start officials and advocates, the ability to offer children a safe, clean, and educational environment in which to develop their cognitive and social skills is essential and at the core of the school-readiness mission. By participating in Head Start, children learn the alphabet and numbers, they overcome shyness and the fear of being away from parents, they cooperate and share, and they learn the basic routines of school. Yearlong participation helps to instill in children the love of learning and reading.

A 1965 study conducted by the Southern California Permanente Medical Group documents how impressionable and knowledgeable young children are when it comes to their surroundings. The study aimed to investigate how children perceive and react to "intense disorganization or threat in the physical and social environment."[62] Most studies up to that point had focused on the emotional effects of children in the aftermath of a natural disaster, but there were very few studies on social upheavals like the Watts uprising. The psychiatrists conducting this particular study decided to interview Head Start children right after the curfew was lifted to get the immediate reaction of children aged four to five years old who resided in or close to the riot area. They interviewed 107 African American, 23 Mexican American, and 52 white children (the white children were a control group from nursery schools in Los Angeles, not the Watts neighborhood) in five- to ten-minute semistructured interviews.[63] The interview questions centered on how the children felt during those days, whether they were aware of what was going on, what they saw, their perception of what people were reacting to, and what should happen to those who rioted. The results illustrated that irrespective of race, all children were aware of what was going on. Of course, African American children responded with much more detail, fear, and anxiety regarding the events that transpired. The white children were quick to demonize and blame the African American community for the uprising, as they explained that it was the Blacks' desire to be equals with whites that caused the uprising. Conversely, African American children expressed that in those stressful days they were "scared they would start [their] house on fire." One child stated,

> They burned my house up. Daddy took us all out. People took things out of stores . . . my dog got loose; he's way off. I was scared at night. We slept in old Mr. Jones's house. . . . I saw big men break in places. They burned Steve's house. They burned my things, burned my TV, burned my toys.[64]

Another shared,

> I saw people taking food from stores and I heard guns. I was afraid. They were shooting guns at night so I couldn't sleep and I was afraid they would stick the guns at night so I couldn't sleep. So I slept with my mother. A store close to my house was burning. They were lighting matches and breaking windows and I thought the whole world was burning.[65]

African American children expressed a great sense of imminent threat. Their level of fear and angst must be taken seriously because at an early age children are cognizant of what is happening around them. Unlike their white peers, who learned of the uprising from a distance, Black children witnessed burning buildings close to their homes—often, right next door. They could not ignore what was going on around them. Children at times could not fully grasp the complexity of what was occurring, why people were taking to the streets, but they could process the immediate fear of someone with a firearm coming to their homes or burning their homes. These fears, while couched within the prism of a particular event, have long-lasting repercussions concerning how children understand communities and neighborhoods.

The responses of Mexican American children to the Watts uprising expressed the tense relations between African American and Mexican Americans in the area. The researchers asked Mexican American children whether they knew who participated in the uprising. Two-thirds of the children expressed "hostility or some negatively stereotypic attitude toward the rioters and Negroes in general."

INTERVIEWER: Who did the fighting?
MEXICAN AMERICAN CHILD: Black people.
INTERVIEWER: Why did they do that?
MEXICAN AMERICAN CHILD: Because they were colored.
INTERVIEWER: Why were they mad?
MEXICAN AMERICAN CHILD: Because they like to burn everything.[66]
Another Mexican American child was asked, "Who was fighting?"
MEXICAN AMERICAN CHILD: Negroes.
INTERVIEWER: Why did they do that?
MEXICAN AMERICAN CHILD: Negroes fight. Just fight because they are Negroes. Negroes just fight.[67]

According to the researchers, these sentiments were dangerous because they expressed a "uniformly hostile-fearful attitude towards Negroes, amounting to a sub-cultural stereotype that Negroes are by nature bad and violent. There are important, and unhappy, implications when a stereotype like this appears so clearly by the age of four or five."[68] These sentiments illustrate both the dangers of living in poverty: African American children expressed genuine fear and concern, while

Mexican American children expressed overtly racist sentiments about African Americans. Mexican American children's racial understandings are a reflection of their parents or elders, and therefore work must be done to educate parents to resist passing on racist ideas to their children. The prospects of future cooperation and understanding between these two groups could start to look dim. However, Head Start programs in Los Angeles—because of its diversity—can assist in dispelling negative racial stereotypes of Mexican Americans and African Americans. Placing Mexican American children in classrooms with African American children increases interaction at a very young age, so Head Start is a place where intergroup relations can and must be, improved. Similarly, the multiracial classroom and space can also serve as an entry point for parents to engage with other parents of different racial backgrounds. Exchange and interaction have the potential to complicate these devastating racist ideas of each other.

This study proved that despite adults' belief that children are "ignorant" and "unfazed" by crises, children as early as preschool age are aware of and affected by social and physical realities. They are also painfully aware of how race operates in social life, as African American children expressed feelings of racially motivated rejection. Head Start offers an environment in which children can engage with children of different racial backgrounds as well as one that attempts to help them begin to navigate their social and economic surroundings. The creation of interracial spaces for children is important because limited economic opportunities, poor-quality schools, and very few afterschool programs have made it difficult for children and youth to avoid violence.

This chapter began by discussing the documentary "Pancho," a film that documented Head Start's promise as well as a larger conversation as to who benefited from War on Poverty funds on the West Coast. President Johnson attended the documentary screening in Washington, D.C., in 1967. Pancho and his mother met the president at the screening as Pancho received the "National Head Start Child of the Year" award (Figure 2).[69] Using Pancho's experience to raise awareness about this program was striking, as the research to support Head Start programming to that point was based on African American children, and the written promotional literature on Head Start largely showed African American children's families. The documentary showed that the beneficiaries of Head Start were not just African American but also Mexican American.

Head Start offers children an opportunity for a childhood, despite its pitfalls of representing the lives of low-income families as lacking stimulation, being "in

Figure 2: Pancho Celebration. On March 13, 1967, U.S. President Lyndon B. Johnson celebrated Frank "Pancho" Mansera for having received the "National Head Start Child of the Year" award in a highly publicized award ceremony in Washington, D.C.
SOURCE: White House Photo Office Collection, Lyndon Baines Johnson Library and Museum, Austin, Texas.

the middle of nothing," having a "dreary life," and likely to be on the "welfare rolls." In fact, the documentary uses the language of the culture of poverty that says poor communities of color are deficient and transmit these ideals generationally, and it does not provide analysis of the economic barriers for better life opportunities. It illuminates why and how mothers of color would have reservations in supporting the poverty program by showing how Pancho's mom, Mercedes, was cautious when opening her home to Mrs. Burt. Unlike the narrative that working class and impoverished communities are ready primed for social services, one element that played a role in the difficulty of establishing centers throughout South Central was that the program had to sell the ways participation would offer children physical, mental, and social development.

Investigating Head Start's beginning in South Central reveals multiple layers of activism beyond a sole understanding of Black and Mexican American relations as tense within the War on Poverty. In fact, the program's origins are much more complicated, and they center on the ways in which South Central delegate agencies had to work creatively to secure funding and bolster support in the program. It was a community effort from the ground up. Community residents, both African

American and Mexican American, were part of this collective effort, an effort that required heart and ingenuity in the midst of uncertainty and racial diversity.

Developing and operating this program required an emotive backdrop of creativity and negotiation by delegate agencies, advocates, and Head Start parents. At every turn, they had to strategically problem solve to cope with political battles in the mayor's office and threats of closure because of inadequate classroom space. They had to convince parents to enroll their children in a government program that people knew very little about. They had to acquire and apply the tools necessary for classroom instruction. As the personal letters attest, even as contested as the ideal of safe childhood is, children and their parents expressed that the program was a transformative moment because children became vocal, open, and playful, and—most especially—felt loved by their teachers. These positive appraisals by parents and children would characterize Head Start in the decades that followed, demonstrating how it became a crucial institution in the community. Chapter 5 focuses on how formative it was to reach out and train teachers from South Central. The program served not only children but also parents who became teachers, teaching aides, and engaged parents. Active parent involvement in Head Start would also embolden a relational community formation that began in Head Start classrooms and extended to South Central's city streets.

This chapter has aimed to illustrate how investigating Head Start opens a space to see the implementation of the War on Poverty as not fitting neatly within solely tension or cooperation narratives. At times, interracial collaboration was difficult, because the scarcity of resources and trials of starting a new program mediated these relationships. Presenting Mexican American children as public examples of Head Start's potential challenges the notion that Black children were the primary beneficiaries of War on Poverty funds and programming. Both locally and nationally, the participation of Mexican American families in Head Start was pivotal to the program's image and support. Uncovering Head Start's beginnings in South Central offered an opportunity to explore the multiracial dynamics and realities of the War on Poverty, and the nascent building of relational community formation.

CHAPTER 3

"THE WAVE OF THE FUTURE"

The Emergence of Community Health Clinics

IN MAY 1966, Leonard Deadwyler, a twenty-five-year-old Watts resident, was caught speeding and running red lights while trying to get his pregnant wife to the hospital. The nearest hospital was twenty miles away. As he was speeding through Watts's city streets, he was pulled over by police officers. He believed they were there to help. Instead, Los Angeles police officer Jerold Bova pointed his gun at Leonard and shot him point blank. As Leonard slumped over and died on his wife's lap, he said, "But my wife is having a baby."[1] City officials feared that this incident would have violent consequences—that people would take to the streets and another Watts uprising would ensue. Residents did not take to the streets as they had done nine months prior, but Deadwyler's death served as another example of state-sanctioned violence: by police, against African American residents. This tragedy, many community residents believed, could have been avoided if there had been a hospital conveniently located in the community.

The Deadwyler incident made community residents and activists painfully aware that the lack of health care providers in the area not only was affecting the physical health of residents but also could lead to death. To many, Leonard was not at fault because he was trying to get his wife to the hospital for her delivery; instead, the state and federal governments were to blame because they were unable or unwilling to understand and satisfy the needs of the community. The lack of proximity of the hospital was not the only issue plaguing Watts residents, who believed "a trip to a county hospital or clinic can be an exasperating, infuriating thing . . . first, there's the condescending attitude of those at the reception desks, and then, a long wait, maybe of three, four or five hours, only to be told to come back when they were sicker." Community residents waited until they were "ten dollars sick" before making trips to the hospital.[2] The fact that sick people had to make these decisions demonstrates the gravity of the problem: one of access as well as what kind of treatment they would receive when seeking those services.

In the wake of the Watts uprising, findings from the 1965 McCone Commission showed that only 106 doctors were available to serve the community of 252,000. There was an alarmingly small number of hospital beds—454—available in the whole area. The commission's findings stressed emphatically "the need to create a new, comprehensively equipped hospital as the other major public hospitals, County General and Harbor General, are distant and difficult to reach particularly given the degree to which the Watts area is underserved by public transportation."[3] The president's task force on the Watts uprising also acknowledged that South Central residents had some of the worst health indexes concerning childhood diseases and adult mortality. The "death rate was about 22 percent higher than that for the remainder of the city" and "death rates among infants in the area were about 40 percent higher, fetal deaths 49 percent higher, and neonatal deaths 37 percent higher than the rest of the city."[4] The real incidence of disease may well have been greater than that reported in the statistics. Low-income families' limited access to medical facilities restricted their contact with physicians and other medical personnel. Recommendations from the report were to create new programs in maternal and child health, venereal disease control, tuberculosis, and chronic disease control and the strategic expansion of medical school facilities and clinics throughout the area to help low-income residents and families. Bringing health clinics and a hospital to the community proved a challenge for activists, residents, and city planning officials, who knew all too well that "nothing comes easy down here."[5] Community activists were encouraged to work toward this goal, as it was not just a matter of creating available health options, but also that the operation of such institutions would significantly expand job opportunities.

This chapter uncovers the dynamic relationship between residents, medical advocates, and elected officials in the struggle for a hospital and government-supported community clinics that provided comprehensive health care in South Central. The historiography on Los Angeles's War on Poverty efforts has mostly focused on the struggle for employment, education, and community empowerment without much attention to health equity. South Central residents and their health allies invested in combating poverty worked toward establishing health centers in the community.

War on Poverty funds provided crucial financial support for the development of community health centers and a hospital in the area. The approach used by community health center advocates was to connect health care funding with economic development and job creation for the community. Nonetheless, discursive community control is easier said than done. The struggle of South Central and Watts residents for community control of health clinics was arduous because it rested on their opposition to medical teaching institutions such as USC and UCLA and conservative government officials, all of whom potentially could have played roles in these health care centers. The level of community control was of utmost concern and has been a source of tension in the discussion of Office of Economic Opportunity (OEO) programs and centers. As was the case with Head Start advocates, establishing and gaining community trust would require work. South Central and Watts residents were extremely wary of becoming patrons of clinics operated by the government and the state because of the long history of unethical and discriminatory practices toward people of color at the hands of medical officials. Implementing the goal of preventive health care through regular medical visits and practices also would have its challenges.

The activism of health care advocates opened a possibility for impoverished residents of South Central, both Black and Latina/o, to have some access to health care options. However, as with everything afforded to impoverished communities of color, and despite activists' best efforts, budget cuts would always leave health care options vulnerable, and at times unable to meet the underlying demand of dignified care. It is in this contested reality of health care that African American and Mexican immigrant patrons in South Central have had to learn to navigate these institutions as best they could. Muted interracial interactions and relations in the waiting rooms of health centers reflects the reality that their experiences are born out of similar treatment and struggle, while both groups continue to seek superior, dignified, and equitable health services.

THE URBAN HEALTH CRISIS

In the 1960s and 1970s, concerns over health care access gained national attention. Locally, the Deadwyler incident, the McCone Commission, the Watts uprising, and the availability of War on Poverty funds through the Office of Economic Opportunity spurred activism to secure financial, political, and social resources for a hospital.[6] Residents and advocates believed that disease accounted for the "deepest problems of the impoverished persons in the center of the Negro area," yet the deep-seated interest in public health did not sideline the struggle for fair employment and housing options.[7] Dr. Hubert Hemsley of Compton argued that the African American community was in the "throes of the problem of our century—the urban health crisis" and believed that "the focal point of training should be community medicine with stress on the total community, rather than isolated observation training in clinics."[8] Following such an approach would mean that U.S. medicine would no longer be "mismatched with the lifestyles of the ghetto poor."[9]

In fall 1966, resident Mrs. Charles Zanders wrote to U.S. Congressman Augustus Hawkins in support of a hospital and community clinics:

> I have been a taxpayer in Watts for years and am strongly opposed to USC using poverty money to build and operate a clinic in our area for tutorial purposes. I do not feel that a private school should compete with our own doctors. Furthermore, Watts needs a hospital not a ghetto type clinic. County facilities have expanded enough in the Watts area to take care of the clinic type patients. If there is a need for a clinic, let our community run it with the help of other medical schools including USC, if they wish to help.[10]

Community residents, along with political official Augustus Hawkins, collectively organized to establish a hospital in Watts and clinics in South Central. Also, Dr. J. Alfred Cannon, associate director of social psychiatry at the University of California, Los Angeles, and members of People in Community Action (PICA, a coalition of seventy-five organizations in Los Angeles) organized the

effort to begin construction of a county hospital in the Watts area. The organization was an interracial coalition of African American, white, and Mexican
American residents and health care advocates who wanted to "shake the power
structure" as well as "get a more adequate representation of the poor on the poverty board."[11] PICA organizers were firm believers in the power of community
residents to create their vision of what the hospital should look like and what
services it should prioritize and offer. They urged for the employment of African
American architects to draw up plans for the hospital. In Cannon's estimation,
it was not enough to have a hospital: "[I]t could be an adequate physical facil-
ity and yet provide the worst of medical care. . . . [T]here are too many hospitals where the attitudes of those staffing it are so poor, that the public would
rather stay home ill than suffer from the poor medical practice." For Cannon,
PICA activists, and community residents, what was of equal importance to the
physical building of the hospital was that the establishment would be a "place
where the poorest and most humble can be treated with respect and feel they
belong"; it should be a "hospital where Negroes and other minority doctors of
excellence have positions of responsibility." The hospital and health care centers
would constitute a way to "rise out of the ashes of Watts."

Community health centers became part of the national landscape in 1965
through the availability of War on Poverty funds. President Johnson passed
government-sponsored health insurance for the elderly and disabled by establishing Medicare and Medicaid when he passed the Social Security Act. This
legislation enlarged the government's role in health care and other social welfare
programs.[12] The debates surrounding health care policy in the late 1960s and
1970s were preoccupied with the task of how to best provide for the medical
needs of the poor and elderly. For decades, the American Medical Association
had successfully "lobbied against plans to establish any form of national health
insurance," but Democratic legislators' "moral leverage (and a congressional
majority in 1964) resulted in the passage of the legislation that created the
Medicare program."[13] Bundled into this legislation was Medicaid, a federally
funded program that provided health care services for those living in poverty,
irrespective of age.[14]

The OEO's initial goals to combat poverty did not place health as an essential feature—it prioritized employment and educational training. However, the
health problems of Head Start children (and the strides being made by Head

Start children through sustained health attention) alerted OEO officials to the need for health programs serving not only children but also their families. The experimental health clinics established in Head Start centers served as "feelers" for approaches to providing health services.[15]

The experimental nature of community health centers meant that the number of centers rapidly increased. In 1966 Congress enacted Johnson's Comprehensive Health Planning and Public Health Services Amendments, which created a partnership for health as an "appropriate and necessary response to the Nation's desire for excellence in health care."[16] By 1971, 150 health centers served cities across the United States. In 1974, Senator Ted Kennedy introduced a bill that would guarantee that the federal and state governments were responsible for providing funds to community health programs. It also mandated that all centers have consumer-majority governing boards, meaning a strong commitment to citizen participation. By 1974 there were 158 grantees nationwide, and in 1980 there were 872 centers. More people received help with this growth, yet most of these centers were small. It was evident that more needed to be done. Per War on Poverty VISTA volunteer Dan Hawkins's assessment of community health centers, "We grew low and slow, under the radar . . . until we were big enough to make our presence known."[17] In the 1960s, community health meant a series of experimental programs, but in the present, these experimental programs have real consequences to the operations of services rendered. Debates surround the differences between public health and community health, with the former being more top-down in approach and the latter driven by residents; in either case, health resources that cater to the community remain of the utmost importance.[18]

The ultimate goal of government-sponsored community health centers on the local level was to have spaces in which "modern science was replete with the most advanced specialty services" and to place them in neighborhoods that had been medically abandoned, with very few doctors available for everyday needs, and where the most elementary public health and preventive care was frequently unavailable. Health care became a symbol of the continuing inequalities in American life. The most-needed measures for health equity were as follows: "[to] provide services when people can take advantage of facilities, [and to ensure] clinics have extended hours, including evenings and weekends, and will be located where the people live. Mobile units will also be employed to take 'health to the people.' "[19] According to a Los Angeles County Health Department report in 1965, the OEO prioritized seven areas for health programs: comprehensive health/neighborhood health, family planning, emergency food and medical services, environmental health, narcotics addiction, alcohol control, and the other community health services.[20]

The OEO believed that the health task force and personnel were most "noteworthy" in the sense that "federal funds have armed an angry, underserved minority community of a major urban area with the tools to effectively negotiate with a series of insensitive providers and governmental bureaucracies with the skill and the methods to document inequities and in-house articulate spokesmen to argue for responsible redress."[21] It is this mismatched narrative that framed the OEO's role in funding community projects. On the one hand, the organization wanted to provide the resources and support for community residents to assert their rights and needs, but on the other, it describes the very people it aims to help as "angry." It was the OEO and political officials' understanding of their role as benevolent in helping the "underserved" that became a source of tension between community residents, doctors, and government officials in South Central and Watts.

The economic and geographic barriers present significant challenges for disadvantaged groups wanting to access health care services in Los Angeles. Public Law 93-641—Appropriateness of Recommended Geographic Regions for Health Planning and Resources Development—required that each health service provider have a population of not less than five hundred thousand or more than three million for each emergency health care provider and neighborhood clinic.[22] The sprawl of Los Angeles County meant that executing this law would prove difficult, as a comprehensive and expensive transportation system was not in place. OEO officials knew that the most indigent of residents were the disabled, mothers with small children, and the economically disadvantaged. Plans for the location of these clinics and services required that the following issues be accounted for, along with the existence of a full-service teaching hospital: the health needs of the population, community interest, natural and human-made geographic barriers, and municipal boundaries.[23] Executive director Frank F. Aguilera wrote a letter to assistant OEO deputy director Saleem A. Farag in which he stated, "Los Angeles County by virtue of the fact that it is . . . a standard metropolitan area, automatically is exempt from the maximum population limit of three million imposed by public law, and will become by far the most populous health service area in the United States."[24] Farag believed that to best serve the health needs of the residents of Los Angeles County required breaking the county into designated areas, with South Central and Watts residents occupying the southeast and central regions. By 1970 the population in these areas, according to health officials, was as depicted in Table 3.

	WHITE	BLACK	SPANISH	OTHER
SOUTHEAST	313,748 (41 percent)	303,482 (40 percent)	129,966 (17 percent)	17,761 (2 percent)
CENTRAL	446,660 (36 percent)	288,208 (23 percent)	408,955 (33 percent)	95,591 (8 percent)

Table 3: Southeast and Central Regional Population, 1970
SOURCE: "OEO Health Task Force," 1965, Box 2, Entry 70, Record Group 381, Community Action Program, National Archives and Records Administration, College Park, Maryland.

The large percentage of whites in the Southeast and Central regions is because these geographic areas cover South Gate, Downtown L.A., and East Los Angeles. This table demonstrates how the county health commissioners set boundaries to disperse health care funds, with the urban health crisis in Los Angeles having an impact on not only African American residents but also a diverse grouping of people.

COMMUNITY HEALTH CLINICS:
THE WAVE OF THE FUTURE

In 1967, the OEO supported the opening of the South Central Multipurpose Health Services Center (SCMHSC) to provide accessible health care options for South Central residents. To build SCMHSC required that five local construction companies cooperate, with the labor coming from local residents. This health center was one of the first forty-four centers built with War on Poverty funds.[25] On the clinic's opening day, September 16, 1967, Sargent Shriver (director of the OEO) attended the dedication services. In his speech he stated,

> Change is coming. The same change that has come to Watts. Not because of
> programs but because of people. Not because of committees, but because of

commitment. For too long, the poor have looked around and asked: "Where is this life we are guaranteed?" They haven't seen it. Instead of being guaranteed life, the poor get a guarantee of death. Not a quick, violent murder. But a slow, quiet death that whittles away life. This is why the OEO is in the business of delivering health services—because health is basic to everything. Health is one of the surest guarantees of "life, liberty, and the pursuit of happiness." This health center in Watts is your answer. You want a commitment to live. A life where good health is not a lucky privilege for a few. But a basic right for all.[26]

Shriver's speech was indicative of how health equity was, in fact, a social justice issue that needed immediate attention, support, and action. Health care is an essential service for everybody, and without it, the poor are vulnerable to slow death. With such ardent support by the OEO director, the clinic opened to serve the needs of poor residents of Watts.

A year after the opening, more than twelve thousand patients registered at the clinic, and it became one of the first antipoverty clinics sponsored, with a $2.4 million grant from the OEO. The large enrollment signaled how many medical services at the community level were sorely lacking. The clinic was a "radical experiment in the health care of the poor. . . . [C]hampions hail the center as a shining example of what interracial cooperation can do to help underprivileged people."[27] The area immediately surrounding the clinic in Watts was composed of fifty-eight thousand residents, of which thirty-five thousand were on welfare. The initial surge of twelve thousand patients meant that less than one-fourth of the resident population was being served—most alarming in a severely depressed area with a high rate of maternal deaths, premature births, infant mortality, tuberculosis, high blood pressure, heart disease, sickle cell anemia, and lung cancer.[28] The tuberculosis death rate was 4 per 100,000 persons, compared to 2.8 for the county. SCMHSC wanted to combat this, and other health issues, head-on. The OEO knew that opening a health center would not eliminate poverty because other factors contributed to the level of poverty; however, through the funding of the SCMHSC, the OEO wanted to foster and create a model that would change how health care was administered and provided for impoverished communities.

Opening SCMHSC and describing it as a modern health center would remove it from the category of charity medicine. However, like many social

providers supported by the OEO, SCMHSC relied on renewal grants, and its
supporters were afraid that the OEO's commitment to the clinic could be removed at any moment, despite the fact that the clinic had been heralded as the
"wave of the future" and set the standard for dignified care for impoverished
residents.[29] SCMHSC would become the Watts Health Foundation (WHF)

in 1973, and it registered as a nonprofit organization to continue its mission of
providing low-cost and high-quality health care to residents of South Central.
The foundation has proven to be an essential resource for the funding and implementation of community health centers in the area over the past four decades. Its
interracial personnel—African American, Mexican American, and white—made
it a unique enterprise that served the Watts and Huntington Park communities.
The Watts Health Foundation's motto was to "render personalized service in a
setting of dignity."[30] The WHF focused on serving the most difficult populations: "the poor, minority groups, new immigrants, the homeless, chemically
addicted, elderly, chronically ill, and teenage mothers."[31] The types of resources
offered by the foundation were community health centers in Compton, Watts,
and Huntington Park; a chemical dependency center, the House of Uhuru (freedom), which provided residential and outpatient treatment of people's alcohol
and substance abuse problems; a preventive health services center for persons
receiving nutritional services, AIDS education, sickle cell anemia testing, and
hypertension testing; and finally a teenage health clinic at two Los Angeles high
schools that offered health education and reproductive health options.[32]

By the mid-1960s, African Americans and Mexican immigrants were no
longer at the periphery of the health discussion in Los Angeles; they were at
its center. Health officials' concern over which diseases had an impact on African American and Mexican immigrants matched concerns over findings that
described why these groups underutilized health services. A resident of Watts,
Dolores Morado, expressed that one of the reasons for underutilization of health
services was the lack of proximity of clinics. Morado, a patron of SCMHSC,
liked this clinic very much because it was close to her home and she no longer
had to make the long commute to the County-USC Medical Center in East
Los Angeles when she needed emergency treatment for her children. Similarly,
Watts resident Paula Tate stated, "It made it more convenient for them to come
here. . . . I liked the whole idea of them coming to the community."[33] Convenience proves important when one is selecting a clinic. Feelings of comfort,

good treatment, cleanliness, and supportive assistance play an equal role. Residents expressed that they did not want to walk into depressing centers, as the sight of a worn building and old machinery would make them feel worse. As neighborhood clinic supporter and Illinois senator Charles Percy explained, "Until the time we can take care of the poor here, we have no business trying to Americanize the whole world."[34]

In addition, health officials believed that race and culture explained Black and Mexican immigrant's utilization of services. In 1974, East Los Angeles Health Systems, Inc. made a study to investigate why the Mexican community was not seeking emergency medical services. They created a bilingual household survey administered in East Los Angeles, with the majority of respondents answering the survey in Spanish.[35] They divided the Mexican population in East Los Angeles into three cultural groups: (1) Mexican Americans who were culturally most integrated into the "American way of life" by either rejecting or simply not knowing or practicing the customs and heritage of Mexico; (2) Mexican Americans, usually second or third generation, who had experienced acculturation into American life and considered the cultures of both Mexico and United States suitable and consistent with their lives; and (3) Mexican Americans who clung tenaciously to Mexican customs and heritage. The third group was the most worrisome to health officials and the hardest for the medical profession to engage, and made up the largest percentage of East Los Angeles residents. In the researchers' eyes, "unassimilated Mexicans" would go to physicians only as a last resort, when all folk medicines and healers have failed. This study listed folk illnesses—*mal de ojo* (evil eye), *empacho* (indigestion), *caida de mollera* (sunken fontanelle), and *susto* (fright)—and explained how *curanderas* (healers) healed these illnesses.

The rationale for the study on the Mexican community's use of medical providers illustrated county health officials' own racist and reductionist understanding of health and health care needs in the Mexican American community. In their view, the assimilated and acculturated Mexican Americans were the easiest to get into the medical clinics and the easiest targets for assistance. The premise that culture and cultural practices are the largest deterrents to seeking medical services illustrates the ineptitude of the medical profession. Medical professionals were quick to blame culture and cultural difference as the sources of people's limited engagement with health care, rather than to reflect on how they, the medical experts and professionals, failed to fit and meet the needs of the particular community or to provide services to patients in a language that was accessible to them, or how in some cases undocumented immigrants avoided government agencies out of a genuine fear of deportation.[36] Director Jose Duarte of the East Los Angeles Health Task Force suggested that those conducting studies should concern themselves more with establishing clinics rather than with highlighting different cultural practices of the community.[37]

Clinics created by the Brown Berets and the Black Panther Party began with the mission of serving the needs of residents. The East Los Angeles La Clínica Familiar del Barrio, coordinated by former Brown Beret member Gloria Arellanes, also built a reputation for serving undocumented immigrant patients without repercussions. The sizeable Mexican clientele had access to bilingual medical staff, sex education, and reproductive health counseling for youth in the community. As part of the clinic's visual landscape, its walls were decorated with movement posters and murals to cultivate cultural pride.[38] La Clínica was a community-driven project that provided health services where state and local social welfare programs failed to do so. Similarly, the Black Panther Party made it a top priority to begin the People's Free Medical Research Clinics, offering an alternative to government-sponsored health clinics. In 1969, the Southern California chapter of the Black Panther Party opened the Bunchy Carter Free Medical Clinic in Los Angeles. This clinic, along with its counterpart in Northern California, examined patients for lead poisoning and high blood pressure, administered immunizations to children, and conducted optometry and gynecological exams. The Black Panthers were very vocal in fighting for clinics that strove to "meet the basic health needs of the communities . . . all ethnic groups, including Mexican Americans and Chinese."[39] These clinics served as a model of how to provide care attuned to community needs without falling into the trappings of cultural deficiency arguments. J. Alfred Cannon and Augustus Hawkins were champions in not only setting up clinics in the community but having them operated by people of similar experiences and sensitivity to the needs of communities of color. Hawkins believed that community input and participation would "improve the poor person's image of himself and his community . . . thereby building a greater sense of community pride and desire to remain in the community."[40]

Hawkins worked arduously to challenge OEO and medical practitioners who wanted to maintain control when they argued that it was difficult to train people from the community. From 1969 to 1974, the number of African American and Mexican Americans trained as doctors each year on a national level hovered between one hundred and three hundred students.[41] Training was another layer that health equity advocacy had to tackle and overcome. Locally, at the WHF, by the 1980s only 36 of the clinic's 252 staff people were from the community and had been trained at the clinic. They were clerks and medical assistants, not doctors and nurses. Poor educational opportunities at the high school level guaranteed that very few people from the community attended college, much less medical school.

Despite Hawkins's best efforts, the small number of employees from the community meant that the vast majority of employees were unfamiliar with the realities of South Central and Watts and arrived with preconceived and often erroneous perceptions of the area's residents and health needs. Not all doctors expressed enthusiasm over working with indigent populations. A doctor at County-USC Medical Center told three medical students on their tour of "charity wards" that "we don't want to make it too nice for the patient here . . . we don't want to make it so pleasant that they'll like it better here than at a private hospital." Such statements went against the promise and goals of community health. Medical officials working at HEW realized that hospitals do a good job treating disease but not when it comes to treating people. HEW began a program to get medical students involved and working with the community because its leaders believed that "a lot of health professionals are surprised that medical students should suddenly be organizing for change. Medical schools and hospitals have been conservative places filled with conservative people."[42] The combination of conservative medical professionals; reduced compensation for working in the community; discrimination in medical school admissions; and minimal educational tools in the form of racial, ethnic, and cultural awareness classes meant that medical students and professionals were not aware of how to serve working poor and working class people of color— a community that already had reservations about seeking medical assistance. This challenge would plague health care options throughout South Central and East Los Angeles. However, there is always hope that doctors like *las doctoras* at San Pedro Family Health Center would begin a practice in South Central with the mentality to be of service and provide expert and dignified care for poor families and individuals.

"LA CLINIQUITA"

Dr. Ann Turner and Family Nurse Practitioner Catherine Bax opened South
Central's San Pedro Family Health Center (SPFHC) in 1981. Nestled in the
corner of San Pedro Place and Main Street, it became a valuable community
resource. Turner and Bax would begin to distribute flyers in the neighborhood
at 5 a.m. and introduced themselves and the SPFHC mission to residents willing to listen. Their efforts mirrored those of community residents embarked
on establishing Head Start centers. By 1986, five years after opening its doors,
the center served over six thousand patients, an increase from five hundred
patients in their first year.[43] By this point, on any given day, by mid-morning
the center exceeded its capacity, with patients in the waiting room having to
stand before being called in to see the doctor. The excellent treatment, care, and
concern of "*las doctoras*" (the doctors), as they were affectionately referred to,
as well as the sliding-scale payment options, made this clinic one of the most
critical resources in the community.[44] In the end, their active canvassing, in
which they staked their reputation and expressed their mission to weary and
skeptical impoverished residents, spoke to Turner and Bax's commitment to
render quality, affordable, and humane health care (Figure 3).

Who were the patients at this clinic? Mothers, children, and young couples
with newborns filled the pleasant, though small waiting room. For the most
part, patients went into the clinic seeking pregnancy tests, family planning,
medical attention for young children's fevers or flu, or general family medicine.[45] Dolores Rosas says of her first visit to the clinic, "I will always have fond
memories of *la cliniquita* (small clinic) . . . *las doctoras* were so nice. The clinic
was humble, warm, welcoming. The waiting room had women waiting to get
back pregnancy results, taking their children when sick. The talk in the waiting room—children and pregnancy. Not to say that we were the only people
there . . . elderly people also were in the waiting room."[46] For almost twenty
years, SPFHC operated on private capital, which began with Bax and Turner
funding the initial investment in supplies and continued with fundraising to
keep the clinic operating. Although SPFHC operated on private funds, outwardly it looked like a federally supported community health clinic. Modeling
itself as a federally funded health clinic made it eligible to become part of the
federal program of community health centers in 2001, and was renamed South
Central Family Health Center.

Figure 3: Dr. Ann Turner Holds a Young Patient. *The Los Angeles Times*'s documentation of the establishment of the San Pedro Family Health Center in South Central Los Angeles prominently focused on the investment in and vision for this community clinic by its co-founders, Dr. Ann Turner and Catherine Bax.

SOURCE: Joe Kennedy, Los Angeles Times, April 16, 1985, copyright 1985. Used with permission.

SPFHC is important in an analysis of the growth of health care options in the neighborhood because it reflects the multidimensional nature of the various health options available in the neighborhood, both government-supported and private. Also important to note is that while SPFHC operated on private donations for twenty years, to become a federally supported health center it had to operate like a federally financed center for over a decade. For community residents, their loyalty to SPFHC was due to its mission of "practicing medicine" as a way to "practice justice" and by default provide dignified care. Also, with many of the initial clientele of *las doctoras* being Mexican immigrant families, the clinic's origins in South Central coincided with the community's demographic shift, as well as with the growth in federal poverty money to curb fears over population growth.

Not all clinics in South Central began as private ventures, as the OEO's sponsorship of the Los Angeles Regional Family Planning Council provided federal, state, and county financial commitment to clinics that offered extensive family planning services, often citing racist studies of women of color's so-called hyperfertility to justify the allocation of such funds.[47] The Neighborhood Adult Participation Program (NAPP) had determined that Los Angeles health concerns should center on reduction of infant mortality rates, prenatal and postnatal services and immunizations for mothers and children, and family planning services for teenage mothers. During the mid-1960s and the 1970s, fears about teen pregnancy took center stage as politicians and researchers grew concerned over overpopulation and the "population boom." The "population explosion" was seen as a global issue that in the U.S. context was tied to the urban crisis; that crisis and the growing flow of immigration led to a racialized ideology in which the prevention of civil disorders rested on minimizing growth in these populations rather than on fixing the inequalities that surface from wealth accumulation.[48]

Family planning in impoverished areas became a focus because health officials believed that a "significant characteristic found in areas of poverty is the number of large families and the resultant need for assistance in proper family planning that will result in properly spaced children and aid in the total well-being of the health of that family."[49] Dealing with the issues at hand would entail "expansion of available services, proper scheduling, and improved follow-up"; this would all add up to a "major attack on the symptoms of poverty through efforts to improve the health of mothers and children, by teaching proper family planning and providing services to pregnant teenagers."[50] By placing the burden on young women, this plan to end poverty fell in line with anti-poor political and social strategies that obscured structural inequalities that have a grave impact on poverty outcomes. The negative racialization of poor women of color only reinforced the tension in the relationship of these communities with the state. NAPP workers understood that this racialized discourse framed the disbursement of War on Poverty funds; thus they argued that they would provide a more humane approach to the delivery of family planning programs with a "neighbor-to-neighbor" approach, in which NAPP aides and volunteers would be "educational helpers" and provide information to patients.

Concerns over the level of government intervention in the family planning affairs of working class and working poor communities of color were warranted. In March 1964, OEO director Sargent Shriver appeared on NBC's *Meet the Press* and explained that sociologists and educators were "convinced that any poverty program that doesn't come to grips with the birth control problem is doomed to failure." The question that followed was, "Is there a place in your program for handling this problem?" Shriver responded by emphasizing "the importance of local choice of such a program operated in conjunction with the total community program, and the program that depends upon local initiatives, local ideas, and local solutions." For Shriver to state the importance of community input was seminal, as two years later, in 1966, he came under intense protest by clergy, members of Congress, and other public officials who wanted clarity as to the role of the OEO with family planning funding. Funding of family planning programs through the OEO had limits, as the money could not be used to advertise birth control options or contraceptives, which conflicted with religious beliefs. Over and over, the reports coming from the OEO discussed how "participation in the family planning component of this program must be entirely voluntary. No coercion or compulsion shall be employed to induce persons to use family planning services funded by this OEO grant." Moreover, and more important, participation or declining to participate in family planning services could not be "prerequisite to receipt of the benefits or participation in another OEO program."[51] The OEO emphasized that "comprehensive health services" were the priority, and family planning could be a part of those services but "will not be given any special attention or priority—despite the department's own estimates concerning the higher cost-effectiveness of family planning in the area of health and its potentials for reducing and prevention of poverty."[52] Despite Shrivers's best efforts, African American women in Los Angeles continued to view family planning services with alarm because of fears of racial genocide. They were amenable to family planning when given information, but a primary concern was "distrust of the county system."[53] This concern would plague family planning funding for decades to come, and demonstrates that in terms of health for patients, it is not just about access but also about the type and quality of care provided.

Both Turner and Bax began their practice in South Central because, as Ann Turner put it, she was "deeply troubled by the overwhelming poverty she was seeing and the inequities that existed between rich and poor." She decided that practicing medicine was for her a way of practicing social justice. She understood that "pretty much the bottom line for us is that we want to provide the kind of health care for these patients that we would want for ourselves or that people in

Mex-Amer — language Serrice +
understandings
Afr. Amer — d. strust — family plan
equals + genocide

more affluent areas would want . . . that does not necessarily mean high-tech. We take time to know the patients and explain as best we can what's going on . . . take care of them."[54] They had to brush up on their Spanish, as the medical chats and interactions would mainly be in that language. Establishing clinics in South Central by the late 1970s and the 1980s required that medical practitioners realize the increased presence and settlement of Latina/o immigrants, and how, similar to African American residents, these immigrants were looking for health care options that would serve their needs with quality and care.

COMMUNITY RESIDENTS BRING A HOSPITAL TO SOUTH CENTRAL

Along with the development of community health centers, establishing a hospital for the community was of critical importance among South Central residents, not only because it was urgently needed but also because it could demonstrate that institutions could have longevity in the community. The first attempt to build a hospital in the South Central area was in 1950. Wells Ford, a Black physician, was the first to organize around the need for a hospital; however, his efforts were unsuccessful. Prizefighter Joe Louis made a similar attempt years later but was unable to secure financial resources. In 1963, Dr. Sol White also worked to bring a hospital to South Central, but as with the efforts of everyone before him, the inability to secure financial support for the project made it difficult for a hospital to materialize.[55]

It took the formidable efforts of a group of women from Watts, including Caffie Greene, Lillian Mobley, Mary Henry, Johnnie Tillman, and Nona Carver, and doctors such as J. Alfred Cannon to make the hospital a reality. Caffie Green was born in Little Rock, Arkansas, migrated to Los Angeles, graduated from Jefferson High School in South Central, and studied cosmetology and culinary arts at Los Angeles Trade Technical College and psychology at USC. During the 1960s she marched and advocated for civil rights in the U.S. South and in Los Angeles. She worked for the Department of Housing and Urban Development and helped organize a local committee to build the Watts Health Foundation. She also was a driving force behind the King/Drew Auxiliary, which raised funds to build the hospital and medical school. Throughout the 1970s, Green was in charge of training and job development programs for youth interested in health careers and was at the forefront of all the affairs regarding King/Drew.[56] Similarly, Mary Henry was critical to the rise of the King/Drew Medical Center and worked on other OEO initiatives, such as Head Start programs. She is described as a spokesperson for children and health care.[57]

Alongside the tenacity of Green and Henry were the tireless efforts of Lillian Harkless Mobley. Born in Macon, Georgia, she married James Mobley and moved to South Central in 1950. She quickly became known as Mother Mobley, and was affectionately known as the "Community Mother" because "she was always there, front and center, to protect and serve, defend in good times and to fight in times of trouble, she was there for the community . . . with the powerful and the powerless."[58] She was a founder of the Black Health Task Force for Los Angeles County. She invested time and energy in the health of Black women, most especially pregnant women.[59] These women along with doctors such as the aforementioned Cannon were instrumental in persuading local and state officials to build what became known as Charles Drew University and Martin Luther King Jr. General Hospital.

The hospital opened its doors on March 27, 1972—the seventh hospital operated by Los Angeles County. The hospital, named after the civil rights leader and visionary, had an attached medical school named after the African American pioneering physician and medical researcher Charles R. Drew. The general hospital was a teaching hospital. The Drew Medical Society was the first established African American medical school west of the Mississippi when it opened its postgraduate medical school. The medical school trained interns and doctors at the hospital. The promise and value of a "teaching hospital" were that it was a cost-effective manner by which to provide care to indigent patients who otherwise could not afford to pay for private care.[60] Opening the hospital and medical school was an achievement; however, convincing community residents to seek services at the hospital was another challenge (similar to those characterized by Head Start centers).

The hospital's first years of operation coincided with revelations of the U.S. government's role in the Tuskegee experiment, a forty-year-old government study that withheld medicine from African American syphilis patients. Community activists needed to find a way to dispel patients' apprehensions about seeking services from a government- and county-sponsored hospital. The hospital sponsored health bazaars and festivals to provide free hypertension, blood pressure, and sickle cell anemia tests. Through these outreach efforts, the organizations attempted to present themselves as concerned medical providers attuned to the particular health needs of the community, as well as to give the hospital a friendly reputation.

The efforts to open MLK hospital meant that community residents and local politicians were protective of the hospital. Government funding for medical centers increasingly became a challenge after the Carter administration, and most especially during Ronald Reagan's presidency.[61] On July 24, 1981, the Los Angeles County Board of Supervisors met to discuss the budget cuts waged against health programs and services in the county. The proposed budget cuts would reduce the number of health clinics from fifty to forty-two. In turn, these closures would mean the layoffs of two thousand county health employees.[62] The county supervisors suggested that the patients from these soon-to-be-closed clinics be moved to the larger comprehensive health centers. Such closures would eliminate the central tenet of having health clinics within a five-mile radius for nearly every citizen in the county. The distance would increase by eight miles. This increase may have seemed minor, but it made a world of difference for a population that had insufficient means of transportation and scarce resources.[63]

All county supervisors attended this meeting (a very conservative county board), along with Maxine Waters (then a member of the California State Assembly who later would serve in the U.S. House of Representatives representing South Central), and county health worker representatives. Throughout the opening comments, Waters was quiet, but once Martin Luther King Jr. Hospital was brought up she quickly voiced her concerns. She was upset over the funding threats to the hospital, as she believed that the hospital bore the brunt of these cuts. The hospital was expected to absorb an additional 10 percent cut over other county-operated hospitals. In supervisor Harry Hufford's assessment of the necessity of such budget cuts he explained,

> [W]e provide a full range of basic health care and public health service as well as a generous range of optional county financed services, such as paramedic services, emergency and major trauma services, and alcoholism and drug services well beyond state funding levels. Our health system is one of the largest and finest in the nation and represents a major investment in staff, equipment, and facilities by the people of this county. The county is also mandated to provide such services as fire protection, elections, law enforcement, justice in the courts, welfare, social services, land use and planning. In addition,

we operate parks, beaches, recreational programs, and library systems. The county's budget must fund all of these services, which benefit all our residents, including the poor . . . this year, there simply isn't enough money to provide all of these services at the level we all agree is desirable.[64]

He also clarified and stressed that health was not the only sector experiencing cuts, and that departments across the board faced similar straits. County supervisors defended this penalization because the hospital was unable to show expenditure receipts and collect patrons' debts. Hufford's discourse of "generosity" and "finest" services in the nation could easily be refuted by many working poor or working class community residents that sought medical attention from any of the county's operated clinics or hospitals. Long waits, poor service and medical expertise, and depressing conditions made an already charged experience all the more depressing and devastating.

Waters's frustration increased when she felt that the supervisors were not answering her questions. For county supervisors, payment for services rendered at Martin Luther King Jr. Hospital was of great concern because the rate of payment was 13 percent below that of UCLA-Harbor Medical. Waters explained that this disparity was an outcome of the different patient populations treated at each of these medical centers. The patients at King Hospital were "indigents": "the working poor use MLK, they are 50 percent of our population, 70 percent in our ob-gyn, those are the people who are trying to pay their bills—the indigents, working poor, who do not have the dollars, and that makes a significant difference in the collection."[65] She further elaborated and took Hufford's comments to task, arguing,

[W]hat we have been doing is maintaining county health services at the expense of other essential county services. . . . What could be more essential than health services? And we know that if you take away services, you take away preventive services, that eventually you're going to have illness, you could have a reoccurrence of communicable disease in this community, and you wouldn't need another year of other services because it'd thoroughly wipe out our population . . . the bias that's obvious there.[66]

Waters's comments were forceful and drove her message home; she was unapologetic and unwavering in her assessment of the situation at hand. She was the only person in the room who spoke out on behalf of the hospital, community clinics, and overall community, and who understood that the funds being cut by the county were of critical importance because they were the last line for the funding of health services. Cutting down on health centers meant that the three largest comprehensive centers in the South Central area, Hudson, Humphrey, and Roybal, would bear the brunt of taking in patients. The influx would mean that waiting rooms, already filled past capacity, would experience increased delays.

Throughout this discussion, most of the indigent patients discussed were thought of predominantly as African American. Sporadically the discussion would address the growing Mexican immigrant population. As Waters put it, "[O]ur undocumented worker population at MLK has increased significantly in the past few years."[67] It is unclear what she meant by this comment because the employee demographics of King Hospital did not suggest an increase in hiring undocumented immigrants. However, she could have been motioning to not only how the employee population was shifting but also how the community's demographics were changing. What is clear is that this comment stands almost as a throwaway statement in her testimony in the meeting. Nonetheless, it does reveal how early into the 1980s medical centers in South Central were serving the needs not only of African Americans but also of Mexican immigrants—overwhelmingly racialized as undocumented immigrants.

The county approved the budget cuts to these medical centers despite the disapproval of Waters and community health advocates. Waters's fervent tenacity and commitment to fighting for the sponsorship of clinics and hospitals—the health needs of the community—make her one of South Central's most visible politicians. These budgetary cuts, increased immigration from Latin America, and economic restructuring framed the social, economic, and political milieu in which community health faced multiple challenges.

Community and neighborhood health centers were touted as "the wave of the future" because they aimed to tackle the health issues plaguing the communities that surrounded them. In South Central and Watts, the struggle to bring these clinics to the community did not bring about large-scale marches but were battles waged between elected officials, doctors, community residents, and county supervisors. The establishment of these clinics was in large part due to the tireless efforts of and collaboration between residents, doctors, and government officials. The WHF serves as one example in a web of government-sponsored community health clinics in the area that had similar beginnings and trajectories. The clinic had community residents as part of its governing board and originated through the ingenious efforts of community residents and doctors committed to serving indigent residents. As documented here, establishing and funding government-funded community health centers in the community has not been an easy endeavor. These clinics made inroads in trying to provide a humane approach to health care; nonetheless, limited funds still meant that patients had to wait months for appointments and routine checkups, the medical buildings were sometimes old and unkempt, and often a sense of sadness was palpable at these clinics.

South Central Family Health Center (SCFHC), previously SPFHC, has been in the heart of South Central since Catherine Bax and Ann Turner began the clinic.[68] Resident Teresa Garcia provides an example of the experience at SCFHC, indicating that while the services at the clinic could be better, they are decent enough considering her other options. She has gone to various clinics, but this one, she believes, is the best. At the very least, she says, it is clean, well lit with big windows, and organized: "Clinics with no lights just make you feel worse. And trust me there are plenty of those clinics here."[69] They also have TVs that broadcast the latest shows on Spanish-language channels such as Univision and Telemundo. She believes that while the clinic provides free to low-cost medical care, it should not minimize its obligation to provide equitable and up-to-date care irrespective of race, class, and gender. The clinic now serves primarily Latina/o immigrants from the community, and this was not always the case; Garcia says, "I do not know what happened to all the Black people who used to go there. Much like my street changing, the clinic, schools, and grocery store patrons have changed too. I guess you can say we are taking over in everything. But I do wonder where have they gone?" Garcia's inquiry is valid, and the best explanation is that SCFHC is located near the section of this community that is overwhelmingly Mexican—the eastern section of the community. It also speaks to the value of having an institution with long-term investment and continuity in the community—residents find comfort in knowing that resources are not always poised for flight in South Central.

Efforts to open community and neighborhood health centers in South Central required community residents, politicians, and health care practitioners to labor collaboratively to match the initial goal expressed by Dr. Julius Hill, the president of a three-hundred-member Black medical society, who said, "We are sick of the dole and the paternalistic attitude. We want to encourage self-esteem and self-sufficiency in the community, and we feel that giving the community the responsibility of supporting its own hospital will instill those qualities."[70] Also, making health care centers accessible would help to eliminate the threat of another Deadwyler incident. The shared racialization of Mexican American and African American residents, and the relational community formation that formed throughout South Central, affected how they approached, built, and used health centers that not only represented the "wave of the future" but also aimed to model dignified care.

both pops. are low income and feel forgotten

CHAPTER 4

BECOMING "BONA FIDE" RESIDENTS

Developing Relational Community Formation

About people choosing a home, feeling
at home, connected & belong, and
not wanting to leave a
familiar home environment, prefer to
adjust to changes around them.

IN FALL 1975, Leticia Zarate left her home in San Martin de Hidalgo, Jalisco, Mexico, to immigrate to "el Norte." Single and without children, she decided to journey to the United States in search of a better future for herself and immediate family. Her mother had arrived in the United States a few years prior and rented an apartment at the intersection of Olympic Boulevard and Figueroa Street in Los Angeles. Leticia fondly remembers this apartment, which was demolished to build the area around the Staples Center. Shortly after arriving in downtown Los Angeles, she eloped with Bernardo Nuno, also from her Mexican hometown, who had been living in the United States since the early 1970s.[1] Like dozens of other single Mexican immigrant men from San Martin de Hidalgo, he had taken residence in South Central, in an apartment building on 49th Street and Main Street. As early as the late 1960s, single Mexican immigrant men from this and other Mexican rural towns made such apartments and homes their first place of settlement. No one remembers who exactly was the first to rent an apartment in the heart of this African American community; however, these men remember the camaraderie and *vacilada* (playful friendship) this cohort of early twenty-something men shared (Figure 4). When asked why they settled in South Central, as opposed to East

Los Angeles or *la embajada* (the nickname used for Glendale, where most fellow Mexican immigrants from their hometown settled), they all explained that
they merely followed their male friends from back home. Most of the Mexican
immigrants living on 49th Street were men, but as the 1970s progressed, most
of the men married in Mexico and later secured the undocumented entry of
their wives so that they could unite in the United States, slowly transforming
49th Street and the surrounding blocks.

Shortly after their elopement, Leticia and Bernardo returned to San Martin and lived and worked there for a couple of years. However, they had not
abandoned their goal of returning to Los Angeles. They made their way back
and considered moving into a neighborhood other than South Central. They
lived in the City of Commerce with a relative and then in Glendale with
paisanos, but Leticia did not like these cities. She felt isolated, removed, and
disconnected from her family, friends, and employment options. She urged

Figure 4: La Palomilla, 1980. When documenting their enduring friendships and
neighborhood life in South Central Los Angeles, recently arrived and settled Mexican
immigrant men took great pride in taking photographs that celebrated their sharing a
good time together after a hard day's work in local manufacturing plants.
SOURCE: Personal archives of Leticia Nuno.

Bernardo to return to South Central, and they rented an apartment on 47th Street and Main Street, just a few blocks from where they had initially been living. Unlike 49th Street where many of their peers lived, Leticia recalls, her street (just two blocks away) did not boast a large number of Mexican immigrants. In fact, the complex she lived in was the only apartment building in the whole block that was diverse, as African Americans occupied the rest of the homes (Figure 5). She lived comfortably in this two-story apartment building for over a decade, but she desired more from her settlement in the United States.

She gained a steady job in downtown Los Angeles's garment industry, where she moved up from her position as a seamstress to patternmaker and designer, and her husband worked on an assembly line in the manufacturing industry. The next logical step was to purchase a home. As she considered where to buy, she never thought of anywhere outside of South Central; this was and had

Figure 5: Latino and Black Homeowner, 1977. Recently arrived Mexican immigrant men lived as tenants and roommates in apartment buildings and duplex homes throughout South Central Los Angeles owned and managed predominantly by African Americans.
SOURCE: Personal archives of Leticia Nuno.

become her neighborhood, her community.[2] She toured homes in East Los Angeles and Huntington Park, yet none met her expectations. She wanted to live in South Central despite its many drawbacks. Leticia and Bernardo purchased a home close to John C. Fremont Senior High School, on a street she said looked like any other middle-class neighborhood. Palm trees and manicured lawns lined the streets, but more important, her neighborhood did not give the outward appearance of being impoverished (Figure 6).

Currently, it is a different story: what was once a well-kept neighborhood has succumbed to the cumulative effects of decades of poverty, neglect, disinvestment,

Figure 6: Leticia Nuno on Car, 1977. Leticia Nuno was among the recently arrived Mexican immigrant women who enjoyed documenting their access to automobiles and driving as they settled and made inroads in South Central Los Angeles.
SOURCE: Personal archives of Leticia Nuno.

and violence. Now, Leticia feels, everyone is "hustling, *batallando* (struggling). I mean we hustled back then, it is a different hustle now."[3] Reflecting on her settlement, she states, "We were bold moving in with Black people. They weren't happy we purchased homes. You could tell they felt as though we were taking something from them, something that was theirs. You would hear them say Mexican, *mojado* (wetback), in a derogatory tone. It was scary."[4] Her anxiety and fear were not because African Americans were inherently intimidating, as she explains, but because the 1970s and 1980s were a time of real transition. Among these changes were middle-class African American flight from the area, deindustrialization and reindustrialization, the drug epidemic, the escalation of the war on drugs and the intensification of police surveillance and incarceration, increased Mexican and Central American immigration and settlement, and subsequent immigration raids at employment sites and around the community. Like that of countless other Mexican immigrants, Leticia's experience involved leaving her Mexican hometown to settle into a community defined by African American history and character. It was this last dimension that would prove the hardest challenge, as African Americans felt a hard-earned sense of ownership when it came to South Central's corridors and streets.

African American and Latina/o relations and interactions in South Central are tense and cooperative, charged and muted, and, at times, uncomfortable as well as full of possibility. It is in this space of possibility that one begins to see the struggle of both communities, collectively and separately, for dignity, strength, and solidarity against all the odds. South Central was a place for which most non–South Central residents (and in some cases the residents themselves) had lost hope. The charged relations between African American and Mexican immigrant South Central residents were a by-product in part of preconceived racial ideas of each other and in part of African American residents' sense of ownership over South Central. By the 1970s and 1980s, there was something poignant, deep, and historical to the African American character of South Central. It is this space's "Blackness," rather than the overt sense of *lo Mexicano*, that marks Mexican immigration and settlement in South Central as distinct. Because of the shared racialization experienced by Mexican immigrants from having settled in a space tied to African Americans, their lives in this space are different from those of Latina/os living in other areas throughout Los Angeles. By purchasing homes to settle permanently in a community marked by disinvestment, violence, and poverty, Mexican immigrant South Central residents became much more protective of their residence in South Central. As these Mexican residents of South Central would attest, the choice to become invested there drew unwanted negative criticism from coethnics living in surrounding and predominantly Mexican enclaves.

Throughout the 1970s and 1980s, South Central's racial configuration was adeptly described as the "fastest turnaround in a city from Black to Latin."[5] The conditions that spurred this demographic shift were in large part the result of economic, political, and social realities on both sides of the U.S.-Mexico border. In 1964, the United States ended the Bracero Program, a binational guest worker agreement with Mexico. The close-to-two-decade program aimed to control the flow of Mexican workers into the United States by providing seasonal guest worker visas to fill supposed agricultural shortages. Not all Braceros returned to Mexico when their permits expired. Many overstayed their permits and risked living in the United States as undocumented immigrants, thus laying the groundwork for increased familial migration and settlement.[6] The end of the program coincided with shifts in Mexico's economic opportunities. In the mid-1960s, the "Mexican Miracle" offered employment opportunities; however, jobs did not match the country's growing population. The gap between the rich and the poor grew dramatically. The Mexican government, with the support of U.S. corporations, invested in the Border Industrialization Program (BIP) in 1965. The BIP's goal was to tackle the growing unemployment problem throughout Mexico and along the U.S.-Mexico border by building *maquiladoras* (factories) that would produce and transfer goods readily between the two countries. Many Mexican migrants left rural towns in Mexico to work along the border in the maquiladoras, but U.S. labor demands and the lure of better job prospects in the United States meant that they often made their way north, most often as undocumented immigrants.[7] The post-1960s migration of Mexicans to the United States meant that by 1980, the Mexican immigrant population would reach 2.2 million, and the Mexican-origin population throughout the United States would grow to 8.7 million, up from 1.7 million in 1960.[8]

Mexican immigrants increasingly put down roots in the United States by settling in South Central—a South Central that would become their community.[9] Neighborly interactions are charged and indicative of how belonging and relational community building take work. Mexican settlement undoubtedly has changed the visual and social queues of the city, yet it has not entirely erased the African American character of this space. A reading of Mexican immigrants as "recent arrivals" obscures the fact that they have settled and lived in this area of the city for over four decades. Envisioning Mexican immigrants as recent arrivals renders them as perpetual newcomers, not long-term residents with rights to claim local community. Discussing the migration of undocumented Mexican immigrants in the 1970s and 1980s does not diminish the remarkable strides made by African Americans but instead enriches perceptions of how Black residents built, constructed, and shaped South Central's reality. After all, they worked to create opportunity in the midst of the most dehumanizing forms of class, gender, and racial oppression and inequality, and in doing so, offer a glimpse of the complex reality of interracial relations in the making South Central home.

The relations between both groups are based on power structures and ever-diminishing resources. These interactions happen not in a vacuum but rather in tandem with economics, police aggression, politics, and poverty, and thus are fragile and precarious. The history of South Central is one of ethnic and racial intermixing, and this chapter centers on how Mexican immigrants come to terms with settlement into an African American space, and how investigating neighborly interactions captures the changing dynamics of interracial relations. It also discusses the various ways in which both Mexican immigrants and Black residents require racial knowledge of what it means to live in an impoverished and disinvested community, as they learn to understand transition as an emotional process of relational community building, belonging, and inclusion.

THE FASTEST TURNAROUND IN A CITY

Similar to Leticia Zarate's immigration to South Central, Maria Concepcion Ruiz's immigration also placed her in the heart of South Central. Originally from Jalisco, Mexico, she settled in South Central in 1975 shortly after marrying her husband, Magdaleno.[10] Like Bernardo Nuno, Magdaleno Ruiz migrated to Los Angeles in the early 1970s, and lived in the heart of downtown. He then moved to Compton for a few years, and finally settled in the same apartment building on 49th Street as other men from his hometown.[11] He moved into this apartment complex because his friends lived there, and by this point he had spent a few years living among African American neighbors in Compton. He did not think much about settling in "Black Los Angeles," as the area afforded him the opportunity to live with a support network that would help him find a job and secure a home for his future wife and children (Figure 7). He described his weekly routine as going to and from work at Douglas Furniture in Hawthorne, California, and on the weekends spending time with his friends.[12] He remembers avoiding African Americans in those initial years because he had heard they were unwelcoming and confrontational.

Throughout the early part of his settlement, Magdaleno focused on work and sending money back home. He returned to Mexico in the mid-1970s and married Maria, and they moved to Los Angeles shortly after. She did not expect to live in South Central, because in her imaginary settling in Los Angeles meant living with people from her hometown. On the basis of what her husband had told her, she had assumed that the majority of her neighbors would be fellow Mexican immigrants. And, on her block, they were. However, her

Figure 7: Magdaleno and Mario Ruiz, 1976. Formative to documenting their settlement in South Central Los Angeles, Magdaleno and Maria Concepcion Ruiz took family portraits marking their dedication and celebration of thriving in this community as a Mexican immigrant family.
SOURCE: Personal archives of Magdaleno Ruiz.

[handwritten margin note: people choose (first) to live with people they know or who are like them.]

block was squarely in the middle of Black Los Angeles. She and her husband decided to rent an apartment close to where he had previously lived, as they wanted to feel connected to people they knew. They never considered moving elsewhere once her husband had established productive networks. A few years later, they purchased a home a block from their first apartment on 49th Street and have lived there ever since.[13]

Countless Mexican immigrants made this same decision, purchasing homes in South Central before they gained the legal residence to remain in the United States. Their status in the United States was not secure, as at any moment they could be picked up by the INS and deported. They did not think of their choices as bold; all they had in mind was creating better opportunities for their families.[14]

Scholarly interest in the racial, economic, political, and social landscapes of South Central has produced numerous studies of the community's needs and concerns. While these studies to some degree illustrate the demographic change of the community, they also show a vacillation on the part of community activists, political officials, and researchers in taking seriously the migration and settlement of Mexican immigrants into South Central before the 1990s. In 1984, twenty years after the McCone Commission released its findings following the Watts rebellion, researchers and policy analysts returned to the community to investigate its condition. In "McCone Revisited: A Focus on Solutions to Continuing Problems in South Central Los Angeles," the team wrote, "[W]e cannot emphasize too strongly the critical nature of the problems described in this report and the implications of continued inaction. We should not have to wait for a second L.A. riot to erupt to bring these problems to serious public attention."[15] The problems discussed in the report were the same problems that affected the community in the 1960s, and the "overall conclusion of those testifying was that conditions in the area are as bad, or worse, in South Central Los Angeles today than they were 19 years ago."[16] One speaker testified, "A basic problem in South Central Los Angeles in 1984, as it was in 1965, is poverty: grinding, unending, and debilitating for all whom it touches."[17] Residents expressed concern about limited job opportunities and few placement programs, education, police relations, and feminization of poverty (women headed one-third of all households with children in South Central).[18]

Much like the 1965 report, the 1984 McCone report illustrated that everything in South Central remained critical: health, police relations, jobs, education, social services, and housing. The dire need for social services has defined much of South Central's history in the post–World War II period, but this report was one of the few that early on mentioned the burgeoning Mexican immigrant population in the community. However, like countless other investigations, it considered their existence secondary to that of African Americans. The report's authors stated, "[D]espite the increasingly Latino population in the original 'curfew area' of the riots, our hearing will concentrate on the Black population, as did the McCone Commission."[19] This focus on the "curfew area" and its revising of the McCone report served to justify the concentration on African American residents (despite acknowledgment of the expansion and growth of the Black population beyond Watts) and the omission of Latina/os' needs. Their final assessment, and most devastating assertion, was that the "main focus of the majority of the problems in South Central Los Angeles does not concern itself to a great extent with people of Hispanic origin" and "those Hispanic people who are bona fide residents should participate in all political action, all endeavors at improved police relations and all competitive opportunities for job placement."[20] These assertions suggested that the problems plaguing South Central were not of concern for Mexican immigrants, when in fact, like their African American counterparts, they also confronted the effects of poverty. The report also indicated that Mexican immigrants had to work toward becoming "bona fide residents," and if they did, then they would have to participate in political action. In this way, it signaled a perception of Latina/o residents as a community unaffected by living in South Central; on the other hand, one could not deny their ever-increasing presence. It is this reality that Mexican immigrants confronted in their settlement and transition to South Central: their acknowledged presence alongside their not having a stake in the community.

The demographic change that studies like the McCone Commission addressed was that in 1970, approximately fifty thousand Latina/os were living in South Central Los Angeles neighborhoods; this was roughly 10 percent of the area's total population.[21] By 1980 the population had doubled to one hundred thousand, or about 20 percent of the total South Central population.[22] One indicator of racial transformation was in the enrollment of students at schools.

Figure 8: Classroom Demographic Change, 1988. Main Street Elementary School's celebration of student academic achievement reflected the growing ethnic and racial diversity among student populations attending South Central Los Angeles schools. SOURCE: Personal archives of Magdaleno Ruiz.

Roughly about fifty elementary and secondary schools in the Los Angeles Unified School District had a student population that was almost wholly African American. These schools were mainly in South Central and Watts. In South Central, 20th Street Elementary School was 69 percent African American in 1974, and by 1978 it was 75 percent Latina/o. Hooper Avenue Elementary School was 98 percent African American in 1974 but by 1978 only 26 percent.[23] These changes over the course of four years show the rapid rate at which Latina/os were settling in the community, but they also paint a picture of the community in which they settled (Figure 8). Demographics at schools, most especially elementary schools, speak volumes about the projected changes in the community.

Mexican immigrant residents actively made sure that political officials were aware of and considered these changing demographics. In early January 1970, Congressman Augustus Hawkins received a letter from South Central resident Lupe Montano. In it, she stated that Hawkins had done much for the community, but in her estimation, "You forget that there are also Mexican Americans in our community." As an advocate for education, she stressed,

Reading over some of the literature you have sent us, we can see you have done much for our community, but I see only one Brown face in this whole thing, that of a child from Miramonte. Of course, the needs for Black teachers are great in South Los Angeles, but what about Chicano teachers. You are not the only person who seems to think Chicanos are unheard of out of East Los Angeles, but we are, we make up a great deal of this community from Compton Ave on. We are the majority in Florence Avenue School. I am writing in hopes that the Florence Community does not forget the Mexican-American population. We realize your main concern is the equality for minority groups. But to get anywhere, we feel the only community that is really concerned with the needs of the Chicano is East Los Angeles, but we should have to leave our community for this. There is a new library in this community; it is located between the Black and Brown population of this community. This library will be used by both. I truly hope when purchasing books, the community does not forget books concerning the struggle of all the minorities. Once again thank you for your concern in this community, and improvement in our community![24]

Montano's letter was meant to suggest not that Hawkins needed to leave behind his commitment to the African American struggle but, instead, that to meet the concerns of the community, he had to consider all groups, not one over another.

Hawkins responded to Montano's letter affirming his equal concern for all minority groups:

I am not only concerned about equality for minority groups but concerned about equality for all groups. It is very true that we sometimes forget to mention those who constitute a large minority among the larger groups. I think your criticism is highly justified, and I assure you that I will give great attention to including them in my newsletter and other aspects of my activities; especially, a greater amount of attention to Chicanos. I would appreciate any information you can send to me which you feel may be incorporated in some of my newsletters.[25]

He was ready to acknowledge the growing presence of Mexicans in the area. He received other letters from Mexican American and Mexican immigrant South Central residents asking for him to understand their needs in the community.

These letters demonstrate that, as early as the 1970s, Mexican immigrants were growing and sharing space and social services with African Americans. Mexican Americans were not asking to ignore the issues facing the African American community. Rather than be forgotten altogether, they stressed that they wanted to *share* in social services—a crucial point. Most letters and calls were about what they wished for during this period: acknowledgment. Mexican South Central residents did not want the complete erasure of services for African Americans but inclusion in those services.

The influx of Mexican immigrants was met with trepidation by community residents. Gertrude Blanche, a twenty-two-year resident of 56th Street, described her community as a "sophisticated ghetto," a community that, while "worse than some parts of the city, was not quite as bad as others."[26] This reading of South Central goes against our understanding of the configuration of an urban ghetto. Blanche was among the many African American and Mexican residents who described the appeal of South Central because of its tree-lined streets and its homes. South Central's physical landscape is not composed of high-rise public housing options; rather, it consists of single-family dwellings, with the highest percentage of homeowners among blighted urban areas. As president of the Neighborhood Watch of her street, Blanche was particularly nervous about what she thought was threatening her community: "[T]hese Mexicans want to take over the country. I'm not talking about the ones who were born here. They're regular Americans. But these illegal aliens don't want to be told anything. They say this is their country and they want it back." She adds, "They're taking jobs and our housing and they're pushing the colored people out. . . . I even had one who told me to go back to Africa."[27] Blanche's assertion about her changing community reflects a time of tense transition. Similarly, David Ramirez, coordinator of the Mexican American Legal Defense and Educational Fund, stated, "Blacks have the feeling that they are being pushed out because housing is so tight down there. Eventually, I think they will be replaced." Ruth Smith put it adeptly when she said, "I guess this is how white people felt? When we moved in . . . like we were takin' over."[28] A twenty-year resident put it this way:

> When I came here this was almost all Blacks. Now there's only five Black families on the block. The Mexicans, they coming in big droves. Goddang it, what gonna become of the people here . . . these people like me on the

street? What if I moved? One of them gonna get this place. If I ever move, they won't ever be another colored man in here. I get along with 'em. They're nice to me and I be nice to them. . . . I got six months to tend to my business and another six months to leave theirs alone. But if you move around here, a Mexican will take your place. You put this down. The colored can't find a place to live in L.A. These Mexicans done taken it over.[29]

This sense of Mexican immigrants taking over was of grave concern to African American residents. Fears of racial succession cause interactions that are antagonistic and fueled by misconceptions. This perspective that Mexican immigrants were here to reclaim their land and take jobs and housing dominated the imaginations of many of the African American residents. When accusations of Mexican immigrants taking over jobs were waged, it was without much consideration for the economic transformations of the city and community. Young social worker Anne Davis mentioned, "I don't know how much the Browns are pushing the Blacks out of jobs and housing. It's not like the jobs and houses we have are that desirable. And even with the awful conditions we have, we should make room for them. We're so materialistic and such a wasteful country and there are people starving."[30]

Attitudes toward Mexican immigrants are varied and complex, as Davis expressed: "[W]hat some Blacks fail to see is the economics of the situation. . . . [T]his is just another case of poor people being exploited, working in inhumane conditions." Davis did not see "the Mexican people as my enemy, when the hand comes down, it comes down on all of us." She believed that African American attitudes toward Mexican people would change, "but it will take education from people in the community who know we're all in the same boat."[31] An attorney for the Greater Watts Justice Center, Larry Williams, further affirmed this sentiment when he stated that the "Black leadership tends to be conservative. Personally, I'd like to see the Blacks and Browns put in a political context. We're really talking about poor people. The masses will take the simplistic approach that Blacks are losing their jobs to immigrants." However, he did not "think that's the fault of the Chicano. That's the priority of the nation, of the government that chooses not to provide housing and jobs."[32]

Not all neighbors expressed apprehension toward Mexican immigrants in the 1980s. Leon Jones, an auto repair shop worker, noted, "You've got so many poor African Americans and poor Mexicans and we're just gonna all have to get along. We African Americans can't afford to go nowhere. If I could, I'd get out. Not because of the Mexicans. I'd just like to get out of the area."[33] Leon's sentiments regarding his inability to leave the community were due to his limited economic opportunities, not racial prejudice. As his feelings demonstrate, both African Americans and recent Mexican immigrants experienced the same circumstance: poverty. Economic vulnerability could prompt coalition building, but it also led to much of the tension and apprehension between these two groups because limited opportunities made cross-racial relationships all the more fragile. Language barriers heightened misunderstandings. As an African American resident aptly put it, "Groups don't quite know what to make of it yet. I'm not prejudiced at anyone myself. I don't think there's a problem once Mexicans start communicating. But over half the Mexicans can't communicate. They can't talk English."[34] African Americans did not know what to make of these demographic shifts. The transformation of South Central would result in changes to the racial character of their residential streets, but also to the political, social, and economic environment of the community.

This demographic change was visually most apparent when by the 1980s, a "flurry of moving vans, pickup trucks, and station wagons" was lining streets across the South Central area as Mexican immigrants unloaded their modest belongings.[35] Elena Santiago was among many Mexican immigrants in the community that moved into the area during that time. Elena and her husband hired a realtor to find housing listings, as she wanted to move out of her apartment and into a home. The realtor found a beautiful three-bedroom home on 53rd Street, a house vacated by a middle-class African American family leaving the area. Elena explained that the appeal of the street was that it had a "middle-class feel," as conveyed by wide corridors beautifully lined by palm trees and manicured lawns.[36] Her neighbor Dolores Rosas elaborated, "In the summer of 1994 when [I] was shown a property on 53rd Street, the street still had a Black feel to it . . . not like the houses I was shown over by Hooper Avenue and Vernon Avenue [near Historic Central Avenue]." She elaborated that those streets seemed more congested and smaller, so she preferred the home on 53rd Street. Countless African American families lived on this street, yet this was not any different from her experience living in South Central. In 1978, she had lived in an apartment on 50th Street and Main Street that had been predominantly African American. The apartment manager, "La Mimi," was an African American woman. Dolores remembers her interactions with Mimi fondly: the manager would watch her children at a moment's notice and be very attentive to the upkeep of the apartments. She was also a bit strict, reprimanding Dolores and others if they line-dried their clothing on days in which they were not allowed to or simply if she was having a bad day. Nevertheless, Dolores and fellow apartment residents remember her with care because she did her best to communicate with her Mexican immigrant tenants through hand signals and the few words she had learned in Spanish.[37] She created a comforting environment.

In 1985, Dolores and her husband, Francisco, purchased a home a block away from this apartment complex. Their choice to stay in South Central was not difficult. Dolores had grown accustomed to living within this two-mile radius, and again, she found herself in a home that was flanked by African American residents. Terry, a long-time African American resident of 49th Street, like Mimi before her, had become her new neighbor and, as Dolores learned early on, their move into a recently vacated African American home was accepted. She recalled that even though Francisco was not fluent in English or Terry in Spanish, they would joke and talk with each other about daily affairs. They had a cordial friendship and relationship, one that never ended in verbal assaults. Terry continues to live at this property, and when Dolores and Francisco go to visit friends on this block, he continues to greet them with the same warmth he had in the mid-1980s. Dolores lived in this home for close to ten years, before selling it and purchasing another residence on 53rd Street. South Central is where she settled when she arrived in the United States. Here she engaged and befriended her first cohort of African American neighbors, found employment, contemplated legalization, and endured the tumultuous days of the 1992 uprising. The 1980s and this home were relevant to her overall trajectory in South Central.[38]

Similarly, in 1983, Reina Maldonado, her husband, and three children lived in a crowded apartment in the Pico-Union neighborhood. She grew tired of the cramped space and decided to purchase a home further south, on 53rd Street. She quickly made this property her home, and in the 1980s the Maldonados were one of the first Latino families to settle there. "When we first came here, it was almost all Black people. Pretty soon it will be all Latino. And then we wondered who will be next to replace us. The Asians?"[39] Like Dolores, Leticia and Maria witnessed and were part of this influx of migrants. Maldonado discusses this change as if it were inevitable and viewed Asian immigrants as the logical next group to take over the community because they formed the majority of the business owners in the community and were the fastest-growing immigrant group in the region. She saw Asian immigrants, especially Koreans, as part of South Central's business culture but not part of the community: she did, however, consider Asian immigrants potentially a part of the community's racial transformation.

In their adaptation to South Central, the interaction of Latina/os with African Americans was varied. As noted before, in many cases African American residents felt threatened by the increased settlement of Latina/o immigrants. Francisco Rosas stated,

> South Central in those days was not the South Central you now know. You see a little Mexico now, everything is accessible, easy. We changed that. Now we really struggled. We didn't know English, without papers. But we wanted to be here; when you come to the U.S. and you like it, it's hard to go back.[40]

Magdaleno Ruiz discussed some of his negative encounters with African American residents:

> It was hard . . . they would call us Mexicans, *wetbacks*, in a tone that was meanspirited. It was a challenge. As an immigrant one comes to suffer, we suffer a lot. Living with other Mexicans doesn't shield you from violence . . . if I only told you how many *palizas, peleas* (beatings), I saw outside the liquor store.[41]

Mexican immigrant men discussed *el sufrimiento* (the struggle) they endured as they learned to reside in South Central. Their oral histories revealed that demographic change is not easy. In some cases, they experienced violent encounters, but these were only a small fraction of long-term residents' recollections, as most shared many more-muted stories of neighborly interaction than stories of theft and violence.

In 1979, the *Los Angeles Times* reporter William Overend captured this reality when he wrote that Mexican women were perceived as anxious and therefore "easy targets for rip-offs because they usually won't go to the police unless their car has been stolen." Mexican immigrant "women are known as 'walking banks.'"[42] Dolores remembers that she was often accosted on the bus on her way to work: "I would put my purse close to me, but that was not good enough. I got my purse snatched a few times."[43] Mexican immigrant women found themselves using public transit to get to work or go shopping, and they expressed at times having unease when riding the bus. Fear did not stop them, as they had no choice, this was the only form of transportation. They merely became savvy and strategic about how to hide their personal belongings and worked on being less visible on the bus and while walking down the street.[44] These encounters demonstrate the complexity Mexican immigrants experienced as they settled into South Central. The broader context of these encounters is that as Latina/o immigrants were populating South Central, it was also a period of sizeable economic decline, a growing drug epidemic, and increased investment in incarceration. These residents noted that the fear of theft was also a by-product of living and commuting in an impoverished neighborhood that was being devastated by the crack epidemic.

Despite having lived in South Central for over four decades, some Mexican immigrants have not been able to get over their initial feelings of anxiety, fear, and prejudice toward African Americans. The process of working collaboratively and becoming neighbors does not motivate South Central resident Juan Rodriguez, who explains, "Why do I have to befriend them, be nice to them? They have never been nice to me. No point in talking to each other."[45] This attitude not only shapes the reality of these middle-aged Mexican immigrants but also can have an impact on their children and grandchildren. The next generation's possible prejudice and unwillingness to look beyond racial difference is most alarming because it could squander progress made toward coalition-building and perpetuates a sense of "us versus them." Magdaleno Ruiz's assertion that African Americans took out their anxiety over changing demographics and settlement on their Mexican immigrant neighbors is in line with what Alfred Smith shared about the African American perspective: "It is hard to see your street overrun by Mexicans. One minute it was just us, then it was them." Alfred further divulged that Mexican immigrants would yell expletives at them in Spanish: "They thought because they were in Spanish we didn't understand, but we understood . . . the gist was that they didn't like us."[46] These sentiments, however, should not overwhelm or shape our conversation about interracial dynamics in South Central. They prove the complicated and fraught nature of these interactions; however, there are thousands of residents who have made efforts to build bridges across racial differences and learn from shared experiences.

To understand these interactions one must not underestimate how racial scripts circulate in both the United States and Mexico. Knowledge about the U.S. African American struggle and experience is limited in Mexico, and what is shared is often negative attitudes.[47] Mexico has its legacy of colonialism that serves to render its Black and indigenous roots invisible. The lack of conversation and discussion around Blackness in Latin America, Mexico, and the United States leads some Mexican migrants such as Josefina Hernandez to believe that African Americans are predisposed to violence. When she arrived in South Central in 1968, she feared them: "When I first came to this country, I was afraid of them. Now I see that they're just like we are. They have a good heart. I've never had a problem with them. I've never been robbed by a Black person. Never."[48] She went on to share, "People look down on them just because they're a little darker than we are."[49] These preconceived notions of violence and ultimate fear of African Americans fit within the larger racial script in the United States of African Americans posing an imminent threat. Josefina embodies the work that it takes to undo these harmful racial scripts and see African American experiences as similar to her own. This shift in perspective is primarily due to daily interactions and an acknowledgment of the shared racialization as a result of living in the same geographic space.

SHARED EXPERIENCE BY LIVING
IN SOUTH CENTRAL LOS ANGELES

The influx of Mexican immigrants has changed the visual landscape in South Central; however, this has not eroded the African American identity and character that people readily associate with the area. *Paleteros* (ice cream vendors), personal cars, and vans would cruise the streets, with high-pitched horns marking the arrival of the "*donas* truck (donut truck)" (Figure 9).[50] Dora Escobedo explained, "You know we have arrived when we have *panaderias* all over the city."[51] Now there are more Spanish-language than English-language Catholic services. In the mid-1970s, Nativity Catholic Church did not offer masses in Spanish, but by the 1990s, it had erected a shrine to la Virgen de Guadalupe as necessary to reach the burgeoning Mexican population. In people's yards, ci-

Figure 9: Ice Cream Trucks, 1992. Driving and operating ice cream trucks emerged as a profitable and desirable race enterprise among recently arrived and settled Latina/o immigrants laboring and living in South Central Los Angeles.

SOURCE: Jose Galvez, *Los Angeles Times*, February 16, 1992, copyright 1992. Used with permission.

lantro, cucumber, tomatoes, and tall stalks of corn lined the gardens. Chickens roaming freely in backyards and roosters crowing early in the morning became commonplace. Spanish spoken in the street became a daily reality. Despite these changes, outsiders, political officials, and activists continued to think of South Central as a predominantly African American community.

It is productive to consider John Marquez's theoretical framing of Latino and African American relations in Houston, Texas, to understand a community in transition.[52] Marquez frames his discussion of Houston with Denise Ferreira de Silva's concept of "raciality" because it "enables an understanding of race as a dynamic"; with that concept, he also refutes the idea "that race is a mere category of difference socially constructed to justify conditions of economic exploitation and displacement." Using Ferreira's concept, Marquez argues that the "racial state of expendability" allows multiple forms of injustice and exclusion. According to Marquez, anti-Black racism and anti-Black violence are critical to the regions' racial formation. His theoretical intervention of "foundational blackness" argues that the "normalization of anti-black violence in the region" is an "essential component of its law enforcement apparatuses and racial/colonial dynamics" that shapes how Latina/os have "experienced the racial state of expendability."[53] The power dynamics of broader society make Black and Latina/o relations—their labor and their existence—precarious.

Turning to foundational Blackness entails grappling with how Mexico's *mestizaje* racial narrative, which privileges the mix of indigenous and European culture, disregards any African influence within Mexico. More recently, there has been a movement to reclaim the African roots that shape a part of Mexico's history and present, yet for too long the modality of understanding race has centered on *mestizaje* and has posed an initial challenge for interracial relations between Blacks and Latina/os within the United States.[54] As Marquez points out, for low-income residents, like those in South Central, there is "no benefit to attaching themselves to whiteness," and it is not that Latina/os identify with Blackness, but rather that foundational Blackness "represents a method and language through which the antiracist critiques from those same groups are developed and politicized" and that the similar expendability faced by Black and Latina/o people "helps fuse Black and Latino/a politics into a hybrid subjectivity, allowing the groups often to act in unison while also providing them with a subject position from which to act."[55]

In the case of South Central Black and Latina/o residents, to build on Marquez's important theoretical intervention, by living in the same geographic space Mexican immigrants in South Central learned that they shared in some similar experiences of racialization and marginalization. That assertion does not mean to erase the particular racialization that Black residents or Mexican immigrants experience, but rather to point out that space, race, and injustice are intertwined and that by living in the same space—community—some experiences are shared and relational, such as police and government surveillance and harassment, diminishing resources, and poor educational opportunities. Investigating Black and Latino relations in South Central allows for an understanding of how being neighbors means a likeness of experience that in turn shapes how they mutually grow and mobilize into a relational community formation.

Relational community formation in South Central required that Mexican immigrants had to learn how to adapt and cope with living in a community bound up with negative and devastating stereotypes such as drug use, violence, welfare dependence, and poverty. These negative stereotypes, part of a long history of discrimination and racism waged against African Americans, were added to the already loaded stereotypes of recent immigrants. As a racialized space connected to Blackness, South Central at times has alienated Mexican immigrants from other Mexican Americans who settled in mostly Mexican American communities throughout Los Angeles. Subsequently, Mexican immigrant South Central residents felt isolated and disconnected from the larger Mexican community. In those days, "East Los Angeles was a novelty."

Friends who settled in other parts of Los Angeles would hesitate to visit Mexican immigrants who lived in South Central. It became a chore to convince them that coming into South Central would not endanger their lives. In many cases, their friends would not vocalize their discomfort with South Central, but their excuses for not going would indicate their feelings. For example, after Denis Anaya informed his friend that he had moved his notary office to Central Avenue, his friend told him, "You're crazy. How can you work and live there? They'll kill you."[56] The unmarked "they" here are African Americans. Josefina Hernandez echoed these sentiments when she said, "My sister's family lives in La Puente and they won't come here because supposedly we live in a Black neighborhood," but of course "They don't know that on this block there are more Latinos than Blacks."[57] Despite such misperceptions, residents such as Maria

Garcia, a plastics-factory worker, purchased their homes in the 1980s right next to or near the Watts Towers. She explained, "We bought the houses with the idea of staying one year and then selling them, so we could move someplace else. But now we're already used to Watts."[58] Ironically enough, in the 1990s, South Central's Latina/o population continued to grow, and it was difficult for Latina/os living outside of South Central to imagine it as an interracial space.

Esther Sanchez realized that she had come of age in a community that others had marked as distinct. In the late 1980s, she took her seat in the bus on her way to school; as she gazed upon her fellow passengers, all she saw were African American faces. She realized that unlike her peers from her hometown in Zacatecas, her family had settled in a "Black neighborhood."[59] The purchase of a home in South Central was the ultimate indicator that living there was not temporary but rather a permanent move. At that moment, anxiety over her and her family's settlement, as well as feelings of being outnumbered by another racial group, inspired a sense of fear and impotence: "Back then we were a bit afraid. If you looked at them wrong, *se te hechaban encima* [they would fight you]. Look away and to the floor. Now [the late 2000s], if something broke out, we could get into a fight with equal numbers."[60] After she uttered those words, she could not help but laugh at the absurdity of her comment, as she admitted never being in a fight or confrontational with fellow African American residents. Her comments instead stemmed from her and her families' feelings of anxiety and fear. The increased presence of Mexican immigrants in the community offered a level of security but, more important, began to give South Central more complex visual clues to who its residents were.

South Central's perceived identity looms large. In popular culture and news reporting, South Central is depicted as an area to avoid at all costs. Fellow Latina/os' rebuff to Mexican immigrants who live there follows in line with a larger societal desire to disassociate from South Central. Such an approach pushes some families to work toward dissociating from these negative stereotypes; others—such as Leticia, Dolores, Maria, and Esther—take them as a prompt to become prouder residents of the community. While anxious about the prospect of living in South Central, Esther often oscillated between viewing African Americans as people "to be reckoned with," because they have a reputation for being loud and boisterous, and considering them a united group worthy of emulation and respect. She expressed negative character traits of African Americans that reproduce negative stereotypes, but she also admitted that they have assisted when she has needed it without expecting anything in return. This duality is the messiness of race relations; they do not fit neatly within the framework of tension, prejudice, or coalition, but in reality are fraught and ever changing. Esther explained, "This is my 'hood. There are African Americans, but this is my 'hood. . . . I have my house here . . . they can't say anything . . . nobody is better than anybody . . . we all came the same, without papers in search of an opportunity."[61] This last statement, that they all arrived in the United States with similar sets of circumstances as undocumented Mexican immigrants, is her refusal to accept that Mexican immigrants who settled in predominantly Latina/o areas versus her settling into South Central made a better choice. Becoming a resident or a "bona fide resident" meant beginning to feel an investment and connection to the space around them. It meant to be proud of a place, a place marked by interracial relational community formation. Residents do not deny that the majority of them are poor, working poor, or working class, and that some engage in extralegal hustles to make ends meet. Many are beneficiaries of social services and public assistance, and violence is part of daily life, but residents *refuse* to be sidelined or have their neighborhood be viewed negatively by default. They would attest that the working class and impoverished character of South Central is the result of economic, racial, and gender inequality. Their lives in South Central, similar to those of African Americans, are marked by limited means and opportunities. This community and its chances (or lack thereof) are products of decades of disinvestment, neglect, and racism. Within this reality, African American and Mexican immigrant residents struggle to create a space worthy of a future.

INTERRACIAL COMMUNITY RESPONSIBILITY AND ACCOUNTABILITY

For some Mexican immigrant residents, anxiety and fear were not reasons to decide to leave South Central at the first opportunity. Although many Mexican immigrant residents did leave South Central to live in communities with larger percentages of Latina/os, families such as those of Leticia, Maria, Dolores, and Esther decided to purchase homes in South Central. Purchasing a home in the community was an indicator of their commitment to this space. They did not leave behind this struggling neighborhood. When they settled with their families and purchased homes in the 1980s, they were not sure how many more Mexican immigrants would settle like them; much less did they realize that one day they would outnumber African American residents.

Community residents took it upon themselves to establish informal networks to help each other navigate this ever-changing community. Ruth Smith and Elena Santiago quickly became cordial neighbors and, subsequently, friends. Despite the larger narratives of South Central being and becoming a site of urban decline and disinvestment, both Ruth and Elena embraced their community as something to be proud of, something worth preserving. Without much deliberation, both women became essential to the overall functioning of their block. No one in the community challenged them because they were considered the matriarchs that held and brought the community together. From the beginning, Elena began to befriend all her Mexican neighbors because she felt that they too were having a difficult time settling into the region because of the looming threat of INS officials, job exploitation and insecurity, and unfamiliarity with school options. Elena took it upon herself, even though she was not fluent in English, to ensure that all the children on her block enrolled in school. She said, "My neighbors want the best for their children . . . that is why we make the dangerous trip over here. I just wanted to help them and make sure they knew where the closest school was, how to enroll their kids, because it's a community effort. . . . [W]e help each other equally, we have to help each other . . . if we don't do it, who will?"[62]

Elena took her role in the education of local children very seriously. In mornings and afternoons, she would walk not only her children (and now grandchildren) to the nearby junior high and high school but also her neighbors' children to their respective schools. She did this with great pleasure. Ensuring children's safety when crossing the street or just making sure that they got to school on time was a high priority among the ways in which she sought to help her community. Little by little, she began to grow concerned for the African American children on her block—while she did not have the same level of interaction with their parents as with her Mexican immigrant neighbors, whenever she saw children on the street she would ask them whether they had done their homework, had gone to school, or would participate in the upcoming school pageant. She became known as the enforcer of education.

Similarly, Ruth played this vital role in the community. She was more attentive to the needs of the African American children on her block, ensuring that they attended their classes, played safely on the block, and, most especially, were staying away from some of the hazards of living in an impoverished community. The "prevalence of crack became an epidemic in the 1980s—it was and continues to plague the community—you could feel it. I wanted to make sure the kids didn't get into any trouble."[63] Her concern for the community was an extension of her work for her church in that she made sure that the church was always clean and well kept; she felt that if the community itself looked beautiful, the morale of the community could be uplifted.[64] Elena's children brokered these women's initial interactions. Elena knew very little English and could not readily communicate with Ruth. This phenomenon of children being the language intermediaries is not new, but as the years went by Elena needed her children much less because in many ways the communication between these women became much more intuitive. Their intentions were best understood though half-articulated sentences. Both women grew aware of the role that each played in her racial and ethnic community. Only by collaborating would they become influential facilitators in the community. Both women agreed that having to work across racial lines would hinder any form of cooperation, but they saw an opportunity for people in the community to work through and work against their racial prejudices. This friendship has developed and grown for over twenty years.

Ruth and Elena were very conscious in asserting their friendship and cooperation—it could hardly be a secret, as their interaction and strategizing occurred primarily on street sidewalks. The street served as more than just a convenient place to talk; it was a visual and physical marker for their neighbors to observe them working across racial lines for the betterment of their shared community. When mutual distrust and animosity between these two racial communities were commonplace, these women's interaction on the street represented a bold racial reconfiguration—a meaningful symbolic gesture—as well as a model of the power of neighborly interaction and concern. Both women prioritized getting to know their neighbors, not through gossip but through engagement with and for the community, and this orientation was a model for interactions based not on claiming turf but on community building, which can operate in the absence of a movement and on a smaller scale. Elena elaborated, "No one owns anything here. . . . I know that when I got here they [African Americans] didn't like my family moving in, but I think this was part of a natural progression."[65] Ruth was crucial to Elena's eventual understanding that African Americans were apprehensive precisely because they "had worked really hard to get the little they have [political representation and the ability to own a home], so to see us move in proves to be a threat to their struggle."[66] We live in an age in which people do not get to know their neighbors, yet these women's friendship, commitment, and service to the community have benefited the overall operation of the community.

Sustaining solidarity is possible when accountability and the recognition of shared interests serve as the foundation for partnerships among different communities. Ruth and Elena grew to understand that their stories overlapped— both were migrants who had similar goals for a better life for themselves and their families. Once they realized their similarities, they extended their goals to their neighbors and the community at large. Their willingness to think critically about the plight of the working class, particularly in a community like South Central, made their interaction possible. These women's connection, activism, and friendship are distinctive and worthy of examination.

Both women believed that only through community support and self-help, and through their mothering practices and politics, could they move beyond seeing motherhood as a politics relegated solely to the domestic sphere. Motherhood became a larger organizing principle, and the concept was, in many ways, their civil rights struggle. For these women, motherhood was not an oppressive or pejorative concept. It served as a method of exerting power, allowing them to work with the community and also complicate negative representations of working class women of color as pathological and part of the undeserving poor. They challenged these discourses and images through their lived experience, education, and organizing. These women's activism reveals that what drives their collaboration is their understanding of gender, motherhood, and family. It signals the importance of interpreting how historically the most disenfranchised of residents created and nurtured unity and belonging and crafted their sense of neighborhood that made room for two racial communities to demonstrate concern for their neighborhood's livelihood.

LANDSCAPES OF RACIAL TRANSFORMATION

The 2000 Census reported that one-quarter of the African American population had moved out of the South Central community during the 1990s. The changing demographics forced many African Americans to question whether they should stay or should go. As *Los Angeles Times* writer Charisse Jones emphasized, "[O]ld memories cannot compete with new realities." New realities involved not only immigrants but a changing landscape. The "exodus" Jones pointed to is complex, in that "while some undoubtedly are leaving because of the neighborhood's changing demographics, most say a larger factor is the area's long eroding quality of life."[67] The rising crime rate has meant that African Americans and Mexican immigrants alike "have lost a sense of freedom in their neighborhood—[they are] afraid to walk to church in the dark, to water their lawns after sunset, to move freely without worry." Artimese Porter, a resident of South Central since the 1970s, had a theory about the shift: "You know why it changed? It's all because of drugs. Other than that you could sit outside in the summertime and talk until midnight."[68] By the 1980s, Neighborhood Watch groups had less of an impact on the safety of the community because young and old residents stopped going to meetings, afraid of gang retaliation. The 1980s proved to be a tumultuous period in South Central: residents discussed not only changing demographics but also economic, political, and social change.

African Americans believed that the "neighborhood feels not lived in, but lived out." As a resident, Valerie Shaw attested, "When I drive through the commercial districts there and elsewhere in Central Los Angeles, everything feels impermanent, poised for flight, like a diner sitting at a restaurant eating a meal but strategically positioned near the back door, ready to beat it at the first sight of trouble."[69] This sense of flight demonstrates the constant movement, the transience of the community. As Mexican immigrants settled, African American residents came to terms with the influx and defined what it meant to be African American in South Central—and also what it meant to hold community power without a critical mass. South Central resident Leroy Shepard expressed the resentment of African Americans over Mexican immigrant settlement when he stated, "Sometimes we get mad at those doggone Mexicans." Sylvia McLymont lamented, "All of a sudden, it seemed like were invaded."[70]

In many African American minds, the 1990s "became the symbol of all that became wrong, and in this period 'Black' has lost currency to the point where

Black politicians and other leaders, mindful of cultivating broader constituent and financial bases, hesitate to characterize anything as exclusively Black."[71] Here is Ezola Foster: "These people are taking food off our tables. . . . [W]e are shocked to see Black leaders like Maxine Waters and Ron Dellums rallying for illegals."[72] For residents like Ezola, this growing tendency of political officials to become more inclusive created the belief that that very inclusion posed a threat to their livelihood. The *Los Angeles Sentinel* columnist Larry Aubry deemed it a "moral dilemma" for African Americans. On the one hand, they understood the struggle—the experience of discrimination; on the other hand, they feared a loss of political power, which was hard to earn.[73]

This dilemma would plague South Central's community formation and politics. Politicians and activists were unprepared to assist recently arrived Mexican immigrants settling into this community, nor could they prepare African Americans for its middle-class outmigration and changing demographics. The transition of Mexican immigrants into South Central was indeed difficult. They were moving into a city that was not their own, having imagined that moving to Los Angeles meant settling among other Mexican immigrants, not African Americans. African Americans were reacting to the feeling that they were being left behind by middle-class peers, to the loss of job opportunities, to the increased presence of drug and gang activity, to increased police aggression, and to diminishing social services. It is this emotive landscape, one that seriously considers the labor involved in and for adaptation, which requires both groups to grapple with the multiple layers of change and its relational power.

A context of power frames interactions between African American and Mexican immigrants: both have limited power in the face of substantial changes in the economic, political, and social landscape. These two communities are living and interacting in relationship with the state, most especially through the prism of the state-sanctioned surveillance of the police, immigration agents, and social service providers. At various levels, these residents' lives and everyday operations are regulated, shaped, and constructed by the state. Both groups continue to work toward building community, solidarity, and possibility, as individuals and as a collective group, despite the multiple layers of oppression. As this chapter has highlighted, over the past few decades, the relations between these communities have been fraught, strained, and contested as a result of individual and collective race, gender, and class notions of identity. These interactions are also primarily shaped by the overall U.S. racialized discourse that depicts poor, working poor, and working class people of color unworthy of public assistance, "leeches to the system," or part of the "immigrant invasion" coming into the United States to drain the country of its resources. African Americans and Mexican immigrants are subjected to racist, sexist, and class-based discrimination. Once they understand this as a point of connection, as they did in Head Start classrooms and health care centers, a community-based politics that is relational in scope can open up the possibility for both groups to articulate and construct a new reality, full of possibility.

CHAPTER 5

TEACHING TOGETHER

Interracial Community Organizing

A MOTHER MADE a gadget board for her young son while attending a Head Start training course. She noticed the classroom had switches, bulbs, and batteries, and with a piece of the board she had found, she fastened the items and used the switch to turn on the light. The course facilitator asked what else could go on the board and suggested that they could add gadgets that were common in the household for parents and children to learn about their use practically and creatively. They decided to add a chain, hook, and zipper to learn about how to latch. This Head Start mother was part of the Creative Environment Workshop, which had the teaching philosophy that "adults, as well as children, learn by doing, by discovery, by trial and error, and by having success with a personal vision" (Figure 10).[1] As a creative space, the classroom was a place where "materials and people are brought together to learn" and create "healthy learning situations," with adults having a setting where they can plan, direct, and value their work.[2] Parents have an important role in shaping learning environments, and these workshops would "whet the appetite" for parents to engage more creatively in the Head Start classroom. The Creative Workshop philosophy served to empower Head Start parents, encouraging them to imagine themselves as crucial to the success of their children and, in turn, the success of the program.

As participants in Head Start, parents were required to volunteer and assist teachers in weekly classroom activities. For some parents, participation in Head Start became much more than volunteering in classroom tasks: they shaped classroom curriculum and blazed a pathway toward becoming teacher aides and teachers. In addition to involving Head Start parents as volunteers, the mandate of recruiting teachers and aides from the local community was a source of celebration, most especially for South Central residents who viewed this program as an opportunity for upward mobility and financial stability. Community participation in the program ensured that impoverished women and families imagined new possibilities because they became central to classroom success.

The Creative Workshop served as a supportive space for Head Start mothers. However, not all mothers were able to participate in such courses. Some mothers were enrolled in state-controlled seminars and classes that aimed to "teach" them how to better feed their children, mend their clothing, and follow various family planning options. These parenting classes, which originated with the premise that women of color were lacking in their parenting skills, required that African American and Mexican immigrant women develop strategies to make these offerings productive for themselves and children. It often meant using the tools learned in these courses and making them their own or diverting resources and time to the collective needs of the group. Women of color were able to transform these racialized courses into a space of opportunity for their educational development.

As discussed in the previous chapter, in the latter part of the twentieth century, South Central's racial character had transformed radically. Head Start classrooms mirrored the residential streets. By the mid-1990s, 55 percent of children attending Head Start were of Latina/o origin.[3] The increased diversity of the city meant that Head Start sites in South Central needed to hire bilingual teachers and adopt a curriculum that spoke to both African American and Mexican American experiences. This shift, while mandated by Head Start officials, still required support by Head Start teachers and parents. The collective efforts and organizing of women of color practiced in these state-sanctioned courses, in parent Policy Councils, or through in-class volunteerism made this transition manageable and possible.

This chapter focuses on how Head Start targeted more than children as potential beneficiaries of the program. In fact, the requirements to have parents

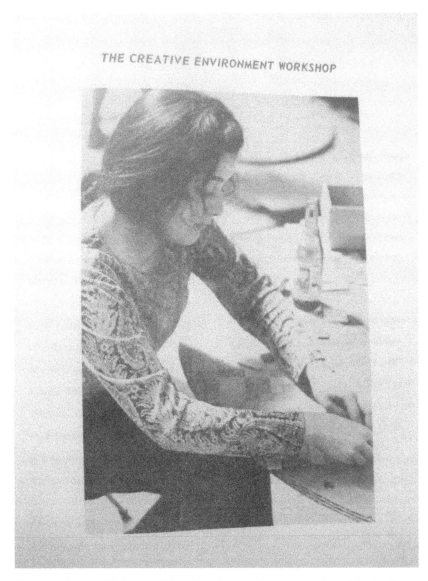

THE CREATIVE ENVIRONMENT WORKSHOP

Figure 10: Creative Workshop. African American and Latina women's participation in Head Start programs was promoted as an employment opportunity for aspiring teachers, teacher aides, and curriculum development officers in communities such as South Central Los Angeles.

SOURCE: Grant Applications/Project Proposals-California Counties Files, Pacific Oaks College-L.A., 1969–1970, Record Group F3751:174, State Office of Economic Opportunity Records, California State Archives, Sacramento.

participate in coursework, volunteer in classrooms, and be active in parent Policy Councils ensured that they would become actively invested in the program. Head Start children's parents—mothers—were heralded as the "vital by-product" of the program, which boasted that their involvement was one of its largest successes.[4] By the latter part of the twentieth century, the positive appraisals of Head Start's place within South Central required an investment by an interracial community of parents. The program's longevity is measured by the ways in which the program enriched "the parent's lives and strengthened family ties as its activities became a project for the involvement of the whole family."[5] This chapter illuminates how parent involvement went beyond acts of volunteerism, as the participation of parents in the classroom required that they, too, modeled and learned from the lessons of inclusion through the infusion of a multicultural curriculum, lessons that would have a reach beyond the classroom space. From its origins in South Central, Head Start has served the needs of a diverse grouping of children, but by the late twentieth century, the increasing racial diversity of the city required that the curriculum and level of parent involvement embrace diversity head-on. The program demonstrated community development through the legacy and growth of a long-standing institution in the community.

THE HEALTH AND NUTRITION NEEDS
OF HEAD START FAMILIES

An initial effort of U.S. government officials in helping poor children was to elevate their health outcomes, a goal in which, they felt, parents were not investing enough energy and concern. For a better educational experience, national health care practitioners believed that children should receive routine medical and dental examinations, screening tests, and immunizations. An important indicator of women and children's health is the infant mortality rate. In South Central, the infant mortality rate was 50 percent greater than the city-wide average. Similarly, a minimal number of children in Los Angeles were immunized against diphtheria, whooping cough, tetanus, smallpox, and polio—entirely different from the rest of the county.[6] As captured in *Pancho*, the documentary film discussed in Chapter 2, Head Start officials believed that introducing children to the importance of visiting the doctor on a frequent basis would set in motion a practice that would extend beyond their participation in Head Start.

Head Start's goal of having all children immunized and undergoing medical examinations was challenging to enforce. The program began blaming impoverished families for inconsistency with regular medical checkups and immunizations for their children. In Watts and South Central Los Angeles, many Head Start delegate agencies reported that "children are gradually undergoing medical examinations," but they were not close to their goal of treating all Head Start children. Officials were ill prepared for the difficulty of scheduling each child for a medical and dental visit.[7] The lack of health care providers in the area produced hardships for families who had to travel long distances to receive medical attention. In response, Head Start programs created mobile medical and dental health care units as important entry points for children's health care.[8]

In addition to medical and dental checkups, Head Start had an ambitious nutritional education program. It followed the model of the Breakfast for Children Program (BCP) developed by the Black Panther Party in Oakland, California, a program that then FBI chief J. Edgar Hoover characterized as an act of subversion. The BCP provided nutritious and consistent meals to vulnerable children facing poverty.[9] Head Start officials similarly believed that "to build strong bodies that grow and develop properly, children need the right food. A child who is fed when he is hungry feels well cared for and secure. A well-nourished child has a better chance to learn."[10] The goal of offering healthy meals appealed to all members of the family. At the Watts Head Start, older children who stayed to help with their younger siblings during class also had an impact on meal and snack time. The increase in child participation was not anticipated; it "created a small problem at snack time and some of the teachers reached into their own purses to buy crackers and milk for the older children."[11] As one teacher put it, "You can't sit there and eat in front of hungry kids."[12] Head Start officials and teachers committed themselves to helping each child establish good food habits and laying the foundation for good lifelong health.

Healthy food and eating, according to nutritionists, would affect many parts of a child's life: "[T]heir bodies would grow stronger and be better able to work and play . . . [and they would] learn about: new foods, how they look, taste, smell, and the different ways foods are served."[13] The hope would be that meals would become pleasant times for families, as children would associate food with pleasure. Teachers and adults would share mealtimes with students to foster among them a better attitude regarding community dining and even to encourage them to learn the concepts of portions and sharing by serving food "family style."[14] As part of their educational efforts, Head Start created an ideal and typical weekly menu for children, which aimed for a balanced and creative diet (Table 4).[15]

	MONDAY	TUESDAY	WEDNESDAY	THURSDAY	FRIDAY
SNACK	Graham crackers w/ peanut butter Juice	Cheese toast Grape juice	Eggs & toast Juice	Hot chocolate Crackers	French toast Grape juice
HOT LUNCH	Meat loaf Cole slaw Canned pineapples Milk Bread w/ butter	Baked chicken Green beans Cucumber in sour cream Pudding Milk Bread w/ butter	Sloppy joes Tossed salad French apples Milk	Grilled liver Mixed vegetables Tomato wedges Peach cobbler Bread w/ butter Milk	Enchiladas Spanish rice Tossed salad Ambrosia Milk

Table 4: Head Start Weekly Meal Menu, 1968
SOURCE: "The Project Head Start Feeding Program," n.d., Record Group F3751:87, State Office of Economic Opportunity Records, California State Archives, Sacramento.

Involving parents in the nutrition program was also paramount for Head Start officials. Unlike the Black Panther Party's free breakfast program, which was born out of a clear understanding of the unrelenting impact of poverty, not individual deficiencies, Head Start tackled the issue of nutrition by not only providing meals to children but also "instructing" mothers in proper nutritional options. The racist and sexist ideologies espoused by Oscar Lewis's "culture of poverty" and Daniel Moynihan's "tangle of pathology," which argued that poverty in families of color was due to individual behaviors and family formation, invaded Head Start's views on poor mothers. The notion that women of color were unfit mothers and that their mothering practices and choices were contributing to the high rates of poverty oriented many parenting classes for Head Start mothers. Head Start officials started with the premise that poor mothers lacked an awareness and knowledge of how to provide healthy meals to their children, rather than by addressing the barriers that shaped limited food options.

The Head Start handbook was a convenient way to disseminate information on proper nutrition and served as the guidebook for instructing mothers.[16] It provided specific guidelines about what time to provide children with meals, daily dietary requirements, the breakdown of food groups, the cleanliness required when serving meals, and, most important, creating a consistent schedule for meal times.[17] Parents inspired by the skills "learned" in the nutrition classes created a recipe book titled "Recipe Collection by Head Start Parents." Increasingly, mealtime was used as a time to teach children how to share and learn about new cultures. Food prepared using recipes of different racial and ethnic communities became commonplace during mealtime. Head Start mothers were proactive in ensuring that the book was accessible not only in English but also in Spanish, and therefore Mexican American and Mexican immigrant parents also contributed to the book. Showcasing recipes such as "Fruited Pork" and "Tropical Pizza" demonstrated how parents were incorporating fruit and vegetables as key ingredients in the meal.[18] Parents attempted to create meals that their children would eat, but with a healthy spin. The recipes created were also reflective of the range of Head Start participants. The cookbook was one way in which parents articulated and celebrated the diversity of families served by Head Start in South Central. In addition, it exercised their version of empowerment through these courses, in that they played a crucial role in shaping the food choices and recipes designed for their children.

In the early twentieth century, Anglo reformers entered Mexican American homes to Americanize and instruct Mexican American families about proper health and nutrition habits.[19] The logic of educating women on proper nutrition rested on the notion of Head Start officials that women were ill-equipped and uneducated, which in some ways aligned with those early twentieth century efforts. However, in the current case, Americanization was not the ultimate goal. The goals of these classes for mothers were born out of a reductionist understanding of low-income families, yet women used these courses as opportunities to come together and discuss their personal, family, and communal

134 TEACHING TOGETHER

needs. They did not let these racialized ideas of being "unfit" deter them from maximizing and utilizing the courses in ways that benefited themselves and their families most effectively.

Mexican and African American women in South Central found creative ways to translate the imposed national nutritional, health, family planning, and sewing courses into something of their own. In the case of Mexican immigrant women, the classes were an opportunity to learn English. Head Start mothers believed that they should learn English for the livelihood of their families in the United States. As one mother expressed, in broken English, "all of them must try to learn the language their children need when they go to school."[20] This call to learn the language became the impetus for volunteering parents to begin English classes formally in Head Starts throughout South Central. In the meantime, Head Start officials hired Spanish-speaking specialists to translate at the meetings and provided materials in Spanish. By the 1980s, Head Start budgets and program proposals committed financially to Spanish translation and English as a Second Language classes.[21]

Both African American and Mexican mothers discussed how their older children were also struggling in class; as a collective, they began to hold remedial afternoon sessions for older siblings using Head Start resources.[22] While these parenting classes were born out of a belief by government officials that as parents they were unable to create educational and effective childrearing spaces, Head Start parents worked within these negative assumptions to build spaces that provided educational opportunities for the whole family. Working poor, working class, and poor women of color at every turn had to find creative ways to assert autonomy in the midst of government officials using Patrick Moynihan's and Oscar Lewis's theories about their abilities as parents. Their ability to do so served to embolden their ability to see themselves as active agents and was key in generating ideas for developing the programming and growth of Head Start in particular, and in South Central broadly.

HEAD START MOTHERS AND FAMILIES: LEARNING, TEACHING, AND EMPOWERMENT

Head Start parents were actively recruited to become teachers and teacher's aides and to be involved in the development of the educational curriculum (Figure 11). Delegate agency employees actively canvassed the Watts community by going "door-to-door to locate children most in need of Head Start, promote the program, and screen prospective assistant teachers and neighborhood aide applicants."[23] Looking for prospective teacher assistants was of critical importance to gaining community trust. At age 21, Carol Chevis's participation in another War on Poverty program, the Neighborhood Job Corps Program, transformed her life. Carol did not complete high school and had been working as a domestic for many years. She never imagined that she could do anything else: "[L]ife seemed good for a while, because I was making almost $100 dollars a week as a domestic. I really didn't know any other way of life—but I felt like I was kind of wasting my time."[24] One day while riding the bus on the way to work, she sparked a conversation with a woman who told her to find a job with a future. The Neighborhood Job Corps would offer training and employment. She was worried about leaving behind a job that offered a solid income. Enrolling in the program "meant a cut in pay, but

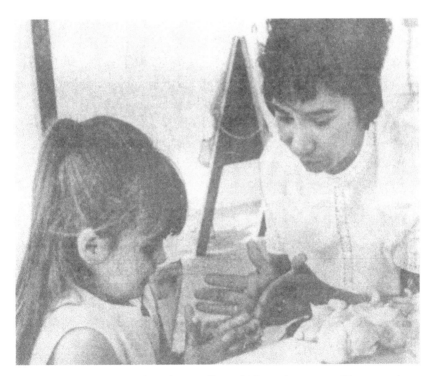

Figure 11: Helping Hand. The volunteer efforts of African American and Latina mothers were decisive in the implementation, longevity, and positive impact of Head Start among participating South Central Los Angeles students and their families.

SOURCE: Ray Graham, Los Angeles Times, November 6, 1966, copyright 1966. Used with permission.

I was really excited about being placed as a teacher's aide with Head Start. I love kids and use to think about being a teacher."[25] Her commitment to children and her dream of becoming a teacher prompted her to return to Manual Arts High School to earn her high school diploma; she also attended Los Angeles City College, earning her degree in child psychology. Efforts toward nurturing residents like Carol to become Head Start teachers would be one of the earliest sources of celebration for the program nationally.

Sargent Shriver and local Head Start centers praised the job opportunities created for local citizens; nevertheless, this local and organic approach toward recruitment had critics. U.S. government officials, especially at the national level, critiqued inner city Head Start centers for failing to provide credentialed and trained teachers, and they claimed that children were at a more significant disadvantage when taught by "inadequately prepared teachers" and that "the use of poorly qualified teachers became commonplace for many summer and year-round Head Start projects."[26] Experts and policymakers initially saw Head Start as a way to overcome the educational limitations of poor children and pointed out that many of these "youngsters soon were to enter Head Start projects taught by semiliterate parents or neighbors rather than professionally trained teachers."[27] Fears of unqualified teachers from the community are connected to the sexist and racist ideologies regarding working poor people's abilities and intellect. Despite claims of their lack of qualifications, women continued to pursue becoming Head Start teachers and aides and used these courses as opportunities to build community.

Head Start agencies in South Central did not report any anxiety over having "unqualified" teachers instructing young children. In fact, they were proud of providing employment opportunities for the community, and these critiques of inadequate training further inspired parents to work as key advocates in the program as teachers and aides. The curriculum for Head Start's local instruction and training focused on personal growth, building classroom content, communication skills, proper supervision and administration through effective communication, familiarization with key ways of assisting in the community, working with parents and volunteers, multicultural education, and basic Spanish.[28] A primary goal of the new teacher curriculum was to engage teachers and aides in reflecting on how their new roles would develop their own "self-confidence as individuals with meaningful purpose." This last point is what Carol Chevis epitomizes the most: that becoming a part of Head Start gave her a purpose and enhanced her communication skills, which would "promote self-confidence in communication with parents, children, and the community."[29] In many cases, this self-confidence facilitated mindful community engagement by teachers coming from the community.

Part of Head Start requirements was the expectation that parents volunteer a few hours per week. These hours translated into helping with classroom duties and managing children. Through volunteering, parents felt welcomed and began to drop by even on days they were not expected. They would be responsible for going on errands, picking up children for school, and reading stories to classes. Lupe Osuna, a Mexican immigrant, became a teacher at the Watts Towers Head Start center operated by the Training and Research Foundation. She was a mother to five children and had begun to volunteer at the local Head Start center in South Gate when her youngest child enrolled. Lupe volunteered daily and even helped the staff clean up at the end of the school year in June by washing the walls and packing the equipment for storage. The following year her child completed the program, but she still returned to Head Start as a volunteer. It was at that point that the teachers urged her to apply for the teacher's aide job; they said, "You're here every day. You know what to do."[30] Convincing Lupe that this route was available to her required work. Her first obstacle was to convince her husband that enrolling in school was a worthwhile cause. As she recalled, when she started school and working, her "husband didn't talk to me for a month after." Her mother-in-law was her biggest advocate and would tell Lupe, "Don't let it worry you. Keep on working. One day he'll leave you and you'll have a job."[31] Lupe felt that her mother-in-law was right. Her husband eventually gave in and began to talk to her since he realized that she was not going to stop working, but sadly Lupe and her husband decided to divorce shortly after. She was thankful for her mother-in-law's advice. There was a hardship in becoming a teacher for Head Start: she had to go to school at night. She recalled, "It would be hard in the winter when I had to get the bus in the rain to go to East Los Angeles College."[32] Sometimes she would take two buses and would have classes from seven to ten at night after a long day of work; she would get home at 11 p.m. and then do what she needed to do to prepare for the next day's work and her children's school day. Her older daughter was of great assistance, helping with her siblings while Lupe was getting her education and setting an example for all of her children.

Lupe's example served to inspire many women, in particular, Mexican immigrant women, to follow in her footsteps. She was very vocal about letting women know that they had options. She knew that some of her peers' husbands were not keen on her encouraging other women away from home to study, but many of the men and husbands ended up budging because Head Start involved their children. Lupe served as a role model not only for her children and those in Head Start but also for the women who volunteered at the center. Her presence and story reaffirmed that if they desired to go to school, gaining employment at a place like Head Start was possible. It was hard work, but possible.

Josephine Garner followed a trajectory similar to Lupe's. An African American resident of Watts, Josephine came to Los Angeles by train from Birmingham, Alabama, in 1962. In a pattern typical of other Head Start teachers, she started volunteering for the program in 1979 because her son attended the Head Start center near the Imperial Courts Housing Project. As a divorced mother, Josephine had to make employment choices that would provide financial assistance and stability for her family. She had worked for fifteen years at an embossing machine plant in Orange County and went back to school to take child development classes, beginning as a teacher's assistant in 1982 at Head Start.[33] She recalled those years as very trying: "Oh yes, I'd get tired. I'd sit in the car between classes and I'd nod off . . . but I knew I wasn't doing myself any good just staying home. I needed to take these fingers and do whatever I can with them."[34] She always had an interest in child education, so her affiliation with Head Start did not come as a surprise. She began as a teacher and quickly ascended to the position of Head Start coordinator. Throughout her trajectory at Head Start she always felt fear: "I wouldn't measure up . . . I'm not good enough."[35] This anxiety over teaching effectiveness was felt not only by Garner but by many Head Start teachers and aides.

Not all women were able to finish the steps necessary to become a Head Start teacher or aide. Elena Santiago followed a path like those of Lupe and Josephine: the volunteering requirement prompted her to start working at the Head Start in 1977. She enrolled her son at the Center Court Head Start near her home. The majority of students were Mexican immigrants, and the teacher was white. Elena's lack of English proficiency did not prove a deterrent to her participation in the classroom: she learned essential English phrases, and the teacher utilized the few Spanish words she knew. She continued to volunteer for the program after her son graduated at the end of the 1977 school year, and in her second year at the center, the teacher was replaced by an African American Watts resident, Ms. Davis. Elena recalls her interactions with Ms. Davis fondly because the teacher was her most influential advocate and supported her in attending night classes to get her GED and teaching credential: "Ms. Davis was super nice, supportive. She wanted the best for the moms. She wanted us to better ourselves. I liked working with her."[36] Elena attempted the coursework, but her husband's hectic work schedule prevented her from pursuing the courses any further because she was not content with leaving her three children unsupervised while she went to school. She did not regret her choice of not pursuing her degree further and recalled those years in Head Start as a meaningful experience to make her feel a sense of community and politically active and engaged, as well as an integral part of her becoming a South Central resident. Understanding parents' participation in Head Start only as volunteerism is limiting, because it fails to capture how Head Start for many parents became much more.

In South Central, the yearlong teacher's aide course ended with a graduation ceremony during which graduates received a diploma of completion and wore caps and gowns as in official commencements. The graduates' families were invited to the ceremony and reception. These ceremonies were communal celebrations in which families and community residents celebrated these women's accomplishments. In her more than thirty years working with Head Start programs, Phillipa Johnson, associate director of King Drew Medical Center Head Start, recorded these celebrations by scrapbooking pictures. The photographs illustrate the happiness, joy, and pride felt by the women and their families as they accomplished this feat. They also show the demographic change of the program. Initially, one sees the boastful faces of African American Head Start mothers, many of whom continue to work at Head Start as coordinators and social workers. By the 1990s, the majority of graduates were Latina women, and like their African American predecessors, they too, joined the ranks of Head Start teachers, teacher aides, and social workers.

These photo albums, while visually illustrative of South Central's demographic change, more importantly capture glimpses of happiness and celebration— visuals that do not readily come to mind when one is considering the lived realities of residents in an impoverished community. In this way, investigating how women and mothers were empowered through the program offers a glimpse into the potential for shared space and experience as well as how Black and Latina/o families drew strength from their education and labor in support of each other.

PARENT POLICY COUNCILS

Undeterred by the underestimation of poor parents' involvement within Head Start, parents carved out a space to voice priorities and concerns through Policy Councils. From the program's origins, Head Start parents have served as the councils' elected officers. The president of the council had to be a Head Start parent and had to be voted in by fellow Head Start parents. These council meetings were held on a monthly basis and became an important step in leadership development. To ease Mexican immigrant women into the program and achieve their active participation, Head Start hired Spanish-speaking specialists to translate at the meetings, provided materials in Spanish, and offered English instruction courses.

Head Start parents raised complaints, concerns, or praises relating to the program. Parents, both African Americans and Mexican immigrants, proved to be vocal about what they felt mattered most. Complaints ranged from the availability of books for every child and ensuring that the bathrooms were promptly fixed to larger grievances such as teacher misconduct or favoritism. In some cases, Mexican immigrant women were the most vocal in their efforts. When they were not able to articulate their concerns in English, these women shared them with a Spanish-speaking social worker or translator who would convey them, in English, to all parents in attendance. Mexican immigrant mothers did not let their lack of proficiency in English or undocumented status deter their commitment to organizing collectively and making sure that their and their children's needs were met. Contrary to the popular beliefs that Mexican immigrants, especially recent immigrants and residents in this community, were not vocal about their needs, Mexican mothers spoke up on behalf of their children because they understood that they were setting an important example for them. The organization of Mexican immigrant women caused some initial tension within the Policy Council and with African American women—there were clear markers of racial division. African American women felt that their children's needs were being shortchanged by the increased activism of Mexican immigrant women. Because both groups understood that their worries were not that different, they promptly quashed their racial divisions. They both wanted what was best for their children, and the fight for classroom maintenance, sufficient books, and toys for the classroom, or for offering more educational opportunities for all women, was a benefit to all.[37] They grew to understand that their activism was rooted not solely in a racial political struggle but also in their identity and politics as working class women of color, mothers, and caretakers concerned for their family's well-being and, in turn, community. Women grew to see and understand their work in Head Start as much more than just taking their children to school and volunteering: this was a real opportunity to shape Head Start's daily procedures.

African American and Mexican immigrant women's activism within the Policy Council extended beyond their local council. The fervor with which Head Start mothers advocated for their children and Head Start programming was powerful. An early example of the power of parent engagement was the work of the Head Start mothers' collective in the summer of 1968. Head Start faced severe budget cuts and a threat of incorporation into the Los Angeles Unified School District. Head Start delegate agencies in South Central grew apprehensive about these looming changes and therefore mobilized their most reliable constituency, Head Start parents. During Policy Council meetings, Head Start parents were encouraged to write letters to Congressman Augustus Hawkins about their disapproval of such moves. The response by African American and Mexican immigrant women was overwhelming, yet in many ways, their perspectives differed. African American women were much more direct about their concerns. Brathei Titicomb wrote, "Dear Congressman Hawkins: Please vote for Head Start programs to remain in their own neighborhoods." Dorothy Turner wrote, "This is in regards to the Head Start program being taken over by the Board of Education. As a South Central community member, I know that this school is already overcrowded and have many problems as a result adding Head Start could only be harmful to our community kids. It should be much better to leave Head Start to the community."[38] Both Titicomb and Turner were expressing that they wanted Head Start to remain community controlled, with the assumption that the school board would not provide adequate attention to the program. Incorporation would eliminate one fundamental tenet of Head Start: community activism and control. Letters by African American residents also expressed unease over the leadership of the program, should the school board take over. The leadership being of the residential community was Head Start's greatest appeal and success, something that would drastically change if the school board took over. African Americans were worried about the future of the program and firmly believed that writing letters to express their dissatisfaction with the future of the program was necessary. Parent involvement through a letter-writing campaign as evidenced in this instance was nurtured and an indispensable feature of the program.

Head Start agencies in South Central have continually faced budget cuts and threats to delegate agency closures. During President Richard Nixon's administration, a period when which the budget for Head Start declined slightly, participants of Head Start wrote to Hawkins again to show their support for the program. As usual, Hawkins made public statements of his commitment to the program and childcare legislation, and most especially, to Head Start being operated by community organizations and delegate agencies. Residents and local Head Start administrators knew they had an ally in Hawkins and that their political engagement through letter-writing campaigns and phone calls was being considered.

Mexican immigrant families voiced concerns over the school board takeover differently. Most Mexican immigrant parents wrote their letters in Spanish. On July 22, 1968, in a letter to Congressman Hawkins, Josefina Velarde wrote, "Honorable Sir: Cordially we request that you support the continued maintenance of the excellent Head Start program that benefits our children greatly, as they are the future of tomorrow."[39] Similarly, Augustina Jurado wrote, "On behalf of the Mexican and Spanish speaking people, I thank you, so much if this great Head Start . . . continue in our community. For the development of our children in this wonderful country in which they will be the future citizens."[40] The majority of letters written by Mexican immigrant families presented Head Start as helping children and families make the transition into U.S. culture. In some instances, these letters appear to have been written by the same person because the handwriting and their message was the same, but they were signed by different members of the community. The letters claimed to speak for the "Mexican" community—a marked contrast from their African American counterparts, who used a much more inclusive language—not, for instance, "the Black community" specifically. Letters written by Mexican families were much more racially motivated. They hardly ever referenced the presence of African Americans in the community or in Head Start, and they spoke to the educational value of the program assisting Mexican immigrant children in adapting to the United States. The discourse around citizenship and nation was overwhelming throughout these letters. They spoke to what this program offered their children, and, in turn, their families: an opportunity for a future in the United States. The utilization of words such as future and citizenship frames how Mexican immigrant women and families conceptualized their citizenship and rights. This discourse follows in line with an assimilationist narrative of immigrant families, in which education is the tool by which the second generation becomes part of the U.S. body politic. The use of future aimed to justify why Head Start in particular, and education more broadly, needed to continue to receive financial support. The Mexican immigrant women's letter-writing campaign illustrates that irrespective of immigration status, they felt they had the rights to fight for the needs of their children and the community.

Nurturing a sense of rights and activism irrespective of citizenship was a part of Head Start's politics in South Central. In total, over three hundred signatures on petitions and one hundred individual letters were written to Hawkins by African American and Mexican immigrant families urging him not to allow the Head Start move to the Los Angeles Unified School District. In the end, the school board did not take over Head Start, and it remained under the purview of the delegate agencies throughout South Central, a victory that these mothers felt was due in part to their activism. Nancy A. Naples's *Grassroots Warriors* provides a theoretical model for understanding Head Start mothers' activism and politicization: she argues that the activism of women of color is connected to a long-term commitment to the community that originates in their residential context. Activist mothering requires nurturing efforts beyond one's kinship group, in addition to the paid and unpaid labor required to fight racism, sexism, and poverty.[41] Naples does not aim to provide an essentialist reading of mothering practices but instead builds on the seminal work of Patricia Hill Collins's theorization of "other mothers," in which activism by African American women extends beyond kinship networks and forms part of the extended network of community mothers.[42] Naples describes such mothering practices as "not natural expressions of a Black women's social or cultural identity"; instead, an analysis of women's community work demonstrates how it develops as a response to a dynamic relationship to historical conditions and is passed on by socialization practices and political struggles.[43]

The multicultural landscape of South Central and Head Start made it such that both African American and Mexican immigrant women crafted their brand of activism rooted in their connections as mothers in the broadest form of identity. The neighborhood, both the streets of South Central and the Head Start classrooms, inspired women of color to make a long-term commitment to community work. The fervor and level of activism by Head Start parents are among the many reasons Head Start is a long-standing institution in communities such as South Central where many social programs are short-lived. The mandatory requirement of parent volunteerism in the classroom opened the door for parents to become active in Policy Councils and provided the space for them to make inroads collectively and interracially as residents invested in South Central as a community, as a place they call home and worthy of such investment.

One prominent political official in South Central, Maxine Waters, began her political career being part of the Head Start program. Born and raised by a single mother in housing projects in St. Louis, Missouri, she moved to Los Angeles in 1961. Her first job in Los Angeles was in the garment industry, and she later made the transition to Head Start. The demand for community representation in poverty boards across Los Angeles politicized Waters. Working in Head Start would catapult her into the political spotlight. She was elected to the State Assembly in 1976. She quickly became "one of the most powerful members of the California Legislature and arguably the nation's most influential black female elected official."[44] She replaced Hawkins in Congress in 1991, and emerged as an effective deal maker and "protest politician." After the Rodney King beating in 1991, "she led rallies demanding the resignation of Police Chief Darryl Gates. In the wake of the 1992 civil unrest, Waters became much more visible on the national stage as a spokesperson for black grievances and justice issues, but she also used her influence to help real estate developers and others . . . to win City Hall approvals and federal grants."[45] Waters continues to represent South Central, despite its increased Latina/o character. In part, this is because of the undocumented immigrant status of the Latina/o population. Her efforts in the community are exemplified most recently by her support of allowing community residents to gain ownership of the largest urban farm in the country: the South Central Farm. It is this level of community engagement sparked through Head Start that is another example of the "vital by-products" of the program.

The political and emotional work by Head Start mothers extended beyond the classroom and parent Policy Councils to their personal relationships and community. They challenged the false separation of reproductive work in the family from work as part of the labor force. For these women, motherhood was not an oppressive or pejorative concept. Instead, it anchored a method of exerting power, allowing them to work with the community as well as complicate negative representations of working class women of color as being pathological and part of the undeserving poor. They challenged these images and discourses through their daily lives, education, and organizing. Women's participation in Head Start politicized them in unforeseen ways, allowing collaborative work irrespective of racial difference. As Head Start mother Maria Garcia stated,

> [E]arly childhood education changed my child's shyness with other kids, but also helped me get over my shyness and work with other women. Before I felt isolated and alone, I spent most of my time at home cleaning, cooking, and caring for others. . . . but going to Head Start I've made new friends, and learned a lot from just talking to other women . . . even Black women. There is a shared sense that we care about our kids. My kid's teacher, she's Black, and she shows no difference amongst the kids. I like her. . . . I use to think that Black women were the worst, but she's changed my mind.[46]

Having recently immigrated to South Central, Maria saw that participation in Head Start transformed not only her child's shyness but also herself. It provided her with a new racial outlook, one that while seemingly minor at that stage in her life could be seen as the beginning of a transformative perspective on the African American community. One would suspect that Mexican immigrant women would prefer to have Latina/o teachers teach their children; however, Mexican immigrant women understood that an essential characteristic of a teacher is commitment and fair treatment of their children.

Parents' activism within the Head Start program facilitated a major transformation, as in some cases it transformed women's lives like that of Maria, not only during their hours inside the Head Start classroom but also in their home life and community. Maria is but one Head Start mother whose racial perspective changed through her participation in the program. However, such change is not an easy feat. Working across racial difference was and is not an easy task for all Head Start teachers and administrators. They, too, had to learn how to let go of their preconceived racial stereotypes and understandings, and open themselves up to the inclusion and increased hiring of Latina teachers and assistants. This transition, while met with some trepidation, was not extremely difficult, however, in that the mission of the program was to help impoverished families of South Central, a mission that parents and Head Start teachers firmly believed in. Nationwide, by 1995, Head Start's students were 36 percent African American, 32 percent white, 25 percent Latina/o, 4 percent American Indian, and 3 percent Asian. In South Central, about 55 percent of children attending Head Start were Latina/o and 40 percent were African American.[47] Demographic change became the backdrop in which to infuse the curriculum with a multicultural approach and mission and to create a model for the grounded realities of diversity.

TEACHING IN A DIVERSE CLASSROOM

Head Start agencies throughout South Central accepted the charge of guiding children and older youth through their multiracial and multicultural futures. They required the curriculum to show that "safe, constructive things to do and places to go are to learn about other cultures in non-conflict situations."[48] It is this racial transformation that forced Head Start directors and officials to make an effort to hire more Latina/o teachers. The hands-on approach of recruiting internally from the community had many benefits. As the demographics in the community changed, administrators such as Josephine and Phillipa looked to their community as a resource for hiring Latina/o teachers and developing an curriculum attentive to diversity that would encourage cross-racial dialogue and collaboration.

As early as 1970, Head Start manuals stated that curriculums must stress "the importance of understanding and appreciating one's own, as well as other people's culture and ethnic background as an essential factor in the achievement of the personal and professional growth for all teachers of young children."[49] Along with the development of a multicultural curriculum is the importance of instructing teachers in conversational Spanish at the very least. The ideal is for full bilingualism, but "conversational Spanish would be meaningful to all Head Start teaching staff who work with parents and children of Spanish descent."[50] Knowing and utilizing conversational Spanish would increase an understanding of the language and culture between Head Start teachers and Spanish-speaking families. By the late 1970s, Head Start centers were mandated by U.S. federal law to ensure that they hired "persons who speak the primary language of the children and are knowledgeable about their heritage . . . at least one teacher or aide interacting regularly with the children must speak their language."[51] This new mandate initially caused anger and discomfort for many African American Head Start teachers, aides, and advocates, as they feared they would soon be displaced by bilingual teachers, mostly Latina/os. Teachers such as Lupe Osuna would not seem like anomalies but would become the norm. This fear in some cases kept African Americans from entirely welcoming and embracing Latina/o residents and fellow Latina/o Head Start supporters, as they feared that their hard-fought efforts for community control and empowerment would come to an end. Such fear of the unknown and what change might engender often leads to interracial tension. Moving beyond fear requires that people embrace these changes, even if they produce bursts of conflict. Often this transition is made by indispensable people encouraging others to be open to their differences.

Head Start teacher Josephine was amenable, although, initially she too had reservations. Reflecting on her childhood experience helped her shape a commitment to a multicultural curriculum. She wanted all the children to learn about different customs,

> so that if they [children] go to another school and meet other children they won't be surprised like I was. We do this so kids can understand other cultures. When I was little, I didn't know Jehovah's Witnesses didn't get Christmas presents and I gave a little boy a present. His father was insulted that I even offered it.[52]

This memory ensured that, from the ground up, Josephine's teaching philosophy incorporated lessons that celebrated difference.

The hiring of Latina teachers was an asset to the overall longevity of the program and, more important, a reflection of how the community had changed. Some Head Start officials embraced Latina teachers entering the classroom because it made their task of being sensitive to the Latina/o experience easier. Josephine spoke very little Spanish, but with assistance from teachers such as Lupe, and by extension mothers such as Elena, she was able to better address the needs of Mexican children and families and to encourage African American children to embrace learning Spanish. She hoped that learning the days of the week, colors, and songs in Spanish would encourage further interest in Mexican culture. Josephine remembers a particular incident with fondness. On a summer day, she encouraged Mexican and African American Head Start parents and students to hold hands in a circle around the table as she led grace and then sang as she always did with the children: "Thank you for my luh-unch, *gracias por las comidas*."[53] The fact that she uttered these words in both languages and that the families around the table were African Americans, Mexican Americans, and Mexican immigrants led her to conclude, "People breaking bread together makes my day."[54]

The need for bilingual Head Start centers arose mainly because the initial wave of Mexican immigrants into South Central were first-generation immigrants who spoke very little English at all. Head Start teachers recounted that "Mexican children go through a six-to-eight-month silent period. They're assimilating what's around them. Ninety-nine percent of them are speaking beautiful English by June."[55] A national study by the National Bureau of Economic Research in 1996 reported that participation by Latina/o children in Head Start has a positive impact on the English-language acquisition by Latina/o children.[56] This study found that Latina/o children of Mexican origin reap the largest gains from programs like Head Start.[57] Bilingual early childhood education is beneficial for Mexican American children because preschool is their "first exposure to English and preschool experiences are likely to enhance cultural assimilation and socialization."[58]

Along with the language barriers that made the relationships between African American and Latina/os most difficult, children had to make sense of society's and their parents' own racial prejudice and attitudes.[59] The initial days at Head Start are primarily marked by segregation, often along racial lines, yet over the course of the school year children become much more willing and able to break down racial walls. Teachers are particularly decisive in this endeavor, as they are conduits of authority and knowledge for these children. While parents might not be open to discussing cross-racial alliances at the dinner table, children's day-to-day encounters with their teachers and other students make for an intervention about how racial difference is not represented only through tension or conflict. Some of the cross-racial friendships that form in Head Start centers might not be long-lasting; however, they do offer an opportunity in a child's cognitive, social, and emotional development to associate racial difference not with negativity but rather with an opportunity to understand the richness in diversity.

The racial transition in the community and Head Start, while not always readily embraced, required centers to find creative ways to make African

American history relevant to Latina/o families and children, and vice versa. By the 1990s, celebrations for Dr. Martin Luther King Jr.'s birthday and Cinco de Mayo had become commonplace in Head Start centers throughout South Central and Watts. A teacher at one center stated, "[W]e ended up with a number of kids wanting to be Dr. King when we have the children portray various Black history figures in February. . . . I remember one Mexican child being King one year."[60] Even after the event, the Mexican child "walked around feeling so proud."[61] Teachers had to find creative ways in which to instruct children that figures like Martin Luther King Jr. advocated for the equality and rights not only of African Americans but also of disfranchised poor people. On Cinco de Mayo, teachers set up a party to celebrate the 1862 Mexican victory over the French in the Mexican state of Puebla. They celebrate Cinco de Mayo with *piñatas* and reenactments that actively involved all the children and parents. Over the years, teachers gathered curriculum and books that helped them make sense of and teach African American and Mexican history and culture for young children.[62] This was made more accessible and possible with the increased presence of Latina/o teachers and parents involved in the program.

In the 1980s, this approach to teaching difference and diversity through an exploration of food, folkways, holidays, and language was part of a broader trajectory of a multicultural curriculum in education. Educators believed that this was a useful tool for celebrating diversity. Critics of multicultural education feared that it represented the social and political fragmentation of national identity, a loss of what is American (that is, white and Protestant).[63] Educators critical of multicultural methods also suggested that such teaching models reify difference and encourage the "normalization of multicultural discourse and its resultant failure to reinvent or confront established categories of knowledge or relations of power," as multicultural curricula add ethnic content to culture.[64] Educators also believed that a multicultural curriculum breaks culture down through a process of categorization, which in turn instructs children to learn through categories and not through structural and power dynamics—in other words, multicultural curricula can eliminate an in-depth analysis of racial inequality.[65] However, advocates of this approach believed that introducing children to some features that characterize different cultures is positive. These multicultural educational resources must not artificially insert culture to "multiculturalize it"; rather what is required is a "holistic and comparative perspective that allows students to draw their own conclusions and abstractions from evidence" to move away from prejudiced, negative, simple, and categorical views and understanding of culture.[66]

Teachers at Head Start attempted as best they could to balance their curricula in light of these critiques and suggestions for multicultural education. They presented and discussed Mexican immigrant and African American experiences through a curriculum attuned to racial diversity and history, and attempted to contextualize what children were studying.[67] Thus "adding culture" was not superficial but thoughtful and mindful of the multiple audiences in the classroom. It also was not only a discursive tool to celebrate racial difference to garner political support and resonance, as the following chapter will discuss, but an attempt to consider diversity as being attentive to the actual on-the-ground realities of the community. Having Head Start teachers from the community was of critical importance: they understood that celebrating culture without understanding lived realities and power structures does a disservice to a multiracial classroom. Head Start teachers understood the difficulty of engaging with power critiques when teaching four- to five-year-olds; however, part of the lesson was not only for the children but also for parents. The lesson plans had to operate on two levels. Discussing what some educators could interpret as superficial categories of culture and difference was a strategic way for these two groups to begin to understand and envision a way to coexist that was not tense, based on conflict, or a threat to their livelihood. At times celebrations in the curriculum became a way to illustrate the promise of interracial community formation. The implementation of a multicultural curriculum in the classroom operated at a different scale than Mayor Tom Bradley's political discourse of diversity, an issue that is discussed in Chapter 6. What both chapters illuminate is that embracing diversity has had its challenges. The context of the Head Start classroom and the development of classroom curricula required that teachers draw connections between lived African American and Mexican American experiences. In many ways, Head Start teachers and parents would prove instrumental in developing an environment where interracial tensions could be minimized and potentially eroded.

"WE WERE THE ONLY GAME IN TOWN"

In the late 1960s, Kedren Head Start Center began as one of the smallest Head Start delegate agencies in Los Angeles County. By the mid-2000s it was one of the largest agencies, with more than twenty-eight centers under its umbrella.

However, in 2014, the L.A. County Office of Education asked Kedren's CEO to close its centers in the midst of controversy about overinflated enrollment numbers and failure to have classroom spaces up to code.[68] With these closures, other institutions picked up where Kedren had left off. However, community trust for continued enrollment and parent participation for new organizations, such as the Children's Institute, did not come easily.[69] In its five decades, teachers at Kedren Head Start centers had labored to gain and retain community trust and engagement. Their longevity, and residents' apprehension about new organizations, illuminate the importance of history, continuity, and the supportive engagement for organizations that have a long-term presence and the support of the South Central community.

In the midst of these changes, perceptions of Head Start continue to be that it is an "oasis of hope." Kedren Head Start centers, like all the others discussed in this chapter, were spaces of hope that were built and achieved through the collective effort of community residents, activists, and government sponsorship. Phillipa Johnson reflected with fondness on when Head Start was the largest and only early childhood provider in the area. As she put it, "We were the only game in town."[70] In 1995, President Bill Clinton signed into law the Early Head Start grants.[71] These grants offered financial assistance for establishing and expanding early childhood education services for pregnant women and children from birth to age three, an age group federal legislation did not cover before. The U.S. government's financial commitment to early childhood development and education created conditions for the proliferation and growth of these types of programs.

In South Central, and across Los Angeles, the growth in early childhood education centers is readily apparent. In addition to the government funding, voters in California voted and approved Proposition 10 in 1998, a fifty-cent tax on cigarette packs and tobacco products that went toward financial assistance for Head Start, First 5 Los Angeles, and St. Johns Well Child and Family Center. These organizations cater to working class families' health, education, and social needs as early as pregnancy. The growth in these organizations (private, public, and government funded) was due in large part to the countless studies that boast the promise and positive effects of early childhood education and the potential for Head Start parents. The growth in early education centers reshaped how Head Start centers approach the recruitment of children and families into the program. Phillipa reminisces that in the early years all they could say to get families involved was to state that Head Start was a free program nestled within the community, but this marker of "free" is no longer enough to get children enrolled, as other programs are also free. Head Start must boost its quality, success, and longevity in the community to get residents in the community to join. The competition from similar centers has dramatically changed the game for Head Start delegate agencies. They have been forced to enter into an organization model to continue to get government funding that frames early childhood education as a business with profits, meaning that studies, reports, and statistics must evidence Head Start's success.

Scholars, educators, and economists agree that Head Start is an asset for child development. Children's growth through participation in the program is a testament to the combination of learning and playing that is fostered. When asked whether she likes Head Start, Maria's young daughter, Paola, meekly nods, "Uh huh . . . I like school . . . I play a lot." Elaborating, Maria says, "She was very shy, she would run away from adults. Head Start has helped her open up and trust others. She loves to count, sing. She also has other little girls to play with . . . she loves her friends and teachers."[72] The premise of Head Start, of trying to correct the "deficiencies" of impoverished children and families, originated from the idea that impoverished families cannot provide for their families due to inherent character flaws. Because it made volunteerism in classroom activities and parent coursework a requirement to guarantee student enrollment, South Central's Head Start became a space that families used creatively to empower themselves for educational and familial growth. The ways in which families engaged with Head Start redefined the value and meaning of volunteerism and maximum feasible participation by the poor. Head Start parents' volunteering their time for classroom management became a springboard for educational opportunity, leadership, and the development of interracial activism invested in children's and community interest. In the end, it was this innovation of volunteerism that ensured that the interracial character of the South Central community and classroom became an asset in the fight to disrupt popular narratives of tension and conflict.

CHAPTER 6

CELEBRATING DIVERSITY
Selective Inclusion in a Multiracial City

ON OCTOBER 19, 1988, Mayor Tom Bradley spoke at the Cultural Diversity Celebration event in the most triumphant tone:

> I am even more proud to be mayor of a city that thrives in harmony while learning from its diversity. I vowed to open the doors of city hall to all our citizens. And I can say our city has been a more racially harmonious place as a result. Entrepreneurs find new products, new markets, and new employees. I remain fundamentally committed to the preservation of ethnic and cultural diversity in the City of L.A.[1]

In his estimation, diversity placed Los Angeles among the most "exciting" and "dynamic" cities in the world. A failure to nurture diversity would "quickly erode the peace and harmony to which we have become so accustomed."[2] He felt that the only way to have fruitful public dialogue was to consider the needs and concerns of the people. Bradley did not suggest that coalition building was easy, since "prejudice and bigotry are not a thing of the past," but he hoped that in the future children would speak to their parents and neighbors in Spanish, Korean, Farsi, Russian, Tagalog, or Hebrew: "To the children, the most important thing is to continue to be playing together, learning together, and making friends. Let us keep it that way."[3]

Bradley feared that discussing relations as "tense" would have a negative impact on the economy because it would "reduce tourism, lead to middle-class flight [regardless of race] out of Los Angeles, and discourage businesses from locating in Los Angeles."[4] He actively tried to create and maintain a positive image of intergroup relations. He wanted to keep the narrative of South Central's interracial relations positive to help prevent the area from seeing "further economic depression as businesses will be hesitant to open there, and philanthropic efforts may choose politically safer places to invest."[5]

Bradley's message of the promise of diversity reflected how he became mayor of Los Angeles. At a young age, he started at the neighborhood level by working on community-based projects with African American leaders. He quickly realized that to be successful in politics he needed to go beyond the African American electorate and forge alliances with Mexican Americans and Japanese Americans in the Crenshaw Democratic Club and its Leimert Park affiliate. He was most adept at working with white leaders, especially Jewish liberals in the Democratic Club movement.[6] To be successful, he had to transcend "minority" candidate status.[7] Bradley used biracial coalition politics to rise to political power. His earliest success in Los Angeles's tenth district proved pivotal, as it was a "biracial meeting ground" between South Central and the wealthier, whiter Westside. This coalition meant that in 1963, Bradley won the city council seat for the then-majority-white tenth district.

During the 1969 mayoral campaign, then Mayor Sam Yorty cast Bradley as a communist and black militant. By 1973, Yorty had become a polarizing mayor, and Bradley's biracial coalition propelled him to the spotlight, and eventually to the mayor's office. It was the first time that white people voted en masse for a black candidate.[8] Bradley's early years in office could be considered L.A.'s feel-good era. For poor residents of South Central and Watts, Bradley was a change of pace in that he was active in antipoverty campaigns and the distribution of community-development funds; he also rid city hall of Yorty's political allies, whom African American and Latina/o advocates had viewed as hindering their political progress in the community.[9] According to Scott Kurashige, Bradley was a "product of a traditional interracial notion of integrationism. Consciously inclusive of whites and recognizing that Blacks were a minority among the minorities, he maintained the image of a racial 'moderate' by comparison with 'Black Mayors' whose careers rose in tandem with the ascension of the Black

Power Movement."[10] Throughout his two-decade tenure that began in 1973, he discussed his beliefs in the ideal of a colorblind society, and in doing so, he was part of a new "effort by civic leaders to celebrate ethnicity."[11]

Bradley believed that governance needed a multiracial commitment. He was hopeful that the infusion of immigrants could have a positive impact on the city:

> Far too little has been said about how we as a community adjust to the grow-
> ing changes in the demographics of this city. We know of course that many
> of the new immigrants are coming from Mexico, Central and South America,
> and the various Pacific Rim nations. Over 80 percent of our immigrants come
> from these regions. If we were wise enough, if we were courageous enough,
> if we were visionary enough, I am confident that we will assimilate, we will
> accept, we will do what we have done as a people and as a nation since the
> very beginning of this country. We are going to make the best of this new,
> enriching infusion of blood and ideas and energy and talent from the vari-
> ous nations around the Pacific Rim and throughout Mexico and Central and
> South America.[12]

It is in this multiracial political landscape that Mexican immigrants, as well as Asian immigrants, settled throughout Los Angeles.

During Tom Bradley's mayoral terms, 1973–1993, his words and vision were an embodiment of the central place of diversity in the city. The Bradley admin-istration became known for its wide-ranging alliance with transnational capital and his successful incorporation of people of color into the public sector.[13] Some Asian immigrants, who came to the United States with economic means and the potential for capital investment throughout Los Angeles, were welcomed and viewed as key to a thriving economy. However, this only tells one version of Los Angeles's story. In the midst of Los Angeles celebrating a Black mayor and his multicultural vision, South Central was undergoing its own demographic and economic changes. These changes, however, were not always seen through the prism of celebration and opportunity. The confluence of increased immigration by people from Mexico, and later Central America, with a national discourse of criminalizing their arrival and presence, meant that the fear of deportation by the Immigration and Naturalization Service (INS) shaped the lived realities of Mexican immigrants in the 1970s and 1980s. Despite Bradley's urging for courage and the welcoming of immigrants, undocumented Mexican immigrants did not always feel the benefits of these calls for the richness of racial diversity and capital development. There was a glimmer of celebration in 1986 when the U.S. Congress announced a one-time legalization program, The Immigration Reform and Control Act (IRCA), which granted Mexican immigrants living in the United States, and in turn, South Central, the ability to gain legal residency in the United States. Not all undocumented immigrants were able to benefit from IRCA, and this resulted in new forms of political, social, and economic constraints and punishments for undocumented immigrants. Simultaneously, in the 1980s, South Central was being affected by the crack cocaine epidemic, the escalating war on drugs, increased unemployment and underemployment, and deindustrialization and reindustrialization in the service sector—all this would have a compounding effect on crime and gang membership in Los Angeles, and ultimately led to the city's 1992 uprisings.

The latter part of the twentieth century was not utterly devoid of the prom- ise of harmonious interracial relations that Bradley espoused. This chapter, however, argues that the celebration of diversity was complicated and should not be seen as overshadowing the complex ways in which South Central resi- dents responded to these changes. Latina/o undocumented immigrants, one of the prime drivers of this diversity, faced immense backlash for their presence in the United States. Korean immigrants who entered South Central as busi- ness owners and investors faced varying forms of rejection. The 1992 upris- ings would illuminate the limits of Bradley's multicultural and multinational boosterism. For South Central residents, the celebration of increased diversity did not adequately capture the various emotive registers people lived through. South Central residents experienced fear and anxiety over deportation, racial nativism, economic restructuring, outside economic investment, criminaliza- tion, and violence. In the end, this chapter demonstrates that city-wide celebra- tions of diversity were unsettled, most especially when by the 1990s the racial dynamics were changing among and between Latina/os, African Americans, and Korean immigrants in the midst of accelerated structural changes.

"LA MIGRA, LA MICA"

Mayor Bradley discussed how "wisdom" and "courage" were required to wel- come immigrants; however, Mexican immigrants arriving and settling in the 1970s and 1980s did not always experience the fruits of this courage and often worried about INS detection and possible deportation. By investigating the lives of undocumented immigrants in South Central, one uncovers the tension between a local public political celebration of diversity and the statewide and national narrative of racial and immigrant "foreignness." This racial script often placed Mexicans as unassimilable and foreign others. Their perceived "foreignness," and the supposed ways in which their presence would taint the fabric of what it meant to be American, strengthened an anti-immigrant racial nativist politics that at every turn expressed that the only way to handle immigrants is to remove them from the nation.[14]

Following the passage of the Immigration and Nationality Act in 1965, immigration from Latin America, Asia, and Africa into the United States grew exponentially. This immigration policy removed previous immigration quotas based on national origin and provided a legal pathway of immigration that prioritized family reunification and skilled labor visas. It placed numerical caps for Latin American immigrants, caps per each of the various qualifying categories, and increased funding for the Border Patrol.[15] By the 1980s, the population of Los Angeles County had grown by 1.4 million, over 90 percent of that growth being Latina/o.[16] Within this growth in immigration in Los Angeles, some Latina/o immigrants benefited from the immigration restructuring, but the vast majority arrived as undocumented immigrants.

In 1979, the California Advisory Committee to the U.S. Commission on Civil Rights conducted a study to document how federal immigration policies treated undocumented immigrants in Southern California upon their arrival in the United States. Its significant findings were that most "anti-alien" attitudes by Americans always cast Mexicans as the foreign others. In the 1970s and 1980s, countless news stories depicted Mexicans entering the country without documentation. They utilized loaded terminology such as "hordes," "border peril," and "invasion" to portray immigrants as a threat. For the authors of the commission's report, such an attitude "paves the way for repressive police or public actions against them [immigrants] because they are portrayed by the media as a menace."[17] They were viewed as a "menace" because of the perception that immigrants came to the United States only to receive welfare benefits. This report found that in the mid-1970s, the level of utilization of social services like AFDC or health care by immigrants was approximately 10 percent of all budgetary costs. The growth in these budgetary requests was due to supplies and salary increases, not the use of services by undocumented immigrants.[18] Despite Bradley's public discourse on the potential assimilation and investment by and for immigrants from Latin America, the larger narrative of invasion and peril was ever present.

The study also signaled that the vast majority of non-Mexican undocumented immigrants apprehended by immigration officials were those who had overstayed their visas. The growth in undocumented immigration meant that the INS and the Border Patrol extended their grasp beyond the U.S.-Mexico border and set up backup stations near San Clemente and Temecula, California. Many undocumented immigrants quickly realized that escaping detection from the INS did not end at the border; *coyotes* (smugglers) had to work to ensure that undocumented immigrants would also cross the San Clemente checkpoint. Immigrants felt that until they reached Los Angeles, they had not yet made it safely into the United States. However, they soon discovered that routine sweeps in the community were common. In 1977, the figure for apprehensions in Los Angeles and San Diego was 432,500, and in 1978 it rose to 571,177. In 1979, the border apprehensions accounted for 40 percent of all apprehensions; thus INS officials found themselves arresting people in other sectors of the community. The majority of these apprehensions involved Mexican immigrants, and the face of undocumented people became associated mainly with immigrants from Latin America.[19]

The increased enforcement experienced by undocumented immigrants meant they were vulnerable to detection throughout all aspects of their daily life, most especially at their worksites. Mexican immigrants living in South Central felt they were not far from INS detection and lived in fear. Undocumented Mexican immigrant residents would hide behind bushes if they saw a UPS truck approach. They had learned that INS officers drove large brown vans, and so many assumed that UPS vehicles—roughly the same color and build—were INS.[20] Similarly, at their worksites, undocumented Mexican immigrants would hear co-workers yell from the front door, "La Migra!" [immigration officers] and see them run past, a sure sign to leave everything behind and run to the nearest exit. Aside from having to deal with the exploitation and fast-paced nature of their worksites, they also had to worry about INS officials. Leticia Nuno recalls that seeing co-workers and residents running scared from INS agents was commonplace, and extremely unnerving and frightening.[21] Living without legal documentation was difficult, as Maria Ruiz explained: "The uncertainty is difficult to live with. You have to be on your feet, because at any moment you could hear someone yell out *migra*, or you would see the vans roll up. It kept you on your toes, alert."[22] Maria further asserted that in the early 1980s they were not sure what their status would be in the long run: "We never imagined amnesty would come into effect. Much less that we would be eligible. Back in those days, you saw your stay as temporary because we were illegal. But amnesty changed that, *la mica* [green card] gave us a permanent stay, gave us some security. A new approach to living in the United States. I mean, many of us became U.S. citizens because we legalized with IRCA."[23] Unlike Maria, Leticia is currently a citizen. However, this is not the case for the waves of Mexican immigrants who arrived and settled in the late 1980s and 1990s. Many of these families continue to reside and work in the United States without the possibility for an immigration pathway to legal residence.

IRCA was a one-time legalization program that affected nearly three million undocumented immigrants throughout the United States. The law itself had five provisions: (1) employer sanctions for those who hired undocumented immigrants knowingly, (2) amnesty provisions for undocumented immigrants who met certain criteria, (3) antidiscrimination measures to appease immigrant-rights groups, (4) H-2 temporary visas, and (5) increased fines and punishment for undocumented immigrants and increased funds for the Border Patrol.[24] The amnesty provisions required that undocumented immigrants show proof of residency in the United States since 1982, through rent receipts, paycheck stubs, and utility bills, as well as evidence of not having received various forms of welfare.[25] Undocumented Mexican immigrant women faced the most significant challenge in presenting this type of documentation because these documents were often in their husbands' names. Immigration officials understood the difficulty of acquiring these documents and accepted affidavits written by neighbors, co-workers, and employers; however, these cases went under intense scrutiny.[26] Los Angeles hosted the largest legalization program in the country and hired a Latina/o workforce to process the paperwork. By the mid-1980s, Mexicans made up roughly half the total share of undocumented immigrants, yet they accounted for over 70 percent of all legalization applicants in the nation, with a higher share coming from California.[27]

As part of undocumented immigrants' pathway to legalization, they had
to participate in English and civics courses. Undocumented immigrants were
expected to take up to forty hours of English preparation courses.[28] As many
South Central undocumented Mexican immigrants recounted, the classes were
a waste of time since they were not long enough to learn English beyond the
basics.[29] At the time, they felt young and able to find work easily in low-wage
manufacturing and garment industries—they never imagined that their lack
of preparation, in the long run, would have negative effects. They would grow
to experience these effects in the wake of the passage of the North American
Free Trade Agreement (NAFTA) in 1994. It eliminated most trade barriers or
tariffs on agricultural and other products, and the already-limited manufacturing sector left Los Angeles.[30] Ten years after NAFTA's passage, when most
manufacturing trade barriers were eliminated, residents became aware of how
NAFTA had reshaped their lives in unforeseeable ways. On a positive note, for
Mexican immigrants yearning for some semblance of life back home, it meant
that they were able to get their favorite goods from Mexico—as these became
easily obtainable and abundant throughout Los Angeles. However, this also
meant that manufacturing and garment industries increasingly relocated to
other countries in search of cheaper wages and less regulation. For many immigrants who spent their laboring lifetimes in the manufacturing sector, the
economic restructuring—or, better yet, eradication—had devastating effects
because their labor skills were nontransferable. By the mid-2000s, many workers over fifty years of age with specialized skills in the service economy could
not easily transfer into professional work. Also, despite having lived here for
over four decades and often having citizenship, many Mexican immigrants in
South Central continue to depend on their children for crucial Spanish-English
translation; if they know any English, it is just the bare minimum needed to
complete necessary transactions and encounters in the community.[31] Amnesty
ushered in a new pattern of migration and settlement in South Central but did
not always transform their employment options.

Speculation and criticism characterized IRCA's initial proposal. Univision television reporter Enrique Gratas, a trusted voice in the community,
was skeptical when discussing IRCA and the promise of amnesty and legalization. A local newsletter, *La Gente* (UCLA's Chicano newspaper), also expressed some of the anxiety over the promise of amnesty. In "Amnesty Law:

A Process of False Hopes," Humberto Benitez highlighted people's reactions, showing that some undocumented Mexican immigrant workers believed that the new employer sanctions would make it more difficult to find jobs. Many undocumented Mexican immigrant workers quickly learned that because they received some form of federal money, such as unemployment benefits or public cash assistance (even if temporary), they were ineligible for legalization. According to Benitez, "false hope is common among many immigrants."[32] Sergio Delatorre, head of the Villa-Zapata Workers Committee, spoke out against amnesty; he believed the law was "extremely limited, the provisions were very demanding, and the law was racist . . . as he estimated that 80 percent of all Central Americans are eliminated under the guidelines." He believed that people needed to organize collectively in support of refugees and undocumented immigrant workers. Another criticism leveled against the law had to do with the "potential breakup of families. Under the law, each person in the family has to apply separately for the amnesty. So . . . one person in the family may qualify for the amnesty. Not everyone."[33] Similarly, critics believed that amnesty was a way for the government to make money, as it was "the best way to get rich in three years by selling amnesty to immigrants," by selling the dream of "La Mica." Undocumented immigrants submitting the paperwork for legalization could have earned the U.S. government a potential two billion dollars. There was much uncertainty regarding this immigration program. Dolores and Francisco Rosas said they decided to apply for amnesty despite their fears and reservations: "We had to try it. We had bought a home in the neighborhood. We had two daughters. We were thinking, we are staying here for a while. Let's try it" (Figure 12).[34]

Many undocumented immigrants who legalized under IRCA look back kindly on President Ronald Reagan and fail to see that IRCA was not a welcoming attempt by the Reagan administration and Congress to become an inclusive nation by legalizing millions of undocumented immigrants. Mexican immigrants often fail to place into greater context the goals of IRCA in relationship to the ways that the Reagan administration ushered in "Reaganomics" with a commitment to tax cuts for the rich, imposed draconian policies toward social services, engagement in the cultural wars, devastating interventions in Central America, and escalation of the War on Drugs that provided increased funding for policing in impoverished communities of color.

Figure 12: Francisco and Dolores Rosas, 1984. Francisco and Dolores Rosas enjoying their first outing to Disneyland. This marked one of the few times in which they ventured beyond South Central. Shortly thereafter they agreed to invest themselves as a family in the United States.

SOURCE: Personal archives of Dolores Rosas.

IRCA's effect on settlement—namely, creating a more permanent immigrant community—meant that immigrants' presence and growth in California could not be ignored. While IRCA provided legalization for an unprecedented number of undocumented immigrants, this did not change the negative perceptions people held for immigrants. In the late 1980s and the 1990s, a series of propositions showcased the anti-immigrant fervor that would take hold in California and the nation. California voters passed Proposition 63, the California English Is the Official Language Amendment, in 1986, and began the anti-immigrant proposition movement in California that would later embolden an English-only movement nationwide. In 1994, Proposition 187, the Save Our State initiative, aimed to prohibit undocumented immigrants from accessing public services throughout the state.[35] It was later deemed unconstitutional by the courts but had already had a profound effect on social services and undocumented immigrants.

Bill Clinton passed the Illegal Immigration Reform and Immigrant Responsibility Act (IIRIRA) in 1996. The act was a "full commitment to the criminalization of immigration and the militarization of immigration enforcement. It increased the Border Patrol's control and allowed the federal government to deputize local law enforcement as federal immigration officers."[36] That same year, Clinton passed the Personal Responsibility and Work Opportunity Reconciliation Act (PRWORA), which would "end welfare as we know it" and extended restrictions to immigrants' access to public services. Not only did this have a negative impact on immigrants, but a large percentage of poor women of color were also affected.[37] That same year, Proposition 209 ended affirmative action in state institutions, which has had a detrimental effect on the opportunities for communities of color to gain meaningful employment in state and government positions, as well as student enrollment in state-operated colleges and universities. Finally, in 1998, Proposition 227, English Language in Public Schools, ended bilingual education in California and was replaced with a one-year English-immersion program.[38]

These propositions and laws were a backlash and retrenchment from the passage of IRCA and the legalization and permanent settlement of millions of undocumented immigrants throughout California. They also signaled the limits to viewing Los Angeles, or the state of California more broadly, as a multiracial paradise. A public commitment to the incorporation of immigrants is not a stable proposition. As the twentieth-first century approached, deportation and immigration enforcement would continue its terror in communities like South Central as it would take on more characteristics that mirrored policing and incarceration features South Central residents knew well.

"BRING A HALT TO THE MADNESS THAT IS SPREADING ALL OVER OUR NEIGHBORHOOD"

Mayor Bradley promoted harmonious interracial relations to prevent capital flight in blighted communities. South Central residents, nevertheless, knew that capital flight was well under way and that deindustrialization's adverse effect was ushering in an increase in violence and drugs. The U.S. government's response was to escalate the War on Drugs. In the absence of meaningful job creation or educational programming, residents in many cases themselves supported such policing mechanisms. However, this did not eradicate their sense of fear or safety and would fuel the criminalization of communities of color in South Central. Understanding South Central residents' genuine fears of violence allows us to consider their complex response to the decline in the welfare state, as well as how in the midst of an era celebrating diversity and growth, impoverished residents in South Central felt left behind.

In 1978, Mayor Bradley was invited to the National Conference of Mayors for Better Cities for a Better Tomorrow. The conference aimed to tackle the urban crisis by emphasizing employment opportunities in cities. The unemployment rate in Watts in 1978 remained as high as in 1965. Most alarming was the growing feminization of poverty, and the fact that youth were bearing the brunt of these problems, "with schools not being fixed, high dropout rates, and graduates graduating without being able to read the morning paper."[39] Unlike many conservative pundits and politicians, Bradley believed in working class people's ability and willingness to create a new reality. He stated,

> You don't have to persuade the poor to believe in work, they've been asking for work all along. Just offer jobs and see what happens. People want to work. What's the first thing you ask a person you've never met before? What do you do? That's how we define each other. When a person can't find a job in American life, it means they may not be very important.[40]

Employment is vital, as people's identities and psyches are bound to their ability to work. Being viewed as idle and jobless is a negative experience, something to avoid at all costs. For South Central residents, this proved particularly challenging because of the lack of resources for locating employment options. Nonetheless, this does not mean that everyone in South Central was without work. Thousands of families were part of the workforce, yet in some of the lowest-paid sectors, such as the garment and service industry. Between 1979 and 1989, the jobs created in Los Angeles, about 40 percent, paid less than $15,000 a year. In that same period, the average earnings for employed Black men fell by 24 percent.[41] South Central's economic landscape as a community is defined by the sizeable working poor population that is working for wages but still impoverished. Many South Central residents found themselves looking for alternative avenues—hustles—to make ends meet. Any resident would attest, "Just 'cuz you live in here, the 'hood, things ain't cheap. We pay higher taxes, stuff just be more expensive and nothing be around here."[42]

The 1970s and 1980s experienced a rise in petty theft, gang violence, and the drug trade, silencing the advocacy for jobs, safe neighborhoods, and quality schools at the core of Better Cities initiatives. The closure of teen service centers and the demise of African American political organizations like the Black Panthers had a negative impacted on the opportunities for Black youth in South Central. In 1972, there were eighteen gang-sets, but by 1982 there were 155, with the last interval coinciding with the sharpest period of decline in local manufacturing. Most young teens in gangs were part of the growing presence of the Bloods and the Crips.[43] The feud between the Bloods and Crips over territory, drugs, and gang membership grew, and the threat of gunfire, violence, and death was a possibility for residents living in South Central and Watts. Homicides became a leading cause of death for men of color, in particular, African American men, as they were nine times more likely than whites to be murdered—Latina/os, four times more likely.[44] These rates and growth in homicide rates in the 1970s provided President Ronald Reagan with evidence to justify increased funds for the War on Drugs, in particular for police and prisons, implementing a military-like approach to policing in inner cities of color.[45] This increased investment would have an impact on the lives of youth of color, as they came under constant surveillance and punishment, and were negatively racialized as potentially criminal.

The homicide rates across the state of California peaked in 1980 and then declined; however, between 1982 and 2000 the California prison population grew 500 percent, with African Americans and Latina/os being two-thirds of the incarcerated populations.[46] Since 1984, California has completed construction of twenty-three major new prisons at the cost of $280 to $350 million apiece.[47] By the late 1980s, our understanding of welfare moved from one of government entitlement to government handouts, in doing so justifying the government's logic for an expansion of the War on Drugs.[48] The failure to provide a meaningful safety net exacerbates the level of poverty and potential violence found in the community. Instead of providing funds for schools and education, California legislators in the latter part of the twentieth century invested funds in prisons and policing and neglected public schools. Over half of male and female youth of color do not earn high school diplomas.[49] The lack of proper schools and employment options means that youth have limited options and in some cases become involved in gangs and drugs, which in turn "justifies," in the eyes of the state, increased police aggression and funding. It is important to consider that the growth in gangs was mostly due to the shift away from large-scale job-training programs, the shift of funding toward the War on Drugs, the educational devastation caused by Proposition 13, and the decline in the Black Power movement.[50]

Many residents and property owners themselves lost sight of structural arguments for poverty and crime, and they, too, internalized the need for policing and enforcement. South Central residents and property owners expressed to Tom Bradley their grievances about the prevalence of violence and drugs in the community. On March 4, 1993, Christina Ainer, a property owner (but not resident) of an apartment complex on 88th Place, wrote to the mayor asking for his help:

> Dear Sir,
>
> We desperately need your HELP! Please! We are apartment owners and operate a business in this area at 547 West 88th Street. Last year, I reported this same problem and after writing the same letter we got some temporary assistance on the block and the robbing, drug dealing, and killing, and shooting stopped for a short period. It was especially effective when a police patrol car stayed parked in the driveway, thank you. But it has gotten real bad again. I sold the bldg last year, but this year I am again the owner because the person who bought the bldg from me was beaten and robbed and nearly killed and finally had a nervous breakdown and had to foreclose and take the bldg back, reluctantly! I am a law-abiding businessperson who have always been a tax paying supporters in L.A. for over 23 yrs. My husband works for the city of L.A. sanitation dept, now for over 25 yrs, we are hardworking, law-abiding productive citizens and certainly an asset to the city of L.A. Don't we deserve some kind of police protection? Please! Please! Help Us. Your observation and advice will be appreciated—please respond to this notice and let me know what can be done here again. *Let's Save Lives!*[51]

She ended her letter by writing the names of the people living in the property. All tenants in the apartment building were of Latina/o origin. Mayor Bradley responded shortly thereafter, assuring her that he had sent her letter for assistance to the Drug Bust Bureau and the Southwest Narcotics Bureau to begin surveillance of the property. This letter by an apartment owner highlighted the various dimensions of life in South Central: the reality of drugs, theft, and violence in the city; apartment and property owners from outside the community; and the urgency of protecting residents. Letters like these are the ones that receive the most attention because they bolster the need for policing and persecution, and continue to describe and perpetuate a narrative of South Central as a dangerous space. This letter captures an element of living in South Central but is not the only reality. Most South Central residents are not involved in the drug trade or are committing violent crimes, but the level on which Bradley responded to this letter had to do almost exclusively with investment in a politics that supports the criminalization and policing of communities of color.

Similar to this letter by an apartment building owner, petitions circulated concerning the prevalence of liquor stores and hotels throughout the South Central community. Community activism against liquor stores has a long history, as South Central residents agree that these businesses do not advance the growth, development, and safety of the community and take up space needed for other businesses and services such as grocery stores and libraries.[52] On September 17, 1992, Alpha Service Petition Members mailed a letter with a petition signed by forty community residents for the closure of the hotel located at 451 East Vernon Avenue. In the letter, they petitioned the L.A. Narcotics Bureau to investigate the hotel. The petition revealed that they wanted to "bring a halt to the *madness* that is spreading all over our neighborhood in the areas of 43rd Place, 43rd Street, Avalon Avenue, and Vernon Avenues. The petition calls for the closing of the hotel at 451 East Vernon Ave, which is a *hotbed* for criminal activities."[53] The hotel was close to the telephone company headquarters where residents would pay their monthly bills, and when completing such tasks, residents stated they experienced fear as they were accosted at gunpoint for their cars and other valuables.

African American and Latina/o residents signed the petition with asterisks highlighting the people who had been assaulted. Residents' use of the words *madness* and *hotbed* illustrated the emotional response of frustration for the presence of these businesses in the community. It captured their sense of urgency and concern for their safety, but also for overall community relations. In this example, one can discern a sliver of Bradley's urging for harmonious coalitions, as residents looked beyond a Latina/o–African American racial divide and rallied together to see the matter as of concern to everyone.

The letter by property owner Ainer reflected that she was also concerned for her tenants and property irrespective of race. The drug trade had taken hold of her property and was threatening the livelihood of both African American and Latina/o residents. Most striking about her letter is not only her plea for assistance and safety but also her method of deploying race. As one reads the letter, one may at first be unaware of the racial identity of tenants, assailants, or Ainer. By the end of the letter, it becomes evident that she is writing to protect her Latina/o tenants, and one can only speculate that she is a white woman from the Westside. Ainer, a "law-abiding business person" who "reluctantly" retook ownership of the property, was uncomfortable, unwilling, and afraid to visit the property herself. Thus she exercised her privilege of not being a resident to write a letter requesting assistance. The Latina/o tenants and the African American and Latina/o residents elsewhere in the community did not have this distance and attempted in different ways to express concern for their safety and that of the community writ large.

The sense that South Central and Watts constituted a dangerous space for residents had a transnational audience when on October 26, 1996, the Mexico City–based newspaper *Reforma* published an article documenting the dangerous community into which Latina/os were settling in the United States. The scope of the article did not align with Bradley's boosterism of Los Angeles as a diverse paradise. The thrust of the article, "Watts: Tierra de Muerte [Watts: Land of Death]," was that Mexican immigrants were not settling in the land of opportunity. Writer Ignacio Rodriguez Reyna began with the story of a drive-by shooting that killed a young boy watching TV in his home. The piece discussed the prevalence of drugs, especially crack cocaine, and how both African American and Latina/o children as young as twelve and thirteen became involved in the drug trade. Resident Rosalio Nava described living in the area: "What is it like to live in Watts? You can't close your eyes. You can easily lose your life. We have to be attentive."[54] Reyna described Watts as "*un ghetto en el 1965 . . . hoy, tres generaciones despues, Watts sigue siendo un ghetto* [a ghetto in 1965 . . . three generations later Watts continues to be a ghetto]." The Mexican immigrant residents and activists he interviewed all would agree that the reason they found themselves living in Watts was that "*la pobreza no perdona. Consume a sus hijos. Son subproducto de una marginacion cronica. Esta es una tierra devastada* [Poverty does not forgive. It consumes your children. They are a by-product of chronic marginalization. It is a devastated region]."[55]

Strikingly, throughout his reporting Reyna utilized terms such as "ghetto," *proyectos* [projects], "shooting," "babies having babies," "crack dealers," and *crack-zombies-los esclavos de la droga* [drug addicts] to describe the community and its realities.[56] This terminology was part of a sensationalized emotional aesthetic meant to attract readership, yet it also resonates as an entry point to understanding Watts and South Central in a transnational context. The article ended by suggesting that most people *"vive al dia,"* because there is no other way for poor residents with limited options. The article provides one sensational scenario for what living in the "land of opportunity" can entail as well as perpetuates a negative image of South Central.

South Central residents themselves make it clear that violence is found throughout Los Angeles and is not particularly unique to South Central. As forty-five-year-old resident Pablo Marquez elaborated, "You know, there were also gang members in Huntington Park and drug dealing? Yes, that too." He stated that it was "even worse sometimes than what he had been seeing here in South Los Angeles." He explained the difference between these spaces: "The answer was obvious: on the Eastside most of the drug dealers and gangsters were Latino. Here on 53rd Street, many of them are Black."[57] These quotes illustrate that violence is not necessarily tied to a particular racial group or neighborhood and it occurs throughout Los Angeles. Nevertheless, South Central gets the notoriety of being an inherently violent space.

Cid Martinez, in *The Neighborhood Has its Own Rules*, demonstrates that when law enforcement fails as the protector against violence or as impartial negotiator in interracial race relations, South Central residents develop alternative forms of governance within churches and schools that rely on localized negotiations between African American and Latina/o residents.[58] There are countless organizations, such as Community Coalition, Concerned Citizens for South Central Los Angeles, and Mothers ROC, that work with the community in a coordinated fashion to politicize residents and challenge the normative response of welcoming law enforcement as an answer to violence. These organizations and activists often talk about "reclaiming the streets," as South Central is home to countless families, both African American and Latina/o, who struggle daily to foster the "possibility for a thriving community" against all the odds and, as this book documents, to move beyond only the narratives of danger, violence, and death. Ultimately, this is often difficult when the police state looms large and does very little to eliminate crime in inner-city communities. In fact, what is achieved is the increased criminalization of people of color, which in many cases ends in death.

BLACK AND KOREAN AMERICAN RELATIONS

To understand the social, economic, and political context before the 1992 uprisings, one must understand not only the increased level of police surveillance previously discussed but also South Central's racial diversity beyond its Black and Latina/o residents. Life in South Central meant that Mexican immigrants and African Americans were neighbors and that they were patrons of liquor and convenience stores owned and operated by Korean immigrants and Latina/os (a different business enterprise than those that will be described in Chapter 7). Korean immigrants, despite coming with high educational degrees, were unable to translate this to white collar work. They pooled their financial resources and thus were able to open businesses throughout South Central and Koreatown.[59] In South Central, this racial diversity would have a significant effect on how residents and store owners would relate to one another.[60]

Leading up to the uprising, African American and Korean relations were strained, as just a year prior, on March 16, 1991, Korean liquor store owner Soon Ja Du fatally shot a fifteen-year-old African American girl, Latasha Harlins. Du argued that she believed Harlins was stealing a bottle of orange juice. The store surveillance video showed that Du grabbed Harlins by the sweater and took off her backpack in efforts to retrieve the orange juice. Harlins hit Du as a response, Du fell to the ground, and upon standing back up she threw a stool at Harlins. As Harlins was leaving the store, Du reached for her handgun and shot her in the head, instantly killing her. During the trial, Du claimed she shot Harlins in self-defense. Eyewitness testimony contradicted her statements, as did the surveillance video of Du shooting Harlins in the back as she was leaving the store. Du was convicted of voluntary manslaughter by the jury. The jury recommended the maximum prison sentence of sixteen years, but the judge, Joyce Karlin, instead sentenced Du to five years of probation, four hundred hours of community service, and a $500 fine.[61] The 1992 Latasha Harlins verdict, compounded with the later Rodney King verdict that acquitted the law enforcement officers charged with beating King, served as a painful reminder that even when a crime is committed against Black people, punishment is nonexistent.

Before 1992, the 1984 Commission on Human Relations report captured the concerns of residents and activists: intergroup tension and conflict, education, employment and affirmative action, minority women and single-parent heads of household, health, police-community relations, and housing.[62] All of these concerns played a role in the uprisings. What set this report apart was that interracial relations took center stage. The goal of the commission was to "promote and improve human relations, civic peace, intergroup understanding, and full acceptance of all persons in all aspects of community life in Los Angeles County."[63] The major grievance cited was that the changing population of Los Angeles County "has produced a significant degree of intergroup tensions and conflict," in which "differences in language, culture, and other behavior in the more recent immigrant and refugee groups and their problems of adjustment to a new society . . . [have] resulted from a misunderstanding, hostility, discrimination, and violence by persons within the majority community and within racial and ethnic minority groups with a long history in the county."[64] Most speakers discussed how this demographic change inspired the "majority group" to express their fear and engage in discriminatory acts against newcomers. The biggest complaint from African American attendees was that landlords preferred Asian refugees and Latina/os to Black people. The report stressed interracial tension in South Central between Korean merchants and African Americans, not among Mexican immigrants and African Americans. The limited discussion about relations between African Americans and Mexican immigrants, at least in the context of this meeting, was one that did not emphasize tension but rather focused on simple coexistence.

This report highlighted African Americans' unease over the "rapid takeover of gas stations and 'mom and pop' stores in the Black community." African American advocates stated that there was relatively little African American ownership as it was, and the presence of Asian-owned shops meant an increase in Asian employees and no meaningful opportunities for African American residents. There was also concern about the failure of some Asian business owners and employees to communicate in English and the apparent rudeness of some toward African American patrons. African American advocates discussed this dynamic not only in the context of employment options but also as a "larger argument of capital opportunities for Korean owners and lack of employment opportunities and unavailability of funds for grocery stores."[65] Moreover, they felt that many "Koreans who are recent immigrants . . . do not fully understand customs and culture, as well as the American way of doing business. Their lack of English language proficiency was causing communication problems and unintentional misunderstandings."[66] These last statements echo larger anti-foreigner attitudes that are not only waged at Korean immigrants but also recently arrived Mexican immigrants. Such sentiments alongside language barriers contribute to relationships and interactions that are tense and fuel misunderstanding and animosity.

It would appear, on the basis of this dialogue, that the primary concern of African Americans regarding interracial relations was the clash with Asian immigrant merchants, as the former felt left behind by investors, entrepreneurs, and employees in their community. Asian immigrant entrepreneurs, and increasingly Latina/o investors, would take advantage of Bradley's, and the broader government's, economic spirit to welcome newcomers through their ability to invest financially. The unequal distribution of economic opportunities is not given enough attention in the consideration of interracial relations. One must not lose sight of how interracial dynamics do not happen in a vacuum but exist in relation to broader political and economic social forces that historically have disadvantaged poor and working class communities of color. The ability for Korean store owners to invest in South Central by opening liquor stores and convenience stores was part of a more extensive economic system.

In the wake of this report, Bradley attempted to make an argument for the need for harmonious collaboration and successful incorporation of newcomers for the growth of Los Angeles; however, on the ground in South Central, those efforts were not successfully carried out. Key to fully grappling with misunderstandings in interracial relations is recognizing that they do not derive from racial prejudice alone. Thus it is not fair to state that African Americans are inherently prejudiced toward Asian immigrants, or vice versa, but rather, as discussed throughout this book, the meanings and emotions attached to racial differences are heightened and further strained when these relationships are shaped by how some groups benefit from particular opportunities while others continually experience the compounding effects of declining investment in

jobs, housing, health, education, and social services, and the increased criminalization of communities of color locally and abroad.

Tensions between Korean merchants and Black residents were heightened
after the Harlins shooting and verdict. In 1992, South Central residents burned
down buildings they felt were not of their own, and thus believed they were at-
tacking outside capital. The reality of the uprising was much more complex, as
between 30 and 40 percent of businesses damaged in the unrest were owned by
Latina/os, not just by Asian immigrants.[67] The 1992 uprising was the nation's
first multiracial rebellion, and it therefore complicated how we discussed and
considered the effects of increased immigration and diversity.

1992 UPRISINGS: A MULTIRACIAL REBELLION

On April 29, 1992, the Black community eagerly awaited the verdict on the four
white LAPD officers charged with beating Rodney King one year prior. Upon
hearing of the officers' acquittal, residents took to the streets in protest. At the
intersection of Florence and Normandie Streets in South Central, a white truck
driver, Reginal Denny, was pulled from his truck and physically harmed. Shortly
thereafter, a Guatemalan immigrant, Fidel Lopez, was also severely beaten.
These televised beatings and the unrest that was developing across the city led
Tom Bradley to declare a state of emergency and order a curfew for the affected
areas. The uprising extended beyond the boundaries of South Central and also
devastated storefronts in Koreatown. It took the presence of the National Guard
and military snipers on rooftops of local buildings to usher in a "sense of calm."
This so-called calm was achieved through the physical exertion of state authority
and violence. African American and Mexican immigrant residents alike never
imagined they could feel as though they were part of a war zone. The demonstration of authority by police, military, and national guards, an extension of
how they had approached the community for decades, signaled that they were
there to restore "order" at any cost. The uprising ultimately ended in fifty-four
deaths, more than two thousand people injured, and more than three thousand
structures destroyed or damaged, with around $1 billion in total damage to the
city. Over half of the people arrested during the uprising were Latina/o, and
one-third of those killed were Latina/o.[68] The INS took advantage of the chaos
during the uprising by arresting Latina/o immigrants for curfew violations and
ultimately deporting two thousand undocumented Latina/os. These rates, in

conjunction with the pictures and television coverage of the rebellion, captured the fact that thousands of Latina/os were not only participants in the event but also residents of "African American South Central Los Angeles." The rebellion extended beyond South Central's boundaries, and it involved a much more diverse set of actors, thus differing from the Watts uprising.

For Angelenos living outside the boundaries of South Central, and for the nation as a whole, this racial transformation was news—a reminder of how isolated South Central's residents were from the rest of the city. For community residents, however, this was not news: they had been living with this reality for over a decade. For Gloria Molina, then the only Latina/o Los Angeles County supervisor, this demographic shift came as a surprise: "All of us have an awful lot of work to do to learn about the changing demographics of South Central Los Angeles."[69] It is imperative to note that while Mayor Bradley acknowledged the changing shape of Los Angeles's demographics, this change was often conceptualized as the forming of segregated communities within larger residential areas.[70] The 1992 uprisings shattered that illusion and made everyone aware that South Central was not just Black, its residents were also Latino, and the business owners were a multiracial group of people. For residents of South Central, this lack of awareness and isolation was one of the many triggers behind the uprisings.

The participation of Latina/os in the uprisings is often seen as arising more out of an "opportunity" rather than outrage. The belief that they were not fully aware of who Rodney King was and became active in the destruction on the third and fourth days when food and essentials were unavailable is used as justification to state that they participated out of necessity.[71] In later discussions, Mexican immigrants did express that they were not fully aware of Rodney King and his case but would say that they understood the feeling of being watched and threatened by a law enforcement entity. In their case, it was INS officials as well as the police. Also, residents still remember the terror that they experienced during those days of unrest, as they were afraid of being caught in the crossfire just by being residents. Magdaleno Ruiz said, "You just didn't know, most people were looting, there was a sense of lawlessness like no one was obeying anything, everything was fair game." He went on to state, "*toda la raza anduvo alli* (everyone was involved)."[72] Whether they participated out of a necessity to survive, or from seeing their neighbors get home with microwaves they were able to take from some of the burned-down shops, all would agree that similar to their African American neighbors, they too needed these goods, as they were barely making ends meet. Residents' reactions to the uprisings were multidimensional, with many directly participating and countless more not participating in the taking of goods from stores, with reasons for not participating including fear of being hurt in the turmoil, fear of being arrested, or their own strategies of how to manifest rage.

Regardless of race, both African American and Latina/o residents experienced unwavering poverty. Just a year after the uprisings, the poverty rate was at 44 percent with a per capita income of $8,159, compared to 15 percent and $16,149 in Los Angeles County as a whole. Owner-occupied housing stood at 39 percent, while for Los Angeles County the comparable statistic was 49 percent.[73] Poverty and working poverty are shared experiences, which can lead any racial group to take to the streets to strike capital in rage by taking a television, a microwave, or food essentials as a response to the state's failure to protect their needs through livable wages, adequate housing options, and the end of police brutality and the criminalization of people of color.

The uprisings were one of the costliest urban uprisings in U.S. history that illustrated the gulf between the wealthy and poor. Director of the Watts Health Foundation Donzella Lee said, "When you don't have any place for kids to work and you don't have any place for kids to play you have a problem. Gangs provide jobs, and a recreational outlet. And not only don't we have jobs for adolescents, but we don't have jobs for their parents. [This] leaves the community very vulnerable—vulnerable to developing an underground community [including] drugs and other criminal activity."[74] This vulnerability is genuine and palpable. Arturo Ybarra, president of the Watts-Century Latino Organization and a resident of South Central since the 1980s, echoed many of Lee's fears: "African Americans and Latinos suffer from the same social and economic neglect, and what is available is not enough for everyone, so this creates some kind of resentment in some groups."[75] He added that the resentment between groups would not exist if both groups were not struggling. Getting both groups to work on the common ground is an essential key to the development of a coalition politics that can be long-lasting.

In response to the uprisings, Mayor Bradley formed Rebuild LA, a five-year project that aimed to infuse the community with investors and business owners. Rebuild LA had eleven task forces with political and economic officials as well as community experts. The task forces focused on finance, construction business development, education and training, racial harmony, insurance, media and communications, philanthropy, urban planning, volunteerism, health, and youth.[76] Rebuild LA came under much criticism for its failure to make inroads in the development of economic capital for the community, although it did manage to secure some investment, such as for large grocery stores. Part of the problem with Rebuild LA was its top-down approach, but others stated that the economic recession had a negative effect on the ability of the organizations to gather the financial capital to establish infrastructure.

One important facet of the Rebuild LA project was its Racial Harmony and Discourse Task Force, established with the help of the Los Angeles City Commission on Human Relations. On February 8, 1993, the task force convened to have an open dialogue, discuss differences, and find common ground. As co-chair of the event, Ki Suh Pak urged that participants "must respect others' perspectives as equally important as our own." Pak warned against "being too nice," noting that it was also important to be honest and listen to each other's points of view without rancor or emotions, and believed they "had to come to grips with what racial harmony is all about. Common language about the city's problems and solutions."[77] Antonia Hernandez, a fellow co-chair, echoed Pak's concern and said that having an open, respectful, and sensitive conversation "is the tough work." Part of the meeting's intent was to allow the community to express grievances so that the task force would understand what was going on in the community and avoid being seen as "do-gooders." The four areas of concern were racial tensions in the schools, community/merchant conflict, Martin Luther King Jr. Hospital, and food distribution.

At this meeting, South Central residents expressed their anxieties over how the disturbances had transformed their daily lives. Residents stated, "economic racism is the root of the problem" and said that they were "living in a war zone and civilians are getting hurt." As important, or enlightening was the sentiment that one resident expressed: "We're all immigrants, some more recent than others," meaning that South Central residents share the experience of having to adapt and settle in the community. As part of the meeting, both residents and officials provided time to look at "communities that have successfully integrated immigrants. What happens in a community that works?" After much debate about approaches to integration, the answer was youth, because "the way to guide youth will be the way the community goes in the future. The youth need safe, constructive things to do and places to go to learn about other cultures in non-conflict situations."[78] Astutely, as residents complained about some of the racial and ethnic problems of the community, they always returned to the understanding that at the root of all problems were economic and political inequalities. Residents were well aware that the problems they faced, while at first glance appearing to be racially motivated, were linked to larger structural forces rather than just unexplored racial prejudice.

The 1992 uprising proved a pivotal moment in the lives of South Central residents, as it was a reaction to the cumulative effects of neglect and racism. Mainstream pundits and journalists viewed the riots as an example of "racial hostility and individual lawlessness," while scholars such as Cornel West viewed them as "neither a race riot nor a class rebellion, but a multiracial, trans-class display of justified social rage . . . it signified the sense of powerlessness in American society."[79] George J. Sanchez argues that the 1992 uprising was a reflection of late twentieth-century racial nativism, as the damage and violence experienced was against Korean merchants and Latina/o residents and business owners.[80] I agree that elements of the uprising are representative of racial nativism, as there were echoes of Asian and Latino immigrants being seen as outsiders and not of the community and worthy of protection. As pointed out in previous chapters, demographic change is complicated and multidimensional, and always triangulated and in relation to larger economic, political, and social circumstances. The Watts Gang Truce's unofficial motto, "Crips plus Bloods plus Mexicans—Unite!" was displayed on city walls throughout Los Angeles during and after the uprisings.[81] In the midst of the violence, this slogan illustrated efforts by some to build institutions and relations in which people could work cross-racially. Understanding interracial relationships throughout various emotive registers, most especially as they relate to large power structures and racial scripts of deserving/undeserving, criminal/model minorities, illuminates how the creation of a relational community formation is a process that does not happen overnight, but takes sustained effort and time. The uprisings were but a punctuated moment that demonstrated how reactions to change do not happen in a vacuum.

The events of the latter part of the twentieth century offer an opportunity to investigate the "lessons of inclusion." In the case of South Central, this would mean understanding that the strains on the community were "more related to the frustrations of people living in poverty" than to just racial or ethnic hatred.[82] Celebrations of diversity often collide with reality, as multiracial spaces require that we consider the difficulties of demographic transitions. The public political discourse of acceptance and diversity obscures how Black and Latina/o

residents experience extreme forms and levels of dehumanization and disinvestment. Understanding the emotive energy of fear and anxiety of residents
illustrates the multilayered experiences of Blacks and Latina/os: the threat of
the INS, drugs, declining job options, the increased presence of law enforcement, and the decline in the welfare state. Also, Asian migrants enter South
Central in the form of store and homeowners and are often scapegoated and
seen as entrepreneurs who are not invested in the community. This is where
tension can and does arise. The effort to bridge racial difference means understanding that racial groups enter the U.S. racial landscape with different access
and under different narratives. The anxiety over undocumented immigration
had a negative impact on Mexican immigrants, yet in many ways shielded
upwardly mobile Asian immigrants, who instead of being viewed as a menace
were seen as part of the model minority. This racialized discourse, augmented
with the increased criminalization of Black and Latina/o people, would have
profound implications for how Black, Latina/o, and Asian Americans related
to each other in spaces such as South Central.

It is imperative that community activists and residents strive to create
space(s) in which they can foster coalition-building in the midst of limited,
differing economic opportunities. This period in Los Angeles is representative
of the promise of multiculturalism, with Tom Bradley being one of its champions. As similarly discussed in Chapter 5, diversity in Head Start classrooms
serves as another way to observe how some welcomed this diversity regarding the
curriculum but also had trepidation in terms of what it would mean for workplace options. These two chapters together provide a nuanced consideration
of diversity's promise, as well as acknowledge that while this celebration is part
of people's realities, it is much more complicated in South Central. Chapter 7
will engage with the ways in which Broadway Federal emerged from the ashes
of the 1992 uprising, and how its leadership had to consider its commitment
to the community in the backdrop of South Central's racial diversity. Effective
incorporation and community building take *work* and go beyond the discursive
tools of acknowledgment and celebration.

CHAPTER 7

BANKING IN
SOUTH CENTRAL
The Limitations of Race Enterprises

BROADWAY FEDERAL BANK stands as one of the few surviving African American–owned banks in South Central Los Angeles. From the outside, it looks like a typical small local bank; however, embedded within its walls is a long history of struggle and pride. Richard Wyatt's vibrant mural, *Sunrise on Central Avenue*, adorns its entryway and celebrates the achievements of architect Paul Williams, gospel singer Mahalia Jackson, jazz musicians Buddy Collette and Duke Ellington, labor activist Cesar Chavez, and the bank's founder, H. Claude Hudson, to illustrate histories of struggle and also point to the bank management's commitment to honoring and nurturing its African American patrons' sense of community, history, and access to savings and loan services.

The 1992 Los Angeles uprising caused massive destruction throughout the Los Angeles region, especially in South Central. During the uprising, "Black Owned" signs on business storefronts served to signal that the business should be spared, as these signs branded the business as locally invested and grounded, not a result of outside investment.[1] One business lost in those tumultuous three days was Broadway Federal Bank, one of the few long-standing economic institutions in the community. Then chairman of Broadway Federal Paul Hudson expressed his commitment to rebuild the bank. He explained that his obligation was to the community, as he promised to continue to provide for the financial needs of South Central residents affected by the uprising.[2] Hudson's choice to stay in the community and not flee as did other businesses demonstrated his commitment and that of the individuals working within Broadway Federal to remain unyielding in serving South Central residents. In the months that followed, the bank opened its doors in a temporary modular building across the street from the original building. On December 5, 1999, the bank moved from this temporary location at the corner of 45th Street and Broadway to its new location at the intersection of Martin Luther King and Figueroa Streets to create a more visible profile. By 1992, and certainly by the unveiling of the new building in 1999, the bank had continued to serve not only long-term African American patrons but also Mexican immigrant patrons.

Reflecting on what happened in April 1992, Paul Hudson speculated that an understanding of the history of the bank and its long-term commitment to South Central Los Angeles residents in general, and African Americans in particular, might have spared the original building from being burned down during the uprising:

> We didn't think it was going to happen. I mean this had happened before . . . in Watts and we didn't have any problems in 1965. I didn't think we were going to have any problems in 1992. But we probably wouldn't have, but it went on for so long, and people were very drunk, very drunk, and the demographic change affected us because the Hispanic population didn't really get the history of the bank, I think they saw us as a federal institution, not a part of the frustration everyone felt, as part of the federal government, so instead of seeing us as a community bank they saw us as a federal bank.[3]

By suggesting that Mexican immigrants were unaware of the bank's history, rather than broadly discussing the chaos of those six days of unrest, Hudson indirectly placed the blame on increased immigration as the reason for the building not being spared. From his statement, it is not clear that he had made a concerted effort to inform Mexican immigrants of what a community bank represents. My oral histories with long-term Latina/o immigrant patrons demonstrate that Hudson had not made the legacy of Broadway Federal legible to them. Nonetheless, what is evident is that the bank's hiring of Latina/o employees, starting in the late 1980s to cater to its growing Mexican immigrant clientele, was not enough to inspire those patrons to consider Broadway Federal as more than just a place to bank, much less something worth being protected.

Paul Hudson's conceptualization of the on-the-ground transformation and the inner workings of Broadway Federal and its place in South Central, along with his relationship to this bank's history, offers an example of how institutions that have a long-standing presence within and commitment to a geographic and racial community fail to confront and deal with demographic change. His framing of the bank's goals through its mission statement provides an opportunity to assess the emergence and growth of the bank and its relationship to African American progress. The mission statement speaks to the bank's intention to provide the "real estate, business and financial needs of customers in underserved urban communities with a commitment to excellent service, profitability, and sustained growth."[4] The bank's goal was to address the needs of communities irrespective of profits and race.

Paul Hudson explained his relationship to the community:

> A community bank is that which is known in the community, is familiar with the leadership in the community, active in social and political activities, and in this case, there is a defined community. In this case, it is the African American community of South Los Angeles. And this has been pretty much throughout the generations. This has been because we have consistently been active on city and county commissions, active in political campaigns, active on non-profit boards. And this is true from 1946 until today. And will continue to be so.[5]

Three generations of Hudsons have served as chairmen over the course of the bank's history. H. Claude Hudson (Paul's grandfather) was one of the founders of the bank in 1947. He served as chairman until 1973, when his son Elbert Hudson (Paul's father) became chairman, serving until 1992. In 1992, Paul Hudson took over as chairman. By 1976, Claude Hudson had become known as "the man they call 'Mr. Civil Rights'" or the "father of Civil Rights." Elbert Hudson followed in his father's footsteps by becoming president of the Los Angeles branch of the NAACP in the early 1970s. His activism, along with that of his wife, Marilyn, ensured that Paul (their son) would commit to rectifying the plight of communities of color. They always supported Paul Hudson's activism in college, law school, and the NAACP (he served as president of the NAACP during the early 1980s). Before Paul took over as chairman of Broadway Federal in 1992, Paul, Elbert, and Claude Hudson had made history as three generations serving on L.A. County commissions. In 1978, it was the first time in the county's history that three generations served simultaneously on various panels. Paul became a member of the County Hospital Commission, his father, Elbert, was part of the Human Relations Commission, while grandfather Claude served for his eighteenth term (at the age of ninety-two) on the Real Estate Management Commission.[6]

The family's commitment to serving the needs of the bank's African American patrons reflects an attitude that at times takes hold in this region's politics when, in the wake of demographic change, leaders, entrepreneurs, and institutions fail to fully understand and grapple with the ways they must adapt and reconceptualize their relationship to the community. As then chairman, Paul Hudson expressed the goal of a community bank in terms of "the African American community of South Los Angeles" and at other times in terms of a broad racial and class category of an "underserved community." He employed language that obscured the active role that Mexican immigrants played in the bank's trajectory and growth (most especially in the past few decades). His language illustrates the complexity of how leaders in a racial community must deploy a discourse that acknowledges the importance of both historical legacy and emergent change. To simultaneously honor his family's legacy and generate profits, as chairman Paul Hudson had to prioritize the retention of long-time African American patronage by emphasizing his, and by extension his family's, historic commitment to South Central Los Angeles's African American community.

Hudson's reflection on the loss of the bank during the uprising demonstrated that he understood and envisioned the bank as much more than an economic center: to him, it was a cultural, political, and social community center for South Central Los Angeles residents that deserved protection. George Lipsitz has identified various ways in which "racism takes place": as mainstream banks started to open branches in the suburbs, working class communities like South Central were left without a banking infrastructure. Lipsitz argues that instead of economic means and "creditworthiness," race is the deciding factor on whether and where bank branches open.[7] Broadway Federal was an essential asset in the community, and as such its role there extended beyond offering loans and savings and checking accounts.[8]

Broadway Federal serves as a prime example for investigating how it is that a business like a bank thrives in a community for over seven decades when other banks historically have shied away from this community due to the limited economic and business opportunities and high levels of poverty. A deep-seated commitment to African American patrons' sense of community and progress contributed to Paul Hudson's complex and often contradictory discourse and understanding of community and change. The placemaking efforts by African American migrants in the early twentieth century that made South Central home, with their entrepreneurial creativity despite overt forms of residential segregation, connect to how Hudson viewed his trajectory within the bank. Nevertheless, by the end and turn of the century, Hudson's leadership was at a crossroads with the bank's long-term patrons and the city's increased racial diversity and settlement. Mexican immigrant and African American patrons of Broadway Federal and residents of South Central were also making sense of not only changes in the city streets but also their relationship and banking practices with an institution whose longevity and commitment had been related directly to the African American community. By placing the banking practices of community leaders, entrepreneurs, and patrons in relationship to one another, one begins to understand the difficulty in letting go of a race-based politics for a broader community-based politics. This opens a space in which to understand how Mexican immigrant settlement in South Central has not only transformed its streets but also ushered in new economic, political, and social realities vested in relational community formation.

BANKING AND INVESTING IN THE COMMUNITY

The 1992 uprising was a pivotal moment for the leadership of Broadway Federal because it forced reflection on the role the bank would play in the community. Many damaged enterprises never rebuilt their business, and others left the community in the aftermath of the uprising. A study by the City of Los Angeles Human Relations Commission revealed that in 1990 South Central had only nineteen bank branches, whereas nonminority areas of equal size to South Central had up to two hundred bank branches operating within city limits. Unsurprisingly, check-cashing centers took the place of bank branches in South Central: 133 such outlets existed there.[9] By 2000, the location of about 60 percent of all check-cashing centers in Los Angeles were in census tracts that

were majority Latina/o.[10] In the wake of the uprising, Paul Hudson rebuilt and
reopened the bank. The absence of the bank would have meant that another
check-cashing center would have opened in its place, but Broadway Federal
renewed its commitment to South Central when it opened a trailer across the
street from where the original building stood.

Similar to Broadway Federal's origins in the community, Family Savings
Bank also emerged as a financial institution by and for the community. Wayne-
Kent A. Bradshaw, president of the organization in the late 1980s and the 1990s,
helped revitalize the struggling bank: high levels of unemployment among its
consumer base, mismanagement and fraud by the previous chairmen, and poor
investments all had taken their toll. Bradshaw believed that the "only way to
turn around the 'trade deficit' in the community is to promote ownership, and
our strategy has been to do that by finding a way to qualify people for loans."[11]
Family Savings, however, did not maintain its autonomy like Broadway Federal.
In 1996, the Watts Health Foundation purchased a 65 percent controlling interest in the bank. The rationale behind such an alliance was that the institution
remained community controlled (especially at a time when larger banks were
absorbing smaller banks), since Watts Health Foundation has its origins as a community institution committed to the needs of the surrounding community. For
the foundation, this was another way for community empowerment that linked
capital and health.[12] The model for such a creative merger was a South Korean
organization that brought together different enterprises such as a university, a
hospital, a bank, and a golf course with the intention of strengthening the local
community.[13] This partnership was short-lived, as OneUnited Bank, one of the
most significant African American–owned banks in the country, currently owns
and operates Family Savings. The origins of Family Savings and its conditions
were like Broadway Federal's, but their fates are vastly different. Broadway Federal's community-centered goals and structure have primarily contributed to its
long-term success, development, and independence.

Considering the plethora of directions from which banks could approach
outside investment, Broadway Federal's approach resonates as mainly grounded
in the community. For example, in the mid-1970s, Broadway Federal launched a
series of advertising campaigns that aimed to attract not only residents of South
Central to invest in the bank but also donors who would become politically and
economically invested in the community. One of the ads situated the reader

within a car as a driver looking out to a freeway exit sign that stated, "Watts Next Right." The headline read, "If you're wondering what it's like in the under-developed areas of the world, get off the freeway and see for yourself." Both the visual markers and the headline appealed to investors and contributors who were not part of the community; they also situated and described South Central and Watts as communities in dire need of financial investment, as suggested by the term *underdeveloped*. Describing South Central in this way blurs the boundaries of how we understand the location of "underdeveloped" and "developed" communities, and potentially muddles how we think of global development. The ad also suggested that the very features that are used to define underdeveloped nations abroad are in our backyard. This type of descriptor for South Central is provocative, most especially in how this bank attempted to position itself as part of the modernizing and capitalist endeavor within the community and one that overtly signaled and deployed race. The bank has moved away from using a discourse of "underdeveloped"—to "underserved"—but both terms point to the fact that South Central's plight is due to the lack of investment in, catering to, and concern for the needs of the residents of South Central.

The advertisement also situated the importance of Broadway Federal in the community in that it stated, "we know what it's like in the 'underdeveloped areas' because that's where we live. . . . we're trying to help rebuild the ghetto areas"; however, the bank did not have "nearly enough money to meet the demands for loans." At the end of the text, the advertisement stated, "You should get off the freeway and see what it's like there . . . and do something about it," which gave a general sense of how potential investors might provide financial support for the community. What is most intriguing is the final line in the advertisement: "Because if you don't come to the ghetto, it may eventually come to you."[14] This ominous final line signaled that failure to invest time, effort, and money in this bank and the neighborhood would undoubtedly lead to problems in other neighborhoods, which, given the tone of the ad, was to be avoided at all costs. This advertising campaign was an effort to drum up support for South Central, to show Broadway Federal's commitment to investing in the community, and to make known that by the 1970s South Central's streets were saddled with a lack of investment and growing impoverishment.

A second ad aimed to garner the support of African American patrons through a different approach. It showed an African American man holding a brick with an angered look; the headline asserted, "How do you break into a white man's world?" The image conjured memories of the civil rights struggles of the 1960s, implying that a brick is one way to break into the white man's world, as "too many young Negroes can't see any other way of crashing the barriers created by poverty, lack of opportunity and frustration." Broadway Federal then offered an alternative to challenge power, not through violence but through economic power—a power that "enables a young Negro to own his own home . . . and develop a community he can be proud to live in." In addition to building individual power through investment in the bank, Broadway Federal builds an economic base, and the bank, in turn, invests in the Black community, and makes "loans that help to regenerate and build it." The discourse of individual economic power was not only about personal fulfillment but also intended to "develop a community he could be proud to live in."[15]

Unlike the first advertisement, which targeted bank investors, this advertisement aimed to get the residents of South Central to invest in Broadway Federal because it offered the path to economic empowerment and independence, and to creating a community to be proud of, not feared. While the first advertisement operated on elements of fear, this one used a different narrative—of hope, empowerment, and direct language—to break down white supremacy. These ads illustrate the varied and multiple ways in which the banks in the 1970s appealed to various sectors, individuals, and communities across Los Angeles.

A third advertisement targeted Black youth and their potential to achieve their dreams of upward mobility, with the tagline, "Suppose he can't sing or dance and he's a lousy athlete. Then what is he supposed to do?" The ad was based on the idea that the only way for Black male youth to make it "out of the ghetto was to excel in athletics," or through a decent education. However, dropout rates were highest in the Black community, and one of the reasons cited was the lack of money. Although there are many more reasons why students drop out of high school or are unable to complete college degrees, for the purposes of this advertisement and to highlight what Broadway Federal could provide in terms of higher education, this tagline was successful in conveying the bank's ability to provide low-interest student loans so that those enrolled in college could excel without finances being a hindrance.[16] According to the ad, this was one of the ways Broadway Federal invested its money, by providing loans to the Black community at a time when other lenders failed to because of their preconceived ideas about the ability of working class and poor residents to repay loans. The ad, again, bolstered the image of Broadway Federal, showing that its relevance to the community went far beyond its central location. These 1970s campaigns were an important effort by Broadway Federal to highlight its commitment to a community that many lenders had long neglected or outright excluded. They utilized a direct racial identity and target audience: the Black community of South Central, where the direct way in which Broadway Federal addressed racial inequality and the bank's commitment to Black opportunity were representative of how the bank saw itself serving the community.

A DIFFERENT APPROACH TO ECONOMIC INVESTMENT IN THE COMMUNITY

Efforts to revitalize South Central Los Angeles have taken different approaches. Caution about the community inhibits investment. The lack of investment has meant that rather than retailers which would provide meaningful opportunities and goods, liquor stores, check-cashing outlets, and dollar stores are key parts of South Central's economic landscape, as discussed in the previous chapter. Broadway Federal stands out as different, with resources that have persevered for over six decades. In the wake of the 1992 uprisings, Earvin "Magic" Johnson announced efforts to revitalize South Central by investing in the community, and he came to embody the potential to usher in a better tomorrow in the Black community. In an astute assessment of Magic Johnson's efforts, Bryant Simon argues that the former basketball star articulated a "vision of civic and community-mindedness" that amounted to "Black-guided capitalism" rather than a new dream for African American Los Angeles.[17] Past Central Avenue businessman such as George Beavers Jr., Claude Hudson, and other "race men" of the early twentieth century were representations of a longstanding faith in race enterprise. Magic Johnson, unlike political officials such as Tom Bradley and Maxine Waters, worked outside of the political arena, and thus South Central residents felt he would understand and engage with the community in a different way. According to Simon, Johnson used the discourse about Black capitalism recycling Black dollars in the community yet lacked the "larger worldview of Garveyism, with its forceful critique of capitalism's brutal relationship to colonialism and the exploitation of Black labor."[18] Johnson's lack of critique and his failure to advocate for anti-discrimination laws led to a strategy that emphasized "style over substance": he did not bring in industrial and unionized jobs that paid well. Nor did he invest in local sources. Consequently, Johnson ushered in "middle-class consumer desires over working families' material needs."[19]

Johnson became known as someone who "helped to revive downtrodden areas." In 1995, he successfully opened a state-of-the-art movie theater in the Baldwin Hills Crenshaw Plaza, despite investors arguing that urban neighborhoods failed to support movie theaters. He would explain to investors that they were "missing out" on the urban market, as limited disposable incomes by poor urban families did not necessarily translate to lack of patronization of movie theaters. Instead, urban residents had fewer entertainment options compared to residents in suburban communities, and therefore the demand was there.[20] Johnson's approach differed from that of others who had come before: instead of looking to form traditional Black-white alliances in the city or looking to politicians of color for support, he sought joint ventures by partnering with well-established and recognizable middle-class brands such as Sony, Starbucks, and TGI Fridays.[21] After opening the Magic Johnson Theaters, he opened Starbucks locations in 1998, expanding the coffee retailer's presence in "ethnically diverse urban and suburban neighborhoods."[22] Johnson advocated for retail justice, which "meant the opportunity, really the *right*, for African Americans to spend like other Americans without having to drive to a white area of the city to do so." This brand of justice, largely conceived of as South Central residents' as having the ability to shop, thus crafted their identity solely as consumers, not as residents worthy of dignified and appealing job and economic opportunities.

While Johnson was able to open these businesses successfully, there were limits to his transformative promise in recycling Black dollars, as he relied heavily on outside "capital that would *not* completely recycle Black dollars into the Black community." Criticisms of investment in spaces that had a built-in middle-class Black clientele (opening his theater next to the Baldwin Hills Crenshaw Plaza) and college-student-age clientele (with Starbucks at USC Village) also circulated. Residents criticized him for not opening restaurants and retail options in some of the poorest regions of South Central and Watts.[23] Similarly, his theater's "code of behavior," which required proper dress and conduct, became another mechanism of policing young men of color. As Ricardo Alvarez recounts,

I did not feel welcome at that "community" theater. I did not think it was right or welcoming for this theater to require a certain dress code to enjoy a movie. Wearing a cap was prohibited, and when walking into the theater, upon trying to purchase a ticket, I was asked to remove my cap or else I could not purchase a ticket-enjoy a movie at this "community" theater. Apparently, what we wore, what the community wore, disqualified us from the community this theater was interested in catering to. This form of policing did not feel right—it felt aggressive, heavy-handed, more of the same, and not what the community needed or was all about.[24]

South Central residents, therefore, felt not openly welcomed as is as patrons of the theater. These ventures also drove up real estate prices for businesses that had existed in the area before Johnson's arrival, showing the early signs of the negative impact of outside investment and capital—what we now describe as gentrification—on communities. Like many entrepreneurs before him, Johnson experienced South Central fatigue, and by the early 2000s he had liquidated all his investments there. By this period, the Black capitalism and "recycle Black dollars" rhetoric had fallen short because in the greater South Central area spending required investment genuinely grounded in the uplift of the community, through not only Black support but also Latina/o patronage.

Not everyone experiences fatigue when working and advocating for the needs of South Central; businesses operated by women and men who are from the community seem to have more staying power. In early 2011, Black and Latina/o business owners along Central Avenue collaborated to advocate for the revitalization of their neighborhood. Latina nail salon owner Virginia Zesati chose to advocate for and help elect Vivian Bowers, a Black owner of a dry-cleaning shop, as president of the newly formed Central Avenue Business Association. Zesati said that Bowers was "an honest person, a very hard-working woman and very dedicated to the community. We're all in this together. Among us there are no differences of color." Fellow business owner Maria Palmas echoed Zesati's sentiments when she said, "Vivian is great at speaking for all of us. That's the most important thing. Because now people are listening to us. . . . With every meeting, we're learning something new." In 1996, Maria's husband was murdered during a robbery in their grocery store. Despite this, she maintained her business along Central Avenue. Bowers remembers Central Avenue's "glory days" when patrons and residents were "distinguished," with pedestrians walking the streets. Alongside her Latina/o allies in the Central Avenue Business Association, Bowers intended to use their collective power to attend city council meetings and advocate for returning Central Avenue to its best days. What they wanted was Central Avenue to return to being "a street that comes alive after dark": "One day, we'll be able to walk outside at night, or take a sip of coffee at a restaurant without being afraid," Maria expressed. "I'm starting to believe it might happen soon."[25] This level of interracial collaboration signals the future of South Central, one that is grounded in *residents* themselves advocating for the future they mutually imagine and work toward, one centered on community, an interracial community.

BANKING AT A MULTIRACIAL FINANCIAL INSTITUTION

Much like the efforts of Maria, Vivian, and Virginia to collaborate cross-racially to revitalize the Central Avenue corridor—and unlike Magic Johnson's ungrounded community approach—Latina/o immigrants have ensured Broadway Federal's longevity in the community through their patronage. The racial demographic shift, along with the rebuilding efforts of the bank and South Central at large, was on the minds of Hudson and the African American and Latina/o residents of the area. Patrons of Broadway Federal and long-term residents of South Central, like seventy-eight-year-old African American Sang Brown, continued to bank at Broadway Federal. The bank was the only institution that allowed Sang to borrow $6,500 to purchase his two-bedroom house in the neighborhood. His commitment to Broadway Federal never wavered: "After the riots and their building was burned down, they stayed. . . . Since they didn't abandon us, I wasn't going to abandon them."[26] Sang also recalled, "I used to see the old man [Claude Hudson] who started the bank right here," which was indicative of how the Hudsons had become a feature of the community across generations. More important, their commitment prompted Sang's commitment. Samuel Martinez reflected that working class people have very few avenues for attaining loans. As working class people, he said, "we get caught in a trap. . . . you can't get credit unless you have it. They [Broadway Federal] were willing to take a chance with me."[27] The lack of banking options and Broadway Federal's willingness to serve the needs of South Central Los Angeles residents made Sang, Samuel, and many Mexican immigrants loyal patrons of the bank, because, as Paul Hudson stated, it has "always been a bank of last resort for people."[28]

Institutions and their leadership must confront the impact of demographic change on businesses' philosophies. Demographic changes led Paul Hudson to assert, "[T]here are a lot of folks who still believe that there is a Black market, and you can make it only in a Black market," yet to be a thriving and growing economic institution you have to have "crossover appeal."[29] By the mid-to-late 1980s, Broadway Federal had begun a new way of banking, hiring bilingual employees to help cater to its growing Mexican immigrant clientele. Similar to the initial recruitment efforts of hiring African American residents from the community, Hudson looked to the community for its pool of Latina/o employees, the first of whom were friends of his or bank patrons themselves. This choice was due in part to convenience but was also an extension of the mission of being a community bank that provides employment opportunities for community residents. Hiring Latina/os from the community proved one of the easiest ways to attract more Mexican immigrant clients since for them the options for cashing weekly paychecks were primarily licensed retail stores such as liquor markets, *loncheras* (lunch trucks), or formal check-cashing outlets. These avenues, however, provided limited options because they were one-time transactions, with fees, and no way to open an account for ongoing savings. Hudson understood that the need for a bank was not only for African American South Central residents but also for recently arrived Mexican immigrants. The conscious choice to hire bilingual employees and seek out new customers is representative of how Hudson and Broadway Federal had to evolve to survive against the backdrop of multiracial Los Angeles.

As Broadway Federal's workforce was slowly making the transition and becoming more representative of the community, Paul Hudson worked as a clerk assisting patrons with cashing their checks, opening bank accounts, and processing home loans. He learned the business from the bottom up, like a typical employee. He remembered his attempts at speaking Spanish to Mexican immigrant patrons: "Yes, I was trying to talk to the Hispanic patrons. I had enough words to negotiate transactions."[30] He expressed this with pride, as he considered this gesture an attempt to include and acknowledge Mexican immigrant patrons. Hudson's presence in the bank did not go unnoticed; as Antonio Sanchez recalled, "The owner's son was working at the bank, well that's what they would say, I did not talk to him . . . if anything it was for basic transactions like to cash my check . . . he would work there like a regular employee . . . but everyone would say that he and his father were involved in helping Blacks."[31] Despite the inability of Mexican immigrants to have conversations with African American employees (because of their limited English skills), information about Hudson and his family's involvement in the African American community circulated among Mexican immigrant patrons. This was always in the form of rumors, or at least that is how it was described. Mexican immigrants heard these rumors from the few in their community who spoke English and from the Latina/o employees of the bank. Not only were Latina/o employees important for satisfying banking needs, they also expanded and sustained information networks concerning the bank owner's identity and incentives.

The pivotal moment when Mexican immigrant men felt as though they were important patrons of the bank was when they won free prizes and rewards for being loyal customers. Francisco, a long-time patron, stated, "I remember that in those days they would give us free tickets to go see a Dodger game—to see Fernando Valenzuela. There was a Latino manager; he was really nice and friendly. He would help us."[32] The hiring of Latina/o employees and the bank owner making a genuine effort to serve their needs in Spanish were sources of comfort for Mexican immigrants because they felt someone had their best interests at heart. Mexican immigrants remember receiving gifts when Latina/o employees began working at the bank. It is uncertain whether the gifts coincided with Latina/o employees or if they had always been part of this bank's practices, but for these Mexican immigrant patrons, the presence of Latina/o employees introduced a generally positive atmosphere of banking at Broadway Federal.

However, hiring Latina/o employees was not positively received by some African American employees and patrons. By 1998, the workforce at Broadway Federal had dramatically changed. The branch manager of the oldest office was from the Dominican Republic, a woman from Belize was in charge of opening new accounts, and Mexican, Salvadoran, and Guatemalan immigrants increasingly worked alongside African Americans as tellers and loan officers. The strategy to hire someone from the Dominican Republic as manager was perceptive as it appealed to both African American and Latina/o patrons. By the late 1990s, Latina/os made up about a quarter of Broadway Federal's fifty-six employees and managed three of the bank's five branches.[33] Latoya Raines saw people from the community working in the bank, and this made the bank stand out to her. While she understood the economic motivation behind hiring Latina/o employees, she also felt that African American employees ostensibly were losing their jobs to make room for Latina/o employees. Latoya explained that the bank was one more institution among many that were responding to the massive influx of Latina/o immigrants. She believed that African Americans were becoming antagonistic toward Mexican immigrants because of what all these changes would mean for the achievements made by the African American community in South Central: "We fought hard for the strides we made . . . to have them cut short by Mexicans." She further elaborated, "I know how hard it is to keep something like a bank around . . . one that cares about Black people . . . who actually gives us loans . . . so to see them hire Mexicans and Mexicans bank here is bad 'cuz I didn't know what that would mean for us."[34] Latoya motioned to the difficulty of patrons to understand what all this change both on her block and in the bank would mean for African American progress.

Francisco thought that African American apprehension about Mexican immigrant settlement in South Central and the ensuing transformation in employment opportunities within the bank and elsewhere was warranted. In his perspective, Mexican immigrants did take jobs away from African Americans: "I saw the change. We didn't take all the jobs because you still see Black people working in the bank, but you see a lot more Mexicans there too. . . . I honestly didn't think it would happen, to see Mexicans outnumber Blacks. Especially because when I came here everything was Black. I understand if they feel threatened."[35] Francisco understands the anxiety of Latoya and other African American patrons and residents about the impact of demographic change on the lives of African Americans, mainly because Black people had had such a stronghold in the community.

Despite the multiracial character of Broadway Federal, the level of interaction between African American and Mexican immigrant patrons was very minimal. They stood in line to cash checks and open savings and checking accounts without really speaking to each other. There might have been a casual hello and goodbye, but for the most part, Mexican immigrants described talking to other Latina/o patrons and employees. In part, this seems to be a function of the fact that Mexican immigrant patrons have or had limited English-speaking skills; communicating with African American patrons would prove difficult. Both Mexican immigrants and African Americans sought particular bank employees, as even on the busiest days they waited to be assisted by employees

of their own racial background. Cultural preferences define this practice, as
Latina/o employees are fluent in Spanish, and Mexican immigrant men would
grow familiar with them and, over the course of their patronage at Broadway
Federal, would have conversations with tellers that extended beyond business
transactions. Similarly, African American patrons also had particular tellers they
frequented. This familiarity meant that both Mexican immigrant and African
American patrons had developed friendships with bank employees and had
learned a considerable amount about each others' lives. Latoya said, "I didn't
talk to the Mexicans. . . . I couldn't even if I wanted to. . . . I didn't understand
them and they didn't understand me. . . . I mean what were we to talk about?"[36]
Francisco expressed that there was some comfort in not communicating with
African American patrons because, in that period, the mid-to-late 1980s, racial
tension in the city streets was at times evident. The bank in many ways prevented
any forms of mutual harassment because it is a professional institution; hence,
the interaction was subtle and illustrates how the community was beginning to
make sense of living in a multiracial and multiethnic space.

Hiring a bilingual workforce proved important because it demystified the
process of applying for and securing bank accounts, as well as learning about
all the services the bank provides. In the 1980s, and even to this day, anxiety
about whether banks would offer resources for Mexican immigrants, both
documented and undocumented, has made Latina/os' engagement with them
tenuous. Not only hiring Latina/os but also training Latina/os from the community remained crucial for encouraging Latina/o patrons to enter and engage
with bank programs.

During Hudson's final years as chairman of the bank, his inclusion of Mexican immigrants meant allowing Mexican immigrants to use a *matricula consular*
(consulate identification card) for opening a bank account, as well as incorporating a Spanish-language section into the bank's website.[37] He also provided
direction on the bank's online presence, with the online Spanish translation of
services providing details on how to apply for a home loan, information on how
to open a bank account, and directions to its various locations. This information
was different from that provided to its English-speaking audience. Sections accessible to English-speaking audiences expanded on the logistics of opening an
account or applying for a home loan, but the "Our Community" segment of
the website provided a section for the history of the bank, including its struggle

to open a minority-owned bank to serve the African American community, and suggestions for places of interest in Los Angeles. These places of interest were a list of historical landmarks in the African American community.[38] The incorporation of a section on the website that speaks to the bank's history and places of interest is indicative of Hudson's conceptualization of community—African American. The website's failure to translate this feature suggests the bank management's inability to envision and treat Mexican immigrant patrons as engaged customers and members of the South Central community.[39]

Paul Hudson acknowledges that during his tenure he did not make efforts to inform Latina/o patrons about the bank and South Central Los Angeles' history. He said, "The history is not a history of the Hispanic immigrant; it's not that type of a history." I would argue that despite it not being the history of the Latina/o immigrant, there is something that could be learned by Latina/os if they were made aware of the difficulties and challenges faced by the African American community. While I am not suggesting that learning the history of the bank would eradicate Mexican immigrants' tensions with and prejudices toward African Americans (and vice versa), it might transform how Mexican immigrants understand banking at Broadway Federal and inform their attitude about interacting in racially and ethnically diverse venues. Informing Mexican immigrants about the political logic of the bank could transform their attitude toward banking at Broadway Federal—to see it as not just a choice made for convenience but one reflective of political efforts.

As Mexican immigrants reflected on their initial experiences at Broadway Federal, they began to question what made this bank unique and set it apart from other banks in the area. On the one hand, the bank is part of a capitalist venture that aims to make a profit. On the other, it saw itself as a relevant cultural, social, political, and economic entity in the community of South Central in general, and of African Americans in particular. At the end of my oral histories with long-time Mexican patrons, I shared the bank's history, commitment, and politics. They realized that Broadway Federal indeed differed from others in the area. Upon discussing this history, they were quick to respond, "It's good to know" or "Things make sense now."[40] Exposing Mexican immigrant patrons to this rich history might lay the foundation for interaction genuinely consistent with creating and nurturing an informed sense of community. They were far more receptive to reflecting on the potential significance of the oil paintings

196   I love this the bank
                story of the
                            BANKING IN SOUTH CENTRAL

of African American men that graced the bank's original building (which had pictures of H. Claude Hudson and Elbert Hudson). Similarly, not all African American patrons are aware of the history and politics behind Broadway Federal. The oil paintings, murals, and quotes are visual markers meant to do some of the cultural work that the bank imagines itself doing. South Central resident Chris Campbell stated that these visual markers made him feel welcome in a way that he does not necessarily feel at Bank of America or a check-cashing center. As a long-term patron, Chris stated that he always found a sense of warmth and history represented through these images. Paul Hudson's attempt to transform building walls into spaces for expressing cultural pride and belonging does work for some African American patrons, but, as Francisco explains, "I would like it if they place a picture of Emilio Zapata, for example. . . . I don't see why not, we are also patrons like African Americans."[41]

Patrons of both racial-ethnic contingencies and Hudson are equally receptive to art's potential to play a symbolic role for the creation of a politics behind banking at Broadway Federal. By making reference to the symbolic function of these images, I do not aim to render the bank's rich African American history as unimportant or irrelevant to the culture and practices of the bank and its patrons; however, if Mexican immigrant patrons see only representations of African American history and progress, that does not in itself introduce the possibility of imagining Broadway Federal as their bank. Mexican immigrant patrons continue to believe that "the bank is for Blacks, we know that."[42] In the initial years of Mexican immigrants banking at Broadway Federal, the bank was still in line with how other institutions treated South Central residents: namely, it catered to the needs of African Americans. This first generation of Mexican immigrants settling into South Central then had to learn how to navigate all institutions, not just Broadway Federal, that worked under this logic. The belief of Mexican immigrant patrons that Broadway Federal catered to African Americans is not surprising, but it is not reflective of Broadway Federal's actual reality. Despite Paul Hudson's attempts to include Latina/os as essential patrons by hiring bilingual employees, the visual and cultural cues and racial discourse make Mexican immigrants feel that Broadway Federal is still primarily a bank by and for African Americans.

Hudson had not invested in features and services necessary to Latina/o immigrant communities, like offering money transfers to nations of origin. In the past few decades, the growth of business in wire and money transfers from the United

States to Latin American countries has grown exponentially because relatives in those countries and towns are dependent on the remittances of family members in the States. In 2004, remittances between the United States and Latin America were $30 billion, with California residents alone sending roughly $10 billion. In that same year, Mexican immigrants in California sent approximately $4.5 billion to Mexico. The money-transfer businesses throughout the state earned $338 million in transaction fees.[43] Businesses such as Western Union, check-cashing centers, and larger banks (for example, Bank of America and Wells Fargo) have proven to be important resources for Mexican immigrant residents of South Central Los Angeles. Broadway Federal's failure to implement a money-transfer option for its patrons foreclosed the possibility not only of generating significant profits but also of understanding how Latina/o immigrant needs might require much more than deposit, checking, and loan options.

Hudson discussed how Broadway Federal has made a conscious effort to market itself to Mexican immigrant patrons, yet upon closer inspection, he still imagined and conceptualized Broadway Federal as a bank for African Americans. His perspective on the role that Latina/os play in his bank is often contradictory—something inherent, perhaps, in the difficult situation confronted by individuals who envision themselves as race leaders in general, and African American leaders in particular. At the very moment in which Paul Hudson became the spokesperson of the bank, the backdrop of the work that his father and grandfather had labored under changed dramatically. The rationale behind his management and expansion of Broadway Federal was reflective of his guarded rhetoric on his process of making sense of demographic change. He believed that including Mexican immigrants in the discourse could have meant a backlash among long-term African American patrons anxious about the Latina/o immigrant population's growing majority. His greatest fear was that this could prompt African American patrons to abandon Broadway Federal, as they would misinterpret the inclusion of Latina/os as a challenge to the bank's longstanding commitment and tradition of helping the African American community.

Broadway Federal's longevity in the community deserves recognition. In a space where investment is limited, or is often brought about by outside investors, Broadway Federal has continued its mission to serve the needs of South Central residents. The 1970s advertising strategies were different from Magic Johnson's efforts throughout the Crenshaw corridor, as they were about creating economic opportunities for residents. Hudson serves as an example of how important it is to have a historical connection to South Central, and his commitment was deep-seated. However, Hudson also represents the tension caused when a business mission of historical connection has to grapple with demographic change and a changing bank structure for revenue and profits. The bank's longevity and success are due to the leadership's unwavering commitment to the community, as well as the spatial geography of the bank, which allows muted relational community engagement, in that interactions are transactional and are taking place within the context of a business institution. African American and Latina/o patrons alike reserve chairs lining this bank's waiting area for the elderly, irrespective of race or gender, and do not object to a disabled or elderly client cutting in line. Chris Campbell explains, "There isn't much in South Central . . . the least we can do is help one another take care of business. Black, Latino—it is up to us to conduct business with respect if we want this bank to make business and stick around."[44] Rosario Cruz's rationale behind her banking practices echoes Campbell's assessment of their situation: "Everyone—Latinos, Blacks, the old, youth—we have to do our part. There is very little around here, it is like an obligation to get along well so that this, the bank, stays here."[45]

Chris and Rosario believe that the continued success of the bank, and of South Central Los Angeles more broadly, lies in the continued interaction between and among African Americans and Mexican immigrants. Broadway Federal has failed to educate its Mexican immigrant clientele on the political and economic importance of a thriving financial institution in an impoverished community like South Central Los Angeles. To put it another way, if one reads this bank's success and growth as going against the grain in terms of perceptions about how minority businesses fail to thrive over generations in an impoverished community (especially a financial business like a bank, as opposed to a check-cashing center), then one must conclude that the bank's success has depended not only on its rich African American history, commitment, and struggle but, in the past few decades, on the support of Mexican immigrants. Such considerations illustrate how Black people and Mexican immigrants can occupy similar spaces and together push forward a new vision and mission.

EPILOGUE

like Richmond
School Dist
after Yamatopez

IN 2003, L.A. city officials felt that changing the name of South Central Los Angeles to South Los Angeles would rid the area of its negative image and connotations. Resident Carol Black hoped that the "name change would mean a new attitude for the people, maybe when the government decides to bring jobs in, they will bring them to our neighborhood, instead of ignoring us," but, as then councilman of District 10 Nate Holden stated, "changing the name doesn't change the circumstances."[1] For many residents, this "new beginning" did nothing to change anything on the ground for their lived reality. In fact, most residents continue to refer to South Los Angeles as South Central, *Sur Centro*, or the 'hood.[2] The change in name, an attempt to provide a fresh start for the area, did not deliver on its promise because society continues to view South Central as an impoverished, working poor, and working class community of color, unworthy of care and attention.[3] Changing the name did not alter the U.S. government's continued reduction of its investment and care for South Central.

In spring 2015, South Central underwent another rebranding attempt, this time in the form of "SOLA." This shorthand supposedly would, as "South Los Angeles" was supposed to do in 2003, rid the community of "negative

see essay, in re businesses
Hernandez sitting gentrification
) og

connotations." The choice to rebrand in 2015 came after a huge development project was announced and approved for Historic Central Avenue; the project was called the SoLA Village. This coincidental rebranding effort after the development announcement made many South Central residents and policymakers wary. They asked, "Whom is this rebranding for? And is it really for the residents who live here now, or is this about gentrification?"[4] Ultimately, resident pushback, community opposition, and reminders of how "South Los Angeles" did little to change life circumstances defeated the SoLA name change proposal. The Latina/o community was quick to point out that *sola* in Spanish means alone, an emotional marker that residents could not and would not support. The refusal to accept such a name change was also indicative of the investment by South Central residents who feared that this project, and others like it, would bring about more outside development, gentrification, and ultimately displacement. Opposition to the name change also captured the emotional landscape of South Central residents, because they know that changing a name does not change circumstances for the better. Being left "alone" was not something residents were willing to consider. The failure of residents to embrace the name change is indicative of how residents continue to organize creatively, to struggle, and to resist (relationally and interracially) the nation-state and society scapegoating of them as if their choices were a result of moral failing.

South Central residents continue to fight against the threat of gentrification and possible resident displacement. Having been born and raised in South Central in the 1980s, and in the midst of the changes discussed throughout the book, I never considered that one day residents in my interracial community could be priced out of living in the 'hood! That my working class, working poor, and poor neighbors would not count on calling these streets their home, their neighborhood. In part, my words echo similar sentiments that African American residents expressed when they started to see and experience the Latina/o population growth and settlement in South Central. My anxiety, however, rests on what these changes would mean for the interracial relations that have taken decades to foster and develop.

This new demographic, one with capital and the ability to develop the community, will bring the strong arm of policing and community "clean-up" that South Central residents distrust and fear. For Mexican immigrant and African American South Central residents, working toward their "American Dream" has been challenging and often has not resulted in upward mobility. Instead, it has entailed creatively making ends meet and investing tirelessly in making South Central their home together. Despite South Central's location in the heart of Los Angeles, it is one of the most isolated parts of the city. The lack of investment in the community opens a space for an underground entrepreneurial spirit among South Central residents. Alfred Smith decided he would put his skills as a mechanic to use and started offering his services to South Central neighbors and friends. The sidewalk became a resourceful place for neighbors to fix cars and sell used clothing or furniture, household garages became places to operate carpentry and welding businesses, driveways were prime locations for *cenadurias* and taquerias, and neighbors' homes and yards became unlicensed childcare centers. Street corners, freeway exits, and bus stops transformed into taco, fruit, hot dog, and flower stands. These are all actions and physical markers of South Central residents' hustle to survive. Hence, a considerable sector of the South Central community is involved in some form of this informal economy. In the Westside and upper-middle-class neighborhoods throughout Los Angeles, this type of entrepreneurial spirit is frowned upon, but in South Central, it seems to be the only way to make ends meet. Gentrification will likely erase this landscape.

Underground economies have a longstanding tradition in working-poor communities; however, in the past few years such "hustles," or *movidas*, have become more visible and prevalent in South Central. There is nostalgia about how beautifully clean the "sophisticated ghetto" looked decades ago, but what once looked like a suburban oasis now looks like a site for employment and business. Alfred's neighbor Elena recounts, "I wake up early to sweep the sidewalk and street because Alfred doesn't pick up the empty motor oil bottles from the day before."[5] She also complains about her struggle to find parking nearby, since he usually parks the multiple cars he is repairing on the street, not in his driveway or garage. Her Mexican immigrant neighbors' carpentry business creates a burdensome loud noise from the saws they use.[6] Her complaints and those of others on the block do not go beyond household conversations or occasional neighborly chit-chat, as most residents realize that in some way or another they too participate in the underground economy or a practice that requires the support of—or at the very least silence from—the community. These neighborly negotiations, sometimes spoken or unspoken, have perhaps always been true of residents of poor urban communities, but these negotiations in South Central occur across racial difference and at times despite language barriers. Elena has never spoken to Alfred about his mechanical negligence, nor he about her occasional childcare service or loud family parties. Despite the occasional neighborhood gossip or complaint about each other's "businesses," none merit reporting to the city. These economies are not based on the drug trade but rather are out-in-the-open transactions that—while not necessarily legal because residents are not paying taxes, securing permits, or paying commercial rents—are services to the community. In order for them to function and operate, both African American and Mexican immigrant residents must work together if they are to help each other out and make ends meet. These are the everyday negotiations of South Central residents in the community, and markers of a relational community formation.

It is a community characterized by decades' worth of disinvestment, poverty, and surveillance, but also home to thousands of families who struggle to find meaning, possibility, and opportunity despite these key visual markers of neglect. Resident lives are monitored and mediated by the state. Surveillance and policing mechanisms will only become accelerated and enhanced by the movement of newly mobile investors and homeowners into South Central. Nonetheless, the evidence discussed throughout this book points to a glimmer of hope, as it is important not to forget or underestimate that South Central residents, both African American and Latina/o, have a long, rich history of struggle and unity.

South Central residents have yet to be paralyzed by change. They continue to organize to show the fruits of interracial relational community investment and formation. In fall 2014, Marqueece Harris-Dawson, former president of Community Coalition (CoCo), a seminal local organization that emerged in the wake of the 1980s community crisis, began his campaign to run for City Council in District 8.[7] By 2015, Harris-Dawson had won and taken office in a district that spans from Baldwin Hills to Watts. This district continues to be considered a Black community, in part because two-thirds of its voters are African Americans. However, as Harris-Dawson quickly learned, the majority of voters in this district may be African American, but its residents, on the whole, are much more diverse. His council meetings readily remind him that active residents are not just Black but also Latina/o. Working with Black and Latina/o constituencies is nothing new for Harris-Dawson because during his time at CoCo he was active in securing town halls and spaces where both Latina/o and African American residents could address and discuss their needs. Harris-Dawson's biggest challenge, political consultants suggest, is finding ways to gain the support and respect of the Latina/o community, which means being attentive to their needs as residents. Otherwise, political consultants such as Dermot Givens say, he runs the risk of becoming the district's last Black politician: "If the Latinos ever wake up and say, we want a Latino . . . then they can take it."[8] However, what sets Harris-Dawson apart is not that he is concerned with being the district's last Black politician, but rather with how best to represent *his* interracial constituency. He ensures that translators are present during town hall meetings and that he maximizes on his limited Spanish-speaking skills. Givens's concern is one of an outsider and one that is not representative of how Harris-Dawson's community roots come from his being born and raised in an interracial South Central. His work and leadership at Community Coalition are emblematic of his lived experience and context in South Central.

There are still ways in which, despite previous efforts to faithfully document the interracial dimensions of South Central, this community and its history continue to be visually rendered as African American. In the summer of 2015, Marisa Zocco, a writer for *Intersections South LA: News and Views from South Los Angeles*, covered the unveiling of a traffic signal at the intersection of Figueroa and 56th Streets. Placing a traffic signal at this location was necessary because South Central residents had complained of the dangers of crossing the busy six-lane intersection. Pictures associated with the story show council member Curren Price and African American residents and children excited about the traffic signal.[9] The choice of residents visually erases the presence of Latina/os. Price's constituency, more so than Harris-Dawson's, boasts a large Latina/o population. As discussed throughout this book, the media are powerful vehicles for rendering, narrating, and framing South Central in particular ways. This event could have showcased the diversity of South Central's residents. The lack of a Latina/o in the photographs renders them invisible, even if they, too, were equally invested in the safety of their community. It is this challenge—of viewing Latina/os as bona fide residents—that at times continues to shape their experience.

Price's choice of attendees for the event is most interesting, given that in his race to win the district seat in 2013, he had to undergo a runoff election with a Latina opponent: Ana Cubas. He narrowly defeated her with a margin of six hundred votes.[10] As quick as election cycles are, by the fall of 2016, Price had become aware that he could not continue to invest in photo opportunities that centered only on Black residents; he began to sponsor know-your-rights workshops and citizenship drives. These programs would provide visual cues that he was aware of the needs of the Latina/o community. His sponsorship of these workshops may appear as though the needs of Latina/os are not relatable to those of African Americans. However, as I have argued throughout the book, relational community formation does not mean that the particular needs of each community are erased or flattened for a coalition politics, but that creating a space for these workshops within South Central is an honest accounting of the lived realities of South Central residents.

Price's sponsorship of these events also emerged as Jorge Nuño, born and raised in South Central Los Angeles, began a grassroots campaign for Price's city council seat in 2017. Throughout Nuño's campaign, he appealed to South Central's voting residents as a native son investing in *his* community; his motto was "Don't move, improve." He highlighted his entrepreneurial and nonprofit efforts, as a resident who attended local schools and whose children are now attending public schools. Despite his best efforts, incumbent Price won the election.[11]

The outcome did not change Nuño's approach or his commitment to his community. He grew up helping his father with his gardening business, and he decided to go to college after the football program at his high school was eliminated. In college, he focused on graphic design and launched his design agency, the NTS Group. As his business gained traction, he knew it was time for it to expand. He had just bought a big, hundred-year-old Craftsman home, with three floors and more than nine rooms, a home he lovingly called the Big House. It was a fixer-upper just a few blocks from where he had grown up on 35th Street, near Jefferson High School (close to Central Avenue). He purchased it as an investment property, with plans to rent it; however, he quickly decided to open NTS on the second floor. Because of its location and Nuño's approach, the Big House became a hub of energy and vision for the neighborhood. Looking out from his office on the second floor, he said, "I'd see tons of kids skateboarding on the street, and thought, Well, I've got this big old lot and decided to build a skate park in the driveway and added an Xbox on one side of the house, and a Playstation on the other, so that kids would have a safe place to play after school."[12] This was the beginning of the Big House's transformation, and the beginning of Nuño's passion project, Nuevo South, a nonprofit that provides technology training opportunities for local youth, and training in civic engagement and leadership development.

He also started having block parties, holiday toy drives, and health fairs to welcome the community beyond the youth who were also tech savvy. These public displays of welcome meant that people started coming out and talking fairly quickly and feeling welcome at the Big House. They started walking down the streets at night. The vibrant atmosphere of the Big House inspired young people to think big about how they could transform their futures. Nuño decided to start his own business and make an attempt at "living in a community where people aren't coming together over funerals, aren't talking about who just got arrested or beat down by the police"; instead, he wanted to create the opportunity for a more humane space, a community, a sense of accountability, and, like generations of South Central residents before him, a sense of home.[13]

The discussion of these political elections is not meant to provide an exhaustive analysis but rather to highlight how in the twenty-first century accountability and community responsibility take on an interracial dimension in South Central. The drive to care for and "improve" South Central for Harris-Dawson and Nuño is coming from a younger generation of residents whose community roots are in their connection to being born and raised in South Central as it was undergoing racial transition. Their commitment to the community through their political engagement and innovative initiatives, whether through Community Coalition, the Big House, and Nuevo South, shows that relational community formation and interracial relations are the normative part of the twenty-first century.

The election of Donald J. Trump to the office of U.S. President renders the interracial efforts of people such as Harris-Dawson and Nuño, and more generally of South Central residents, critically important to the well-being of interracial communities like South Central. The Trump administration has emboldened and empowered the outward and vocal reemergence of white nationalist groups who have embraced his anti-immigrant and anti-refugee rhetoric and a referendum on the two-term African American president Barack Obama.[14] The Trump administration has ramped up its "zero tolerance policies" against immigrants and refugees, and in doing so, created a dangerous family separation crisis that undoubtedly will inflict lifelong trauma on children, women, and men brutally and indefinitely separated and detained in U.S. ICE (Immigration and Customs Enforcement) detention cages. The administration's implementation of its travel ban against Muslim-majority countries, neoliberal policies that foreclose the possibility of economic security among working class and middle-class families, the housing affordability crisis, attacks on constitutional rights to protest, police brutality going unpunished, and the ushering in of new forms of vetting for U.S. naturalized citizens and legal permanent residents are bound to intensify feelings of insecurity among people in U.S. society, most especially among immigrants and populations of color.[15] These devastating political, social, and economic realities require communities like South Central to continue through interracial collaboration to fight against white supremacy and its systemic underpinnings.

The goal of *South Central Is Home* has been to present the messy reality of life in South Central. As we move further into the twenty-first century, the interracial dynamics of the community are not neatly settled but demonstrate the promise of interracial relationships. The lessons of the past are the necessary stepping stones to the possibilities of the future. This is where Marqueece Harris-Dawson's and Jorge Nuño's stories become particularly resonant: their engagement illustrates the promise of relational community formation vested in accountability, the assertion of South Central as home, and a vision for the future. Uncovering the relational aspects of community formation, and considering the ways in which communities are similarly racialized, requires that we consider seriously the daily interactions of South Central residents in city streets: children and parents attending Head Start classes, patients seeking medical care at community clinics and local hospitals, responses to Los Angeles's multiracial celebrations, and locals becoming patrons of longstanding entrepreneurial investments such as a minority-owned bank. The lives of South Central residents are affected by the bifurcation between middle-class and working class families, increased levels of concentrated poverty, violence, a declining welfare state, increased vilification, condemnation, and a growing police state. In light of these realities, *South Central Is Home* illustrates the creative, productive, and even at times unsuccessful ways in which African American and Latina/o people actively and publicly invested in challenging the oppressive interaction between race, economics, and politics in an emotion-laden community.

It is the public investment in community of South Central's African American and Latina/o residents that should be prioritized when one strives to view, understand, and describe *this* working class and working poor interracial community of color. In the end, by documenting the complex terrain that African American and Latina/o residents have inhabited and shared as they cope with decades of disinvestment, limited economic opportunities and government resources, and failed immigration reform with a pathway for legalization, it becomes clear that even under the most oppressive of circumstances, these community residents endure and take heart together in challenging the state in their pursuit of a more just, stable, and equal home.

NOTES

INTRODUCTION

1. Ruth Smith (a pseudonym), oral history conducted by the author, Los Angeles, November 21, 2008.

2. I use the full name "South Central Los Angeles" to describe the community, despite its name change to "South Los Angeles" in 2003. I use this older term because the majority of residents have expressed that the name change did nothing to change their daily lives, as well as because they continue to use "South Central" when discussing their community.

3. Smith, oral history.

4. Josh Sides, *L.A. City Limits: African American Los Angeles from the Great Depression to the Present* (Berkeley: University of California Press, 2003).

5. Dolores Rosas, oral history conducted by the author, Los Angeles, September 23, 2009.

6. Ibid.

7. Sides, *L.A. City Limits*.

8. David Fabienke, "Beyond the Racial Divide: Perceptions of Minority Residents on Coalition Building in South Los Angeles," *Tomas Rivera Policy Brief* (June 2007), 2.

9. Ibid.

10. Sides, *L.A. City Limits*; Douglas Flamming, *Bound for Freedom: Black Los Angeles in Jim Crow America* (Berkeley: University of California Press, 2005); Darnell Hunt and Ana-Christina Ramon, eds., *Black Los Angeles: American Dreams and Racial Realities* (New York: New York University Press, 2010).

11. João H. Costa Vargas, *Catching Hell in the City of Angeles: Life and Meanings of Blackness in South Central Los Angeles* (Minneapolis: University of Minnesota Press, 2006).

12. George Lipsitz, *How Racism Takes Place* (Philadelphia: Temple University Press, 2011), 52.

13. Ibid., 56.

14. Gaye Theresa Johnson, *Spaces of Conflict, Sounds of Solidarity: Music, Race, and Spatial Entitlement in Los Angeles* (Berkeley: University of California Press, 2013), PDF e-book.

15. Ibid.

16. Lipsitz, *How Racism Takes Place*, 52.

17. Albert Camarillo, "Cities of Color: The New Racial Frontier in California's Minority-Majority Cities," *Pacific Historical Review* 76, no. 1 (February 2007): 3. Beyond the urban city framework, Wendy Cheng develops the theory of regional racial formation to unearth the experiences of Asian Americans and Latina/os in the Los Angeles suburb of the San Gabriel Valley. Cheng astutely illuminates how regional racial knowledge developed through the overlapping of local racial scripts, family experiences, and regional and global economies and migrations to further explore the community and ethnic identities that form and relate to homeownership rights, racial privilege in schools, intimate partner relationships, and child and youth leisure culture. Wendy Cheng, *The Changs Next Door to the Díazes: Remapping Race in Suburban California* (Minneapolis: University of Minnesota Press, 2013).

18. Tarso Lu Ramos, "L.A. Story: Who Gains from Framing Gang Attacks as 'Ethnic Cleansing'?" *Colorlines*, May 29, 2007, https://www.colorlines.com/articles/la-story.

19. Ibid.

20. Ibid.

21. Anthony Ocampo in *The Latinos of Asia* presents this argument most poignantly in the context of the greater Los Angeles area. School administrators play a role in the development of racial hierarchies within schools with the placement and tracking of Asian Americans in college preparation courses, versus the more significant share of Latina/os and African American students not placed in these courses. Setting up schools in this way undoubtedly creates a context of schools being racially segregated and fuels the conditions for racial misunderstandings and hierarchies. Ocampo's scholarly intervention goes beyond school tracking to discuss the complex racial and ethnic identity formation of Filipino Americans in relationship to Latina/os and Asian Americans. He shows how institutions and community dynamics are key to unearthing the complexity of identity and race relations. Anthony Ocampo, *The Latinos of Asia: How Filipino Americans Break the Rules of Race* (Stanford, CA: Stanford University Press, 2016).

22. Cid Gregory Martinez, *The Neighborhood Has Its Own Rules: Latinos and African Americans in South Los Angeles* (New York: New York University Press, 2016).

23. Many studies have demonstrated that Black-Latina/o tension was common in California and Texas throughout the twentieth century. See, for example, Neil Foley, *Quest for Equality: The Failed Promise of Black-Brown Solidarity* (Cambridge, MA: Harvard University Press, 2010); Brian Behnken, *Fighting Their Own Battles: Mexican Americans, African Americans, and the Struggle for Civil Rights in Texas* (Chapel Hill: University of North Carolina Press, 2011); Nicolas Vaca, *The Presumed Alliance: The Unspoken Conflict Between Latinos and Blacks and What It Means for America* (New York: HarperCollins, 2004); Vargas, *Catching Hell*; George J. Sanchez, "Face the Nation: Race, Immigration, and the Rise of Nativism in the Late Twentieth Century," *The International Migration Re-*

view 31, no. 4 (Winter 1997): 1009–1030. Scholars such as Luis Alvarez, Scott Kurashige, Anthony Macias, Natalia Molina, Laura Pulido, Gaye Theresa Johnson, and many others have provided important interventions and challenges to understand Black and Latina/o relations as inherently competitive, through their nuanced analyses of labor participation, public health discourse, interracial activism and politics, and leisure and youth culture as critical sites for investigating interracial and interethnic community formations. See, for example, Josh Kun, "What Is an MC If He Can't Rap to Banda? Making Music in Nuevo L.A.," *American Quarterly* 56, no. 3 (September 2004); Laura Pulido, *Black, Brown, Yellow, and Left: Radical Activism in Los Angeles* (Berkeley: University of California Press, 2006); Natalia Molina, *Fit to Be Citizens?: Public Health and Race in Los Angeles, 1879–1939* (Berkeley: University of California Press, 2006); Scott Kurashige, *The Shifting Grounds of Race: Black and Japanese Americans in the Making of Multiethnic Los Angeles* (Princeton: Princeton University Press, 2007); Luis Alvarez, "From Zoot Suits to Hip Hop: Towards a Relational Chicana/o Studies," *Latino Studies* 5, no. 1 (Spring 2007): 53–75; Luis Alvarez, *The Power of the Zoot: Youth Culture and Resistance During World War II* (Berkeley: University of California Press, 2008); Andrew Diamond, *Mean Streets: Chicago Youths and the Everyday Struggle for Empowerment in the Multiracial City, 1908–1969* (Berkeley: University of California Press, 2009); Victor Rios, *Punished: Policing the Lives of Black and Latino Boys* (New York: New York University Press, 2011); Brian Behnken, ed., *The Struggle for Black and Brown: African American and Mexican American Relations During the Civil Rights Era* (Lincoln: University of Nebraska Press, 2012); Johnson, *Spaces of Conflict*; Josh Kun and Laura Pulido, eds., *Black and Brown in Los Angeles: Beyond Conflict and Coalition* (Berkeley: University of California Press, 2014); Lauren Araiza, *To March for Others: The Black Freedom Struggle and the United Farm Workers* (Berkeley: University of California Press, 2014); John Marquez, *Black-Brown Solidarity: Racial Politics in the New Gulf South* (Austin: University of Texas Press, 2014); Frederick Opie, *Upsetting the Apple Cart: Black-Latino Coalitions in New York City from Protest to Public Office* (New York: Columbia University Press, 2014); Brian D. Behnken, ed., *Civil Rights and Beyond: African American and Latino/a Activism in the Twentieth-Century United States* (Athens: University of Georgia Press, 2016); Martinez, *The Neighborhood Has Its Own Rules*; Max Krochmal, *Blue Texas: The Making of a Multiracial Democratic Coalition in the Civil Rights Era* (Chapel Hill: North Carolina Press, 2016); Perla Guerrero, *Nuevo South: Latinas/os, Asians and the Remaking of Place* (Austin: University of Texas Press, 2017).

24. Robert Bauman, *Race and the War on Poverty: From Watts to East L.A.* (Norman: University of Oklahoma Press, 2008) 34–36.

25. For extended discussions of how the NAFTA deal was achieved and its impact on Latina/o immigration to and from the United States, see David Bacon, *The Children of NAFTA: Labor Wars on the U.S./Mexico Border* (Berkeley: University of California Press, 2004); Maxwell Cameron and Brian Tomlin, *The Making of NAFTA: How the Deal Was Done* (Ithaca: Cornell University Press, 2002); Jason de Leon, *The Land of Open Graves: Living and Dying on the Migrant Trail* (Berkeley: University of California Press, 2015).

26. Sides, *L.A. City Limits*, 184.

27. Oscar Lewis, *Five Families: Mexican Case Studies in the Culture of Poverty* (New York: Basic Books, 1959).

28. Daniel P. Moynihan, *The Negro Family: The Case for National Action* (Washington, DC: U.S. Government Printing Office, 1965).

29. Robert Self, *American Babylon: Race and the Struggle for Postwar Oakland* (Princeton, NJ: Princeton University Press, 2005), 199.

30. Robert Self, *All in the Family: The Realignment of American Democracy Since the 1960s* (New York: Hill and Wang, 2013), PDF e-book; Laura Briggs, *How All Politics Became Reproductive Politics: From Welfare Reform to Foreclosure to Trump* (Berkeley: University of California Press, 2018).

31. Ana Y. Ramos-Zayas, *Street Therapists: Race, Affect, and Neoliberal Personhood in Latino Newark* (Chicago: University of Chicago Press, 2012), 6; 19.

32. The scholarly interest in the War on Poverty has moved beyond studies that discuss the legislative aspect of the program to showing the ways in which it was implemented in cities nationwide. See, for example, Bonnie Lefkowitz, *Community Health Centers: A Movement and the People Who Made It Happen* (New Brunswick, NJ: Rutgers University Press, 2007); Susan Youngblood Ashmore, *Carry It On: The War on Poverty and the Civil Rights Movement in Alabama, 1964–1972* (Atlanta: University of Georgia Press, 2008); Bauman, *Race and the War on Poverty*; William Clayson, *Freedom Is Not Enough: The War on Poverty and the Civil Rights Movement in Texas* (Austin: University of Texas Press, 2010); Behnken, *Fighting Their Own Battles*; Gordon Mantler, *Power to the Poor: Black-Brown Coalition and the Fight for Economic Justice, 1960–1974* (Chapel Hill: University of North Carolina Press, 2013).

33. The power and allure of political strategies that were based on claims to whiteness by the Mexican American community in the 1940s and 1950s foreclosed collective organizing with African Americans. Neil Foley, *Quest for Equality: The Failed Promise of Black-Brown Solidarity* (Cambridge: Harvard University Press, 2010); Behnken, *Fighting Their Own Battles*.

34. Scholars have demonstrated that the activism of the 1940s and 1950s opened the possibility for the activism that followed among African Americans and Latina/os. Two key texts that discuss domestic postwar liberalism throughout California are Shana Bernstein's *Bridges of Reform* and Mark Brilliant's *The Color of America Has Changed*. They collectively demonstrate how the reform agendas of the 1930s through the 1950s shaped the national civil rights movement and activism. Shana Bernstein, *Bridges to Reform: Interracial Civil Rights Activism in Twentieth-Century Los Angeles* (New York: Oxford University Press, 2011), 15; Mark Brilliant, *The Color of America Has Changed: How Racial Diversity Shaped Civil Rights Reform in California, 1941–1978* (New York: Oxford University Press, 2012), 14.

35. Alvarez, "From Zoot Suits to Hip Hop," 55.

36. Mae Ngai, *Impossible Subjects: Illegal Aliens in the Making of Modern America* (Princeton, NJ: Princeton University Press, 2003); Natalia Molina, *How Race Is Made in America: Immigration, Citizenship, and the Historical Power of Racial Scripts* (Berkeley: University of California Press, 2014).

37. Ibid.

38. Molina, *How Race Is Made in America*, 6.

39. Ibid.

40. Marquez, *Black-Brown Solidarity*; Johnson, *Spaces of Conflict*; Alvarez, "From Zoot Suits to Hip Hop; Alvarez, *The Power of the Zoot*.

41. Marquez, *Black-Brown Solidarity*, 52.

42. Ibid. Also, to the erasure of the presence of Black people and culture throughout Mexico, Sylvia Zamora argues that Mexican immigrants learn the racial scripts of the United States through either lived experience or stories of racial incidents that are shared and circulated through what Zamora theorizes as racial remittances through Mexican towns. These remittances then shape how both immigrants and non-immigrants view and understand the Black community in the United States, often affirming anti-black perspectives. These perspectives then shape how Mexican immigrants interact with U.S.-born Black people in the United States. Sylvia Zamora, "Racial Remittances: The Effect of Migration on Racial Ideologies in Mexico and the United States," *Sociology of Race and Ethnicity* 2, no. 4 (2016): 466–481.

43. Kurashige, *Shifting Grounds of Race*, 289.

44. Susan Gonzalez Baker, "The 'Amnesty' Aftermath: Current Policy Issues Stemming from the Legalization Programs of the 1986 Immigration Reform and Control Act," *International Migration Review* 31, no. 1 (Spring 1997): 15; Dolores Ines Casillas, "Sounds of Surveillance: U.S. Spanish-Language Radio Patrols La Migra," *American Quarterly* 63, no. 3 (September 2011).

45. For more, see Daniel Martinez HoSang, *Racial Propositions: Ballot Initiatives and the Making of Postwar California* (Berkeley: University of California Press, 2010).

46. Martha Escobar, *Captivity Beyond Prisons: Criminalization Experiences of Latina (Im)migrants* (Austin: University of Texas Press, 2016), 51.

47. Ramos-Zayas, *Street Therapists*, 19.

48. Both the 1965 and 1992 uprisings produced countless studies about the structural inequities in the community. For more on the 1992 uprising, see Jervey Tarvalon and Cristian A. Sierra, eds., *Geography of Rage: Remembering the Los Angeles Riots of 1992* (Maryland: Really Great Books, 2002); Darnell Hunt, *Screening the Los Angeles "Riots": Race, Seeing, and Resistance* (Cambridge, UK: Cambridge University Press, 1996); Robert Goodwin-Williams, ed., *Reading Rodney King/Reading Urban Uprising* (New York: Routledge, 1993); Edward Chang and Jeannette Diaz-Veizades, *Ethnic Peace and the American City: Building Community in Los Angeles and Beyond* (New York: New York University Press, 1999); Min Song Hyoung, *Strange Future: Pessimism and the 1992 Los Angeles Riots* (Durham, NC: Duke University Press, 2005); Mark Baldassare, ed., *The Los Angeles Riots: Lessons for the Urban Future* (Oxford, UK: Westview Press, 1994).

49. The migration of Central Americans is complex and multidimensional. The immigration experiences and status of Salvadoran, Guatemalan, Honduran, and Nicaraguan people were vastly different from those of Mexican immigrants or Cuban refugees, in that President Ronald Reagan considered them economic migrants rather than refugees. The massive deportation campaign against Central Americans led to one of the most significant sanctuary movements across the nation. It was not until the early 1990s, with the passage of temporary protective status, that their experience in the United States would change. For more on Central American migration to Los Angeles, see Nora Hamilton and Norma Stoltz Chinchilla, *Seeking Community in a Global City: Guatemalans & Salvadorans in Los Angeles* (Philadelphia: Temple University Press, 2001); Cecilia Menjivar, *Fragmented Ties: Salvadoran Immigrant Networks in American* (Berkeley: University of California Press, 2000); Maria Cristina Garcia, *Seeking Refuge: Central American Migration to Mexico, the United States, and*

Canada (Berkeley: University of California Press, 2006); Steven Osuna, "Intra-Latina/o Encounters: Salvadoran and Mexican Struggles and Salvadoran-Mexican Subjectivities in Los Angeles," *Ethnicities: Latino Formation in the U.S.: Laboring Classes, Migration & Identities* 15, no. 2 (2015): 234–254; Leisy J. Abrego, *Sacrificing Families: Navigating Laws, Labor, and Love Across Borders* (Stanford, CA: Stanford University Press, 2014).

50. For a detailed exploration of the transnational, neoliberal, and racialization of Latina/o immigrants and its impact on Salvadoran-Mexican immigrant identity, see Osuna, "Intra-Latina/Latino Encounters."

51. Pierrette Hondagneu-Sotelo and Angelica Salas, "What Explains the Immigrant Rights Marches of 2006?" in Ramon A. Gutierrez and Tomas Almaguer, eds., *The New Latino Studies Reader: A Twenty-First-Century Perspective* (Berkeley: University of California Press, 2015).

52. Alfred Smith, oral history conducted by the author, Los Angeles, October 19, 2009.

53. The level of foreclosed homes in South Central also attracted investors hoping to make a profit from flipping homes. Alejandro Lazo, "Flipping Houses Is Back in South Los Angeles," *Los Angeles Times*, April 24, 2010. For a poignant and meticulous discussion of the foreclosure crisis nationally, see Matthew Desmond, *Evicted: Poverty and Profit in the American City* (New York: Broadway Books, 2017).

54. Failure by Congress to offer comprehensive immigrant reform led President Obama to pass the executive order Deferred Action for Childhood Arrivals (DACA) in 2012. It was a measure that would not have an impact on the bulk of undocumented people in the United States but would allow individuals who arrived in the U.S. as children the ability to have a two-year renewable work permit and deferred action against deportation. Roberto G. Gonzales, *Lives in Limbo: Undocumented and Coming of Age in America* (Berkeley: University of California Press, 2014), 25.

55. Keeanga-Yamahtta Taylor, *From #Blacklives Matter to Black Liberation* (Chicago: Haymarket, 2016).

56. Steve Lopez, "Finding L.A. Real Estate Gold Rush in Compton, Watts, and South Los Angeles," *Los Angeles Times*, December 9, 2017.

57. Merdies Hayes, "'People's Plan' Rejects Gentrification of South Los Angeles Neighborhoods," *Our Weekly: Los Angeles*, November 21, 2017.

58. Lopez, "Finding L.A. Real Estate Gold Rush."

CHAPTER I

Passages from Chapters 1 and 7 appeared in a different form in "Banking on the Community: Politics, Identity, and Interracial Interaction in a Historically African American Bank in South Central Los Angeles, 1947–2007," in Laura Pulido and Josh Kun, eds. *Black and Brown in Los Angeles: Beyond Conflict and Coalition* (Berkeley: University of California Press, 2014), 67–89. Reproduced with permission by the University of California Press.

1. M. Earl Grant, November 12, 1966, Oral History Collection, African American Oral Histories, Pollack Library, California State University, Fullerton.

2. Ibid.

3. Ibid.

4. Ibid.

5. Josh Sides, *L.A. City Limits: African American Los Angeles from the Great Depression to the Present* (Berkeley: University of California Press, 2003), 172.

6. Sides, *L.A. City Limits*.

7. Douglas Flamming, *Bound for Freedom: Black Los Angeles in Jim Crow America* (Berkeley: University of California Press, 2005), 14.

8. Ibid, 45.

9. Ibid., 8.

10. Scott Kurashige, *The Shifting Grounds of Race: Black and Japanese Americans in the Making of Multiethnic Los Angeles* (Princeton, NJ: Princeton University Press, 2008), 67.

11. Sides, *L.A. City Limits*, 11.

12. Sides, *L.A. City Limits*, 15. Augustus F. Hawkins was elected to the California State Assembly in 1935. In 1963, he would become the first African American congressional representative elected west of the Mississippi and provided a national public representation of the city he represented, South Central, as largely African American. He retired in 1991, and in his place, Maxine Waters was elected to the U.S. Congress and continues to be the public political face of South Central. Both Hawkins and Waters have been attentive to the community's demographic change. They view Latina/os as a constituency to speak to in South Central; however, the convergence of race and political representation continues to give the outward vision of South Central as a Black community.

13. Sides, *L.A. City Limits*, 15.

14. Flamming, *Bound for Freedom*, 73.

15. Ibid., 72–73.

16. Ibid., 71.

17. Tom Larson, "An Economic View of South Central Los Angeles," *Cities* 15, no. 3 (June 1998): 199.

18. For a national conversation on the ways in which race-restricted covenants affected residential community formation, see George Lipsitz, *How Racism Takes Place* (Philadelphia: Temple University Press, 2011).

19. Josh Sides, ed., *Post Ghetto: Reimagining South Los Angeles* (Berkeley: University of California Press, 2012), 13.

20. Kurashige, *Shifting Grounds of Race*, 72.

21. For information in addition on the impact of the Great Depression on the Chicano community, the impact of the Japanese internment on residential neighborhoods in Los Angeles, and the impact of real estate restrictive covenants on Chicano, Japanese, and African American residential opportunities, see George J. Sanchez, *Becoming Mexican American: Ethnicity, Culture, and Identity in Chicano Los Angeles, 1900–1940* (Oxford, UK: Oxford University Press, 1993); Kurashige, *Shifting Grounds of Race*; Flamming, *Bound for Freedom*.

22. Sides, *Post Ghetto*, 3.

23. Ibid; Kurashige, *Shifting Grounds of Race*, 72; Lipsitz, *How Racism Takes Place*.

24. Clora Bryant, Buddy Collette, William Green, Steve Isoardi, and Marl Young, eds., *Central Avenue Sounds: Jazz in Los Angeles* (Berkeley: University of California Press, 1999), 4.

25. Flamming, *Bound for Freedom*, 104.

26. Ibid.

27. Bryant and others, eds., *Central Avenue Sounds*, 4.

28. Flamming, *Bound for Freedom*.

29. Anthony Macias, *Mexican American Mojo: Popular Music, Dance, and Urban Culture in Los Angeles, 1935–1968* (Durham, NC: Duke University Press, 2008).

30. Flamming, *Bound for Freedom*, 377. This increased policing meant that what was once a vibrant interracial community was by 1960 about 95 percent black.

31. Lipsitz, *How Racism Takes Place*.

32. Kurashige, *Shifting Grounds of Race*, 71–72.

33. H. Claude Hudson, November 29, 1966, Oral History Collection, African American Oral Histories, Pollack Library, California State University, Fullerton; Douglas Flamming, *Bound for Freedom*, 117; 258.

34. Sides, *L.A. City Limits*, 38.

35. Ibid.

36. Ibid., 190.

37. Hudson, oral history.

38. "Hearing of Application: Permission to Organize a Federal Savings and Loan Association," n.d., Records of the Federal Home Loan Bank System, Record Group 195, National Archives and Records Administration, College Park, Maryland.

39. Hudson, oral history.

40. "Loan Bank Praised as Opening Set Saturday," *Los Angeles Sentinel*, January 9, 1947.

41. Ibid.

42. Hudson, oral history.

43. Hudson, oral history; Flamming, *Bound for Freedom*, 291.

44. Flamming, *Bound for Freedom*, 271.

45. Ibid., 270–281. The "beach wars" consisted of a group of five or six African American men and women who wanted to challenge beach segregation in Los Angeles. They went to Manhattan Beach, a racially segregated beach, and were arrested and put in jail because they violated the law. The case was eventually thrown out, and African Americans were allowed to go to the beach in Los Angeles.

46. Flamming, *Bound for Freedom*, 212–214, 270.

47. Ibid., 351.

48. Hudson, oral history.

49. "Broadway Federal 'Like a Big Happy Family,'" *Los Angeles Sentinel*, April 23, 1959, B13.

50. "Helps Families Obtain Homes at Broadway," *Los Angeles Sentinel*, September 19, 1957, A7.

51. "Accountant Lauds Bdwy. Fed Staff," *Los Angeles Sentinel*, January 22, 1959, A8.

52. "She's Proud of Association with Broadway Federal," *Los Angeles Sentinel*, August 29, 1957, B5.

53. Hudson, oral history.

54. For a detailed discussion of the growth of African American employees in the banking industry throughout the United States, see R. D. Corwin, *Racial Minorities in Banking: New Workers in the Banking Industry* (New Haven: New College & University Press, 1971).

55. Paul Hudson, oral history conducted by the author, Los Angeles, October 16, 2007.

56. Lila Ammons, "The Evolution of Black-Owned Banks in the United States Between the 1880s and 1990s," *Journal of Black Studies* 26, no. 4 (March 1996): 467–489, 473–475.

57. "Minority Banks" and "Letter to Corporate Institutions, April 1970," Box 91, Collection 1642, Augustus F. Hawkins Papers, 1935–1990, Department of Special Collections, Young Research Library, University of California, Los Angeles. In this folder are multiple copies of letters sent out by Hawkins to local corporations requesting them to invest in minority banks in the region. Corporations often replied by informing Hawkins of the dollar amount they invested in the bank through shares. The average investment was for $50,000. Edward Roybal, the representative for the Mexican American community in East Los Angeles, similarly put out a call for local community members and corporations to invest in minority banks. Roybal urged for investment in Eastland Savings and Loan Association, which Roybal served as president for the initial four years of the bank's history. See Box 11, Collection 847, Edward Roybal Papers, 1947–1962, Department of Special Collections, Young Research Library, University of California, Los Angeles.

58. "Correspondence from Litton Industries, September 8, 1971" and "Correspondence from Avery Products Corporation, August 9, 1971" Box 91, Augustus F. Hawkins Papers, 1935–1990, Department of Special Collections, Young Research Library, University of California, Los Angeles.

59. "Minority Banks," Augustus F. Hawkins Papers.

60. Sides, *L.A. City Limits*, 201.

61. Bauman, *Race and War on Poverty*, 34–36.

62. Sides, *L.A. City Limits*, 201.

63. Ibid., 180.

64. Bauman, *Race and War on Poverty*, 31; Paul Bullock, ed., *Watts: The Aftermath: An Inside View of the Ghetto* (New York: Grove, 1969), 30–36.

65. Ibid.

66. Charisse Jones, "Old Memories Confront New Realities in South L.A. Neighborhood," *Los Angeles Times*, February 17, 1992, A1.

67. Ibid.

68. Sides, *L.A. City Limits*, 201.

69. Jones, "Old Memories Confront New Realities."

70. Ibid.

71. For more, see Alice O'Conner, *Poverty Knowledge: Social Science, Social Policy, and the Poor in the Twentieth Century* (Princeton, NJ: Princeton University Press, 2002).

72. Bauman, *Race and the War on Poverty*; Robert Self, *American Babylon: Race and the Struggle for Postwar Oakland* (Princeton, NJ: Princeton University Press, 2005).

73. Bauman, *Race and the War on Poverty*, 17.

74. Ibid., 20.

75. Ibid., 21–22.

76. Quotes in this paragraph are from "Poverty United Needed," *Los Angeles Sentinel*, June 10, 1965, A6.

77. Ibid.

78. Bauman, *Race and the War on Poverty*, 22–23.

79. Ibid., 35.

80. Jack Jones, "L.A. Gets More Poverty Funds Than Any Other City—Shriver," *Los Angeles Times*, June 15, 1966, A3.

81. Bauman, *Race and War on Poverty*, 37.

82. "Report of the President's Task Force on the Los Angeles Riots, August 11–15, 1965," September 17, 1965, papers of Ramsey Clark, Box 129; Folder President's Task Force Report, Lyndon B. Johnson Presidential Library, Austin, Texas.

83. Ibid.

84. Ibid.

85. Ibid.

86. Ibid.

87. Ibid.

88. Ibid.

89. Sides, *L.A. City Limits*, 136.

90. Robert Bauman, "The Black Power and Chicano Movements in the Poverty Wars in Los Angeles," *Journal of Urban History* 33, no. 277 (2007): 282.

91. Rudy Acuña, *A Chronicle of Chicanos East of the Los Angeles River, 1945–1975* (Los Angeles: Chicano Studies Resource Center, 1984), 124, 132.

92. Carlos Munoz, *Youth, Identity Power: The Chicano Movement* (New York: Verso, 2007), 83.

93. Bauman, "Black Power and Chicano Movements," 295.

94. "Neglect of Mexican American Group in Poverty War Charged," *Los Angeles Times*, August 1, 1966, A3. See also "Economic Hardships Faced by ELA Neighborhoods," *Eastside Sun*, August 26, 1965; "Equal Opportunities Demanded by Rep. Roybal in House," *Eastside Sun*, September 23, 1965.

95. Bauman, "Black Power and Chicano Movements," 292.

96. Ibid., 293.

97. Opal Jones, "How to Work with People of All Ethnic Groups," n.d., NAPP Papers, Special Collections, University of Southern California, Los Angeles.

98. Ibid.

99. Ibid.

100. Gordon Mantler, *Power to the Poor: Black-Brown Coalition and the Fight for Economic Justice, 1960–1974* (Chapel Hill: University of North Carolina Press, 2013), e-book.

CHAPTER 2

1. *Pancho*, documentary film written, directed, and photographed by Robert K. Sharpe, 1967.

2. Ibid.

3. Ibid.

4. Ibid.

5. Ibid.

6. In the film, only one African American child, Rachel, is shown. Rachel does not say anything, but we see her sitting in the doctor's office ready to go through her physical examination. It is unsurprising that the documentary featured few to no African American children, given the choice of a location such as Nipomo; Black people were a small part of the population there.

7. Jack Jones, "Head Start Off to a Good Start," *Los Angeles Times*, July 23, 1965, A1.

8. Ibid.

9. William Estes, "Head Start Provides Step Up in Learning," *Los Angeles Times*, July 8, 1965, SF1.

10. "The Office of Economic Opportunity During the Administration of Lyndon Baines Johnson, Administration History, November 1966–January 1969" Box 107, Entry 14, Record Group 381, Community Action Program, National Archives and Records Administration, College Park, Maryland.

11. Maris Vinovskis, *The Birth of Head Start: Preschool Education Policies in the Kennedy and Johnson Administrations* (Chicago: University of Chicago Press, 2005).

12. Vinovskis fails to provide a broader picture of why Republicans supported early childhood education, but one could surmise that part of their support was the belief that the OEO's commitment to education had two advantages within the Great Society context: "it did not threaten middle-class assumptions about success, and it presumed the existence of almost unlimited opportunity for those willing and able to seize it." Vinovskis, *Birth of Head Start*, 67.

13. Vinovskis, *Birth of Head Start*, 9.

14. Vinovskis, *Birth of Head Start*.

15. Ibid., 145.

16. Edward Zigler and Sally J. Styfco, *The Hidden History of Head Start* (Oxford, UK: Oxford University Press, 2010).

17. Vinovskis, *Birth of Head Start*, 76.

18. Ibid., 10.

19. Ibid., 46.

20. "Head Start Report, Spring/Summer 1966," Box 1, Los Angeles Area Federation of Settlement and Neighborhood Centers, Special Collections, University of Southern California, Los Angeles.

21. "The Office of Economic Opportunity."

22. Kazuyo Tsuchiya, *Reinventing Citizenship: Black Los Angeles, Korean Kawasaki, and Community Participation* (Minneapolis: University of Minnesota Press, 2014), 18.

23. Natalie M. Fousekis, *Demanding Child Care: Women's Activism and the Politics of Welfare, 1940–1971* (Champaign: University of Illinois Press, 2013), PDF e-book.

24. In 1969, under President Richard Nixon, Head Start was transferred to the Department of Health, Education, and Welfare and became part of HEW's Office of Children Development.

25. Vinovskis, *Birth of Head Start*, 151.

26. Fousekis, *Demanding Child Care*.

27. Ibid.

28. Ibid.

29. Ibid.

30. Ibid.

31. Laura Briggs, *How All Politics Became Reproductive Politics: From Welfare Reform to Foreclosure to Trump* (Berkeley: University of California Press, 2018), 48.

32. Jack Jones, "On a Year-Round Basis: 6,780 Children Begin Head Start Classes," *Los Angeles Times*, September 22, 1966, A8.

33. Ibid.

34. Ibid.

35. Wesley Brazier, "Your Urban League," *Los Angeles Sentinel*, September 16, 1965, A6.

36. "Memo: When Did Head Start Become Part of HEW?, August 1, 1968," Box 2, Entry 70, Record Group 381, Community Action Program, National Archives and Records Administration, College Park, Maryland.

37. Ibid.; Vinovskis, *Birth of Head Start*, 67.

38. "Head Start Report."

39. Jones, "Head Start Off to a Good Start."

40. "Head Start Spring/Summer 1966 Proposal," Box 1, Los Angeles Area Federation of Settlement and Neighborhood Centers, Special Collections, University of Southern California, Los Angeles.

41. "Press Release: Governor Brown, January 28, 1966," Box 187, Alexander Pope Papers, Special Collections, The Huntington Research Library, San Marino, California; "Largest Head Start Program Announced by Governor Brown," *Los Angeles Sentinel*, February 3, 1966, A2.

42. Wesley Brazier, "Your Urban League," *Los Angeles Sentinel*, September 16, 1965, A6.

43. "Head Start Program Seeks Adult Volunteer Assistants," *Los Angeles Sentinel*, July 7, 1966, A8.

44. "Head Start Delegate Agencies, July 20, 1966," Box 1, Los Angeles Area Federation of Settlement and Neighborhood Centers, Special Collections, University of Southern California, Los Angeles; Jack Jones, "Precedent Feared: Portable Classrooms Pleas Stall Head Start," *Los Angeles Times*, September 14, 1966, A1; Jack Jones "New Exemption Pushed for Head Start Sites," *Los Angeles Times*, September 15, 1966, A12.

45. Jones, "Precedent Feared," A1.

46. Phillipa Johnson, oral history conducted by the author, Los Angeles, November 14, 2009.

47. "Head Start," n.d., Record Group F3751:86, State Office of Economic Opportunity Records, California State Archives, Sacramento; "Photo Standalone 3," *Los Angeles Sentinel*, September 22, 1966, A4.

48. "Head Start," Record Group F3751:86.

49. Jack Jones, "Let's Get Them Off to a Headstart!" *Los Angeles Times*, June 24, 1965; "What Is Head Start?" *Los Angeles Times*, January 18, 1968.

50. "Head Start Report," n.d., Box 2, Los Angeles Area Federation of Settlement and Neighborhood Centers, Special Collections, University of Southern California, Los Angeles.

51. "Letter," n.d., Box 94, Collection 1642, Augustus F. Hawkins Papers, 1935–1990, Department of Special Collections, Young Research Library, University of California, Los Angeles; Jones, "Head Start Off to a Good Start."

52. "Parents' Improvement Council Letter to Hawkins, September 25, 1965" and "Head Start Reports" n.d., Box 94, Collection 1642, August F. Hawkins Papers, 1935–1990, Department of Special Collections, Young Research Library, University of California, Los Angeles.

53. "McCone Commission Population Reports, 1966," Box 184, Alexander Pope Papers, Special Collections, The Huntington Research Library, San Marino, California.

54. Sides, *L.A. City Limits*, 117.

55. Ibid., 118.

56. Ibid., 118.

57. Ibid., 120.

58. Ibid., 117.

59. "Parents' Improvement Council Memo," n.d., Box 94, Collection 1642, Augustus F. Hawkins Papers.

60. Jim Cleaver, "Poverty Program Defended," *Los Angeles Sentinel*, June 12, 1969, A1.

61. Ibid.

62. Ralph Dunlap, Astrid Beigel, and Virginia Armon, "Young Children and Watts Revolt: Reactions of Negro, Mexican American and White Pre-School Children to the August 1965 Los Angeles Race Riots, 1966," Southern California Permanente Medical Group, Box 187, Alexander Pope Papers, Special Collections, The Huntington Research Library, San Marino, California.

63. Ibid.

64. Ibid.

65. Ibid.

66. Ibid.

67. Ibid.

68. Ibid.

69. "Here and There: Successful Story," n.d., Box 29, Office Files of Ceil Bellinger, Office Files of the White House Aides, Lyndon Baines Johnson Library and Museum, Austin, Texas.

CHAPTER 3

1. Jennifer Bihm, "King/Drew Medical Center and the 1965 Watts Revolt," *Los Angeles Sentinel*, August 11, 2005; "California: The Deadwyler Verdict," *Time*, June 10, 1966.

2. M. Frankel, "In the Watts Health Center, the Customer Is Always Right," *NTRDA Bulletin* 55, no. 2 (1969): 14.

3. Darnell Hunt and Ana-Christina Ramon, "Killing 'Killer King': The Los Angeles Times and a 'Troubled' Hospital in the 'Hood,'" in Ana-Christina Ramon and Darnell Hunt, eds., *Black Los Angeles: American Dreams and Racial Realities* (New York: New York University Press, 2010), 286.

4. "Report of the President's Task Force on the Los Angeles Riots, August 11–15, 1965," Box 129, Personal Papers, Papers of Ramsey Clark, Lyndon Baines Johnson Library and Museum, Austin, Texas.

5. Ibid.

6. "Violence in the City: An End or a Beginning?, December 1968," Box 94, Collection 1642, Augustus F. Hawkins Papers, 1935–1990, Department of Special Collections, Young Research Library, University of California, Los Angeles.

7. Jack Jones, "Political Fighting Slows Up Health Programs: Politics Impedes Health Programs in Watts Area," *Los Angeles Times*, July 19, 1967, A1.

8. Charles Baireuther, "A Doctor's Opinion: MLK Hospital will Fail Without Community Stress," *Los Angeles Times*, April 23, 1970.

9. Ibid.

10. "Letter by Mrs. Charles Zanders," n.d., Box 73, Collection 1642, Augustus F. Hawkins Papers, 1935–1990, Department of Special Collections, Young Research Library, University of California, Los Angeles.

11. "County Hospital Construction in Watts: Group's Objective," *Los Angeles Sentinel*, March 3, 1966. The other quotes in this paragraph are also from this article.

12. Alondra Nelson, *Body and Soul: The Black Panther Party and the Fight Against Medical Discrimination* (Minneapolis: University of Minnesota Press, 2011), 13.

13. Alondra Nelson, "Black Power, Biomedicine, and the Politics of Knowledge" (PhD diss., New York University, 2003), *Dissertations & Theses: Full Text*, ProQuest, 3.

14. Nelson, *Body and Soul*, 4–5.

15. Bonnie Lefkowitz, *Community Health Centers: A Movement and the People Who Made It Happen* (New Brunswick, NJ: Rutgers University Press, 2007), 6.

16. "Legislative History of the Partnership for Health, July 1968," Box 5, Papers of Lyndon Baines Johnson, President, 1963–1969, Administrative History, Lyndon Baines Johnson Library and Museum, Austin, Texas.

17. Lefkowitz, *Community Health Centers*, 25.

18. Valery Riddle, "Reducing Social Inequalities in Health: Public Health, Community Health, or Health Promotion," *Promotion and Education* 14, no. 2 (2007): 63–70.

19. "Intensified Health Services Program," Los Angeles County Health Department, April 1965, NAPP Papers.

20. "OEO Health Task Force," 1965, Box 2, Entry 70, Record Group 381, Community Action Program, National Archives and Records Administration, College Park, Maryland.

21. Ibid.

22. Frank F. Aguilera, "Letter to Saleem A. Farag, Assistant Deputy Director, March 10, 1975," Entry 70, Record Group 381, Community Action Program, National Archives and Records Administration, College Park, Maryland.

23. "OEO Health Task Force."

24. Aguilera, "Letter."

25. "The Office of Economic Opportunity During the Administration of Lyndon Baines Johnson, Administration History, November 1966–January 1969," Box 107, Entry 14, Record Group 381, Community Action Program, National Archives and Records Administration, College Park, Maryland.

26. "Speech by Sargent Shriver at the Dedication Ceremonies, South Central Multi-Purpose Health Services Center, Sept. 16, 1967," Box 64, Collection 293, Mayor Tom Bradley Administrative Papers, 1973–1993, Department of Special Collections, Young Research Library, University of California, Los Angeles.

27. Harry Nelson, "New Watts Clinic Fights to Survive Many Problems," *Los Angeles Times*, July 8, 1968, A1.

28. E. Richard Brown, et al., "Inequalities in Health: The Sickness in the Center of Our Cities," in *South Central Los Angeles: Anatomy of a Crisis*, Lewis Center for Regional Policy Studies, Working Paper No. 6 (June 1993): 79–81.

29. Ibid.

30. "Watts Health Foundation Fact Sheet—July 23, 1987," Box 3653, Folder 7, Collection 293, Mayor Tom Bradley Administrative Papers, 1973–1993, Department of Special Collections, Young Research Library, University of California, Los Angeles.

31. Ibid.

32. "Office Memorandum," n.d., Box 3653, Folder 8, Collection 293, Mayor Tom

Bradley Administrative Papers, 1973–1993, Department of Special Collections, Young Research Library, University of California, Los Angeles.

33. John Kendall, "Health Center in Watts Visited by Senator Percy," *Los Angeles Times*, July 7, 1969.

34. Ibid.

35. "Proposal to Study the Cultural Barriers to Utilization of Emergency Medical Services—May 23, 1974," Record Group 381, Community Action Program, National Archives and Records Administration, College Park, Maryland.

36. Ibid.

37. Ibid.

38. Dionne Espinoza, "'Revolutionary Sisters': Solidarity and Collective Identification Among Chicana Brown Berets in East Los Angeles, 1967–1970," *Aztlan* 26, no. 1 (Spring 2001).

39. Nelson, *Body and Soul*; "Black Panther Party Plans Health Clinics," *Los Angeles Times*, November 25, 1969, A24.

40. "Hawkins Writes Open Letter to Economic Youth Opportunities Board, March 14, 1966," Manuel Ruiz Papers, Special Collections, Stanford University, Palo Alto, California.

41. "East LA Health Task Force," Record Group F3751, State Office of Economic Opportunity Records, California State Archives, Sacramento; "Chicano Health—A Statistical Nightmare," *NCHO Newsletter: Salud y Revolucion Social* 3, no. 5 (January 1974).

42. "Students Health Project Fights Medical Tradition and Poverty," *Los Angeles Times*, July 22, 1968, B1.

43. Gladys Garcia, "Our Story," accessed January 29, 2018, www.scfhc.org/history.

44. Kathleen Hendrix, "Health Center Practices Justice by Practicing Medicine," *Los Angeles Times*, April 16, 1985, G1.

45. Ibid.

46. Dolores Rosas, oral history conducted by the author, Los Angeles, September 23, 2009.

47. Jenna M. Loyd, *Health Rights Are Civil Rights: Peace and Justice Activism in Los Angeles, 1963–1978* (Minneapolis: University of Minnesota Press, 2014), pdf e-book.

48. Ibid.

49. "Intensified Health Services Program, April 1965," Los Angeles County Health Department, NAPP Papers.

50. Ibid.

51. "The Office of Economic Opportunity During the Administration of Lyndon Baines Johnson, Administration History, November 1966-January 1969."

52. "OEP Guidelines for Family Planning Grants, 1967," Papers of Lyndon Baines Johnson, President, 1963–1969, Administrative History, Lyndon Baines Johnson Library and Museum, Austin, Texas.

53. Harry Nelson, "Drive to Launch Among Poor to Test for Cervical Cancer," *Los Angeles Times*, May 30, 1968, B1.

54. Hendrix, "Health Center Practices Justice."

55. Malaika Brown, "Sweat and Pride Help Keep ML King Hospital Alive," *Los Angeles Times*, January 13, 1994.

56. Elaine Woo, "Caffie Greene Dies at 91; Activist Was a Leader in Creation of King/Drew Hospital," *Los Angeles Times*, June 7, 2010.

57. Carol Williams, "Mary B. Henry Dies at 82; Civil Rights Activist Improved Education, Healthcare in L.A.," *Los Angeles Times*, August 16, 2009.

58. Yussuf J. Simmonds, "A True Community Treasure Passes On," *Los Angeles Sentinel*, July 21, 2011.

59. Libby Clark, "A 'Taste' of History: Living Legends: L.A. Sentinel's 'Mother of the Year'", *Los Angeles Sentinel*, January 26, 2012; "Lillian Mobley 'Community Mother' Embraces Young and Old," *Los Angeles Sentinel*, May 12, 1999, C10.

60. Hunt and Ramon, "Killing 'Killer King,'" 289.

61. Lefkowitz, *Community Health Centers*, 18.

62. "Hearing on Los Angeles County Budget Cuts in Health Programs and Services," Assembly Committee on Health, Sacramento, California, 1981, 1.

63. Ibid., 53.

64. Ibid.

65. Ibid., 28.

66. Ibid., 33.

67. Ibid., 27.

68. The clinic on San Pedro Street was broken into in the midst of the 1992 uprising. In the spring of 1993, the clinic changed locations, and Dr. Turner and Bax decided to move back to Portland, Oregon, and leave SCFHC, as the clinic had become self-sustainable.

69. Teresa Garcia, oral history conducted by the author, Los Angeles, November 12, 2007.

70. Loyd, *Health Rights Are Civil Rights*.

CHAPTER 4

Passages from this chapter appeared in a different form in "Raising a Neighborhood: Informal Networks Between Black and Mexican American Women in South Central Los Angeles." Reproduced from *Struggle in Black and Brown: African American and Mexican American Relations During the Civil Rights Era*, ed. Brian D. Behnken, by permission of the University of Nebraska Press. Copyright 2011 by the Board of Regents of the University of Nebraska.

1. Leticia Nuno, oral history conducted by the author, Los Angeles, August 6, 2009.

2. Ibid.

3. Ibid.

4. Ibid.

5. William Overend, "South Central L.A.: Minority Meets Minority," *Los Angeles Times*, August 19, 1979, A1.

6. Ana Elizabeth Rosas, *Abrazando el Espíritu Bracero: Families Confront the US-Mexico Border* (Berkeley: University of California Press, 2014), 90; 207.

7. Jimmy Patino, *Raza Si, Migra No: Chicano Movement Struggles for Immigrant Rights in San Diego* (Chapel Hill: University of North Carolina Press, 2017), 50–51.

8. Ibid., 50.

9. Overend, "South Central L.A."

10. Maria Concepcion Ruiz, oral history conducted by the author, Los Angeles, October

20, 2009; Josh Sides, *L.A. City Limits: African American Los Angeles from the Great Depression to the Present* (Berkeley: University of California Press, 2003), 113.

11. Magdaleno Ruiz, oral history conducted by the author, Los Angeles, July 15, 2008.

12. Ibid.

13. Maria Ruiz, oral history.

14. Maria Ruiz, oral history; Magdaleno Ruiz, oral history; Francisco Rosas, oral history conducted by the author, Los Angeles, September 4, 2009; Nuno, oral history.

15. "McCone Revisited: A Focus on Solutions to Continuing Problems in South Central Los Angeles, January 18, 1985," Box 952, Collection 293, Mayor Tom Bradley Administrative Papers, 1973–1993, Department of Special Collections, Young Research Library, University of California, Los Angeles.

16. Ibid.

17. Ibid.

18. Ibid.

19. Ibid.

20. Ibid.

21. "Beyond the Racial Divide: Perceptions of Minority Residents on Coalition Building in South Los Angeles," *Tomas Rivera Policy Brief* (June 2007), 2.

22. Ibid.

23. "Elementary Schools," n.d., Box 2066, Collection 293, Mayor Tom Bradley Administrative Papers, 1973–1993, Department of Special Collections, Young Research Library, University of California, Los Angeles.

24. "Letter from Lupe Montano, January 1970," Box 92, Augustus F. Hawkins Papers, 1935–1990, Department of Special Collections, Young Research Library, University of California, Los Angeles.

25. "Letter from Augustus Hawkins, February 24, 1970," Augustus F. Hawkins Papers, 1935–1990, Department of Special Collections, Young Research Library, University of California, Los Angeles.

26. Overend, "Minority Meets Minority."

27. Ibid.

28. Ruth Smith (a pseudonym), oral history conducted by the author, Los Angeles, November 21, 2008.

29. Overend, "Minority Meets Minority."

30. Ibid.

31. Ibid.

32. Ibid.

33. Ibid.

34. Ibid.

35. Hector Tobar, "Latinos Transform South L.A.," *Los Angeles Times*, February 16, 1992, A1.

36. Elena Santiago (a pseudonym), oral history conducted by the author, Los Angeles, November 19, 2008.

37. Dolores Rosas, oral history conducted by the author, Los Angeles, September 23, 2009.

38. Ibid.

39. Tobar, "Latinos Transform South L.A."

40. Francisco Rosas, oral history.

41. Magdaleno Ruiz, oral history.

42. Overend, "Minority Meets Minority."

43. Dolores Rosas, oral history.

44. Maria Ruiz, oral history.

45. Juan Rodriguez, oral history conducted by the author, Los Angeles, September 14, 2007.

46. Alfred Smith, oral history conducted by the author, Los Angeles, October 19, 2009.

47. Sylvia Zamora, "Racial Remittances: The Effect of Migration on Racial Ideologies in Mexico and the United States," *Sociology of Race and Ethnicity* 2, no. 4 (2016): 466–481.

48. Ibid.

49. Ibid.

50. Tobar, "Latinos Transform South L.A."

51. Dora Escobedo, oral history conducted by the author, Los Angeles, March 2, 2009.

52. John Marquez, *Black-Brown Solidarity: Racial Politics in the New Gulf South* (Austin: University of Texas Press, 2014), 44. Also see Denise Ferreira de Silva, *Towards a Global Idea of Race* (Minneapolis: University of Minnesota Press, 2007).

53. Ibid., 32–33.

54. Ibid., 56–57.

55. Ibid., 52.

56. Hector Tobar, "Latinos Move to South-Central Los Angeles," *Los Angeles Times*, May 3, 1990, A1.

57. Ibid.

58. Ibid.

59. Esther Sanchez, oral history conducted by the author, Los Angeles, August 12, 2010.

60. Ibid.

61. Ibid.

62. Santiago, oral history.

63. Smith, oral history.

64. Rene P. Ciria Cruz, "To Live and Let Live," NACLA Report on the Americas (May/June 2007): 38.

65. Santiago, oral history.

66. Ibid.

67. Charisse Jones, "Old Memories Confront New Realities in South L.A. Neighborhood," *Los Angeles Times*, February 17, 1992, A1.

68. Ibid.

69. "Lost Soul: A Lament for Black Los Angeles," *Los Angeles Weekly*, December 2–10, 1998, South Central Los Angeles Documentation Collection, Southern California Library for Social Science and Research, Los Angeles, California.

70. Sides, *L.A. City Limits*, 204.

71. Larry Aubry, "Urban Perspective: Illegal Immigration and the African American; A Moral Dilemma," *Los Angeles Sentinel*, December 28, 1994, A7.

72. Ibid.

73. Ibid.

CHAPTER 5

1. "The Workshop Way of Learning," n.d., Record Group F3751:174, State Office of Economic Opportunity Records, California State Archives, Sacramento.

2. Ibid.

3. Kay Mills, *Something Better for My Children: How Head Start Has Changed the Lives of Millions of Children* (New York: Plume, 1999), 18.

4. Jack Jones, "Community Participation: Many Head Start Classes Producing Vital By-Product," *Los Angeles Times*, November 6, 1966, E1.

5. "Head Start Is for Parents Too: Education and Involvement Guide," *Los Angeles Sentinel*, January 29, 1970, C1.

6. "Head Start: Spring and Summer, 1968," Box 1, Los Angeles Area Federation of Settlement and Neighborhood Centers, Special Collections, University of Southern California, Los Angeles.

7. A. Frederick North Jr., "Health Services in Head Start," in Edward Zigler and Jeanette Valentine, eds., *Project Head Start: A Legacy of the War on Poverty* (New York: Free Press, 1979), 240.

8. "Head Start: Spring and Summer, 1968."

9. Robyn C. Spenser, *The Revolution Has Come: Black Power, Gender, and the Black Panther Party in Oakland* (Durham, NC: Duke University Press, 2016).

10. North Jr., "Health Services in Head Start," 229.

11. Jack Jones, "Head Start Off to Good Start," *Los Angeles Times*, July 23, 1965, A1.

12. Ibid.

13. Ibid.

14. "The Project Head Start Feeding Program" and "Meal Time Calendar," n.d., Record Group F3751:87, State Office of Economic Opportunity Records, California State Archives, Sacramento.

15. "The Project Head Start Feeding Program."

16. Parents were given food guides on a regular basis. As nutrition standards changed, parents received the most updated information possible. From the nutrition program's inception, Head Start created a film explaining its nutrition programs. The film was widely distributed, screened, and nominated for an Academy Award. See "Parent Education in Nutrition, June 8, 1966," Record Group F3751:87, State Office of Economic Opportunity Records, California State Archives, Sacramento; North Jr., "Health Services in Head Start," 246.

17. "Parent Education in Nutrition."

18. "Recipe Book Tells What's Cooking in Anti-Poverty," *Los Angeles Sentinel*, May 16, 1968.

19. George J. Sanchez, *Becoming Mexican American: Ethnicity, Culture, and Identity in Chicano Los Angeles, 1900–1945* (Oxford, UK: Oxford University Press, 1993), 103.

20. Jones, "Community Participation."

21. Phillipa Johnson, oral history conducted by the author, Los Angeles, November 14, 2009.

22. Ibid.

23. "Head Start Report," n.d., Box 2, Los Angeles Area Federation of Settlement and Neighborhood Centers, Special Collections, University of Southern California, Los Angeles.

24. "Determined LA Mother Learns to Achieve Goal," *Los Angeles Sentinel*, September 14, 1967, A8.

25. Ibid.

26. Maris Vinovskis, *The Birth of Head Start: Preschool Education Policies in the Kennedy and Johnson Administrations* (Chicago: University of Chicago Press, 2005), 151.

27. Ibid.

28. "Pacific Oaks Intensive Training Program," n.d., Record Group F3751:87, State Office of Economic Opportunity Records, California State Archives, Sacramento.

29. Ibid.

30. Mills, *Something Better for My Children*, 20.

31. Ibid., 77–78.

32. Ibid., 78.

33. Ibid., 10.

34. Ibid., 10.

35. Ibid., 25.

36. Elena Santiago (a pseudonym), oral history conducted by the author, Los Angeles, November 19, 2008.

37. Johnson, oral history; Maria Garcia, oral history conducted by the author, Los Angeles, January 2, 2010. See also "Future T.A.'s for Head Start in Training at Phillips Temple," *Los Angeles Sentinel*, February 24, 1966, A3; Jones, "Community Participation."

38. "Letter by Brathei Titicomb, July 19, 1968," and "Letter by Dorothy Turner, July 19, 1968," Box 94, Collection 1642, Augustus F. Hawkins Papers, 1935–1990, Department of Special Collections, Young Research Library, University of California, Los Angeles.

39. "Letter by Josefina Velarde, July 22, 1968," Box 94, Collection 1642, Augustus F. Hawkins Papers, 1935–1990, Department of Special Collections, Young Research Library, University of California, Los Angeles.

40. "Letter by Augustina Jurado, July 23, 1968," Box 94, Collection 1642, Augustus F. Hawkins Papers, 1935–1990, Department of Special Collections, Young Research Library, University of California, Los Angeles.

41. Nancy Naples, *Grassroots Warriors: Activist Mothering, Community Work, and the War on Poverty* (New York: Routledge, 1995), 15.

42. It is important to note that Patricia Hill Collins discusses African American family structures as defined by shared mothering practices ("bloodmothers," "othermothers," and "community mothers"). The communal strategy of raising children challenges the conceptualization of parenting and family as an independent and private endeavor. Patricia Hill Collins, *Black Feminist Thought: Knowledge, Consciousness, and the Politics of Empowerment* (New York: Routledge, 1999).

43. Naples, *Grassroots Warriors*, 191.

44. Leland Saito, *Race and Politics: Asian Americans, Latinos, and Whites in a Los Angeles Suburb* (Champaign: University of Illinois Press, 1998), 147–148.

45. Ibid.

46. Garcia, oral history.

47. Mills, *Something Better for My Children*, 18.

48. "Racial Harmony and Discourse Task Force, February 8, 1993," Box 1179, Collection 293, Mayor Tom Bradley Administrative Papers, 1973–1993, Department of Special Collections, Young Research Library, University of California, Los Angeles.

49. "Pacific Oaks Head Start Program."

50. Ibid.

51. Janet Currie and Duncan Thomas, "Does Head Start Help Hispanic Children?" *National Bureau of Economic Research Working Paper no. 5805*, October 1996, 5.

52. Mills, *Something Better for My Children*, 80.

53. Ibid., 86.

54. Ibid.

55. Ibid., 157; Jones, "Head Start Off to a Good Start."

56. Currie and Thomas, "Does Head Start Help Hispanic Children?" 5, 25.

57. Ibid.

58. Ibid., 4.

59. Johnson, oral history.

60. Currie and Thomas, "Does Head Start Help Hispanic Children?" 155.

61. Ibid.

62. Ibid.

63. Diane Hoffman, "Culture and Self in Multicultural Education: Reflection on Discourse, Text, Practice," *American Education Research Journal* 33, no. 3 (Autumn 1996): 545–569.

64. Ibid., 547.

65. Ibid.

66. Ibid., 555.

67. Johnson, oral history.

68. Stephanie Monte, "LA County Office of Education Forced Kedren Head Start Closure, says Waters," *Intersections South LA*, March 20, 2014, intersectionssouthla.org.

69. Stephanie Monte, "Children's Institute to Take Over Head Start Centers in South LA," *Intersections South LA*, March 20, 2014, intersectionssouthla.org.

70. Johnson, oral history.

71. Mills, *Something Better for My Children*, 226.

72. Garcia, oral history.

CHAPTER 6

1. "Cultural Diversity Celebration, October 19, 1988," Box 3686, Collection 293, Mayor Tom Bradley Administrative Papers, 1973–1993, Department of Special Collections, Young Research Library, University of California, Los Angeles.

2. Ibid.

3. Ibid.

4. "Memo: Issues Group, August 26, 1991," Box 3692, Collection 293, Mayor Tom Bradley Administrative Papers, 1973–1993, Department of Special Collections, Young Research Library, University of California, Los Angeles.

5. Ibid.

6. Raphael Sonenshein, *Politics in Black and White* (Princeton, NJ: Princeton University Press, 1994), 10.

7. Ibid., 50; Scott Kurashige, *The Shifting Grounds of Race: Black and Japanese Americans in the Making of Multiethnic Los Angeles* (Princeton, NJ: Princeton University Press, 2008), 279.

8. Ibid.; Robert Gottlieb, Regina Freer, Mark Vallianatos, Peter Dreir, eds., *The Next Los Angeles: The Struggle for a Livable City* (Berkeley: University of California Press, 2006).

9. "The Killing of South Central," *L.A. Weekly*, 1989, Box 25, South Central Los Angeles Documentation Collection, Southern California Library for Social Science and Research, Los Angeles, California.

10. Kurashige, *Shifting Grounds of Race*, 279.

11. Ibid.

12. "Los Angeles 2000 Human Relations Conference, 1985," n.d., Box 3692, Collection 293, Mayor Tom Bradley Administrative Papers, 1973–1993, Department of Special Collections, Young Research Library, University of California, Los Angeles.

13. Danny Widener, *Black Arts West: Culture and Struggle in Postwar Los Angeles* (Durham, NC: Duke University Press, 2010), 224.

14. Natalia Molina, *How Race Is Made in America: Immigration, Citizenship, and the Historical Power of Racial Scripts* (Berkeley: University of California Press, 2014); George J. Sanchez, "Face the Nation: Race, Immigration, and the Rise of Nativism in the Late Twentieth Century," *The International Migration Review* 31, no. 4 (Winter, 1997): 1009–1030.

15. Zaragosa Vargas, *Crucible of Struggle: History of Mexican Americans from the Colonial Era to the Present* (Oxford, UK: Oxford University Press, 2010); Dolores Ines Casillas, "Sounds of Surveillance: U.S. Spanish-Language Radio Patrols La Migra," *American Quarterly* 63, no. 3 (September 2011).

16. Sanchez, "Face the Nation," 1018.

17. "A Study of Federal Immigration Policies and Practices in Southern California by California Advisory Committee to the U.S. Commission on Civil Rights, June 1980," Record Group 453, Records of the United States Commission on Civil Rights, National Archives and Records Administration, College Park, Maryland.

18. Ibid.

19. Ibid.

20. Magdaleno Ruiz, oral history conducted by the author, Los Angeles, July 15, 2008.

21. Leticia Nuno, oral history conducted by the author, Los Angeles, August 6, 2009.

22. Maria Concepcion Ruiz, oral history conducted by the author, Los Angeles, October 20, 2009.

23. Ibid.

24. Ronald Mize and Alicia C. S. Swords, *Consuming Mexican Labor: From the Bracero Program to NAFTA* (Toronto: University of Toronto Press, 2011), 91.

25. Susan Gonzalez Baker, "The 'Amnesty' Aftermath: Current Policy Issues Stemming from the Legalization Programs of the 1986 Immigration Reform and Control Act," *International Migration Review* 31, no. 1 (Spring 1997): 15.

26. Ibid.

27. Ibid.

28. Ibid.

29. Magdaleno Ruiz, oral history; Nuno, oral history; Maria Ruiz, oral history; Francisco Rosas, oral history conducted by the author, Los Angeles, September 4, 2009.

30. David Bacon, *The Children of NAFTA: Labor Wars on the U.S./Mexico Border* (Berkeley: University of California Press, 2004).

31. Magdaleno Ruiz, oral history; Nuno, oral history; Maria Ruiz, oral history; Francisco Rosas, oral history.

32. Humberto Benitez, "Amnesty Law: A Process of False Hopes," *La Gente Newsmagazine*, May 1987; See also Javier Rodriguez, "Amnesty: Billion Dollar Business," *La Gente Newsmagazine*, March/April 1987.

33. Benitez, "Amnesty Law."

34. Francisco Rosas, oral history.

35. Elena R. Gutierrez, *Fertile Matters: The Politics of Mexican Origin Women's Reproduction* (Austin: University of Texas Press, 2008).

36. Mize and Swords, *Consuming Mexican Labor*, 92.

37. The restructuring of welfare assistance meant that families receiving cash assistance needed to enter the workforce after two years, and benefits were available for up to five years. The removal of welfare recipients from the "welfare rolls" was fueled by politicians and public officials crafting the image that poor people of color were abusing the system. Ronald Reagan described public assistance recipients as "welfare queens . . . driving Cadillacs" and committing fraud against the government to receive aid. These racist and gendered representations of welfare recipients have had a negative effect on the public perception of people on welfare. Many women would attest that the job "opportunities" afforded paid less than a livable wage and were entry level without much mobility. Thus, as a consequence, many women and families found themselves negatively affected by the implementation of PRWORA. They were left even more vulnerable than when they were on welfare assistance. These changes were an open assault on the life chances of undocumented Mexican immigrants as well as the working poor and low-income families throughout the United States. See Laura Briggs, *How All Politics Became Reproductive Politics: From Welfare Reform to Foreclosure to Trump* (Berkeley: University of California Press, 2018).

38. For a nuanced and astute analysis of the multilayered and dynamic efforts of interracial coalitions to pass or reject various ballot measures throughout the state, see Daniel Martinez HoSang, *Racial Propositions: Ballot Initiatives and the Making of Postwar California* (Berkeley: University of California Press, 2010).

39. "1978 Conference: Better Cities for a Better Nation," National Urban League Papers, Library of Congress, Washington, DC.

40. Ibid.

41. Sanchez, "Face the Nation," 1022.

42. Alfred Smith, oral history conducted by the author, Los Angeles, October 19, 2009.

43. João H. Costa Vargas, *Catching Hell in the City of Angeles: Life and Meanings of Blackness in South Central Los Angeles* (Minneapolis: University of Minnesota Press, 2006), 179–180.

44. E. Richard Brown et al. "Inequalities in Health: The Sickness in the Center of Our Cities," in *South-Central Los Angeles: Anatomy of an Urban Crisis*, Lewis Center for Regional Policy Studies (June 1993), 77.

45. Ruth Wilson Gilmore, *Golden Gulag: Prisons, Surplus, Crisis, and Opposition in Globalization California* (Berkeley: University of California Press, 2008).

46. Ibid., 7.

47. Ibid.

48. For more, see Jordan Camp, *Incarcerating the Crisis: Freedom Struggles and the Rise of the Neoliberal State* (Berkeley: University of California Press, 2016); Elizabeth Hinton, *From the War on Poverty to the War on Crime: The Making of Mass Incarceration in America* (Cambridge, MA: Harvard University Press, 2016).

49. Brown et al. "Inequalities in Health," 102.

50. Widener, *Black Arts West*, 220.

51. "Letter to Bradley, March 4, 1993," Box 303, Collection 293, Mayor Tom Bradley Administrative Papers, 1973–1993, Department of Special Collections, Young Research Library, University of California, Los Angeles.

52. For more information on the activism around the closure of liquor stores in the area, see Regina Freer, "From Conflict to Convergence: Interracial Relations in the Liquor Store Controversy in South Central Los Angeles" (PhD diss., University of Michigan, 1999).

53. "Letter and Petition to Bradley, September 17, 1992," Box 303, Collection 293, Mayor Tom Bradley Administrative Papers, 1973–1993, Department of Special Collections, Young Research Library, University of California, Los Angeles.

54. Ignacio Rodriguez Reyna, "Elecciones EU 96: Watts: Tierra de Muerte," *Reforma*, October 26, 1996, 18.

55. Ibid.

56. Ibid.

57. Hector Tobar, "Blacks, Latinos Coexist in a Peace Tempered by Fear South L.A.," *Los Angeles Times*, February 19, 1992, A1.

58. Cid Gregory Martinez, *The Neighborhood Has Its Own Rules: Latinos and African Americans in South Los Angeles* (New York: New York University Press, 2016).

59. Sanchez, "Face the Nation," 1018.

60. The interaction between African American residents and Korean merchants has been a source of tension for both groups and has preoccupied the scholarly literature on Black and Korean relations. These interactions cannot be ignored in the broader scope of the history of South Central, as there was tension among both groups during and in the aftermath of the 1992 Los Angeles uprising, as Korean and Asian merchants were some of the targets of the destruction in those tumultuous days. I do not explore African American-Korean relations in greater detail, but rather discuss it in terms of highlighting how in the 1980s interracial relations in South Central Los Angeles were multifaceted. For more on Black-Korean relations, see Kazuyo Tsuchiya, *Reinventing Citizenship: Black Los Angeles, Korean Kawasaki, and Community Participation* (Minneapolis: University of Minnesota Press, 2014); Brenda Stevenson, *The Contested Murder of Latasha Harlins: Justice, Gender, and the Origins of the LA Riots* (Oxford, UK: Oxford University Press, 2015); Nancy Abelmann and John Lie, eds., *Blue Dreams: Korean Americans and the Los Angeles Riots* (Cambridge, MA: Harvard University Press, 1997); Edward Chang and Jeannette Diaz-Veizades, *Ethnic Peace in the American City: Building Community in Los Angeles and Beyond* (New York: New York University Press, 1999); Pyong Gap Min, *Caught in the Middle: Korean Communities in New York and Los Angeles* (Berkeley: University of California Press, 1996).

61. Stevenson, *Contested Murder of Latasha Harlins*.

62. "Today's Conflict, Tomorrow's Challenges: A Report on Five State of the County Hearings by the Los Angeles County Commission of Human Relations, January 1984," Box 64, Augustus F. Hawkins Papers, 1935–1990, Department of Special Collections, Young Research Library, University of California, Los Angeles.

63. Ibid.

64. Ibid.

65. Ibid. For more on the hazards of liquor stores in the community, see Didra Brown Taylor, "Knowledge, Attitudes, and Malt Liquor: Beer Drinking Behavior Among African American Men in South Central Los Angeles" (PhD diss., California School of Professional Psychology, 2000); Freer, "From Conflict to Convergence."

66. Ibid.

67. Maria Newman, "After the Riots: Riots Put Focus on Hispanic Growth and Problems in South Central," *New York Times*, May 11, 1992, B6.

68. Manuel Pastor Jr. "Economic Inequality, Latino Poverty, and the Civil Unrest in Los Angeles," *Economic Development Quarterly* 9, no. 3 (August 1995): 238.

69. "In the Neighborhood Watts: Demographics and Culture, but Poverty Persists," *Los Angeles Times*, February 22, 1993, A4.

70. Sanchez, "Face the Nation," 1023.

71. Gloria Alvarez, "20 Years Ago: For Many Latinos, the L.A. Riots Were Not About Outrage," *Eastern Group Publications*, April 26, 2012.

72. Magdaleno Ruiz, oral history.

73. "In the Neighborhood Watts."

74. Ibid.

75. Ibid.

76. Alex Alonso, "Rebuilding Los Angeles: A Lesson of Community Reconstruction," University of Southern California: Southern California Studies Center, 1998.

77. "Rebuild Los Angeles Racial Harmony and Discourse Taskforce Meeting Minutes, January 4, 1993," Box 1179, Collection 293, Mayor Tom Bradley Administrative Papers, 1973–1993, Department of Special Collections, Young Research Library, University of California, Los Angeles.

78. Ibid.

79. Jane Twomey, "Searching for a Legacy: The Los Angeles Times, Collective Memory, and the 10th Anniversary of the 1992 L.A. 'Riots,'" *Race, Gender & Class* 11, no. 1 (January 2004): 63–80.

80. Sanchez, "Face the Nation," 1009.

81. Roberto Rodriguez, "An Unnecessary Conflict: Black/Latino Relations," *Black Issues in Higher Education* 11, no. 16 (October 1994).

82. "In the Neighborhood Watts."

CHAPTER 7

1. Brenda Stevenson, *The Contested Murder of Latasha Harlins: Justice, Gender, and the Origins of the LA Riots* (Oxford, UK: Oxford University Press, 2015).

2. In the months that followed the uprising, African American leaders in South Central

were placing pressure on national banking institutions to help rebuild the community through not only short-term relief but also long-term economic investment and programs that would best serve the community, in the form of business development programs and establishment of bank branches. See James Bates, "Large Banks Pressed to Hasten Rebuilding with Flow of Credit Money: Riots Renew a Dispute Between Bankers and Community Activists Who Accuse the Institutions of Not Doing Enough for South Los Angeles," *Los Angeles Times*, May 5, 1992, pg. 3.

3. Paul Hudson, oral history conducted by the author, Los Angeles, October 16, 2007.

4. Broadway Federal Bank, "Mission Statement," accessed July 2010, www.broadway federalbank.com.

5. Hudson, oral history.

6. "Like Father, Like Son: The Hudsons Are Civil Rights Fighters," *Los Angeles Sentinel*, May 20, 1971; "Three Hudsons Serve County," *Los Angeles Sentinel*, September 28, 1978, A3; "Three Generations of Hudson Men Make Mark in Los Angeles," *Los Angeles Sentinel*, June 29, 1978, A3.

7. George Lipsitz, *How Racism Takes Place* (Philadelphia: Temple University Press, 2011), 11.

8. The scholarly literature on minority-owned banks has primarily focused on the economic longevity and growth of African American banks and Asian American banks, respectively. This scholarship has centered on discussing the importance of race as the organizing principle in the success of minority-owned banks, with little attention to how demographic change has an impact on minority-owned banks' politics and management. In the case of Los Angeles, the past four decades has seen a growth and proliferation of Asian American banks throughout Southern California. This growth parallels the mass immigration and settlement of Asian immigrants across the region. Unlike those of their Asian immigrant counterparts—in particular Korean and Chinese immigrants—African American banks do not have the same commercial growth or financial backing. African American–owned banking institutions must rely on the federal government for support, but the financial support of Asian American banks is intimately tied to capital back in their sending countries. The presence of these banks has proven extremely important to the growth of community business and institutions in Asian American suburbs and neighborhoods across Los Angeles. The link between the Pacific Rim and global commerce has set apart Asian American banks from the business opportunities and ventures of Broadway Federal. See Lila Ammons, "The Evolution of Black-Owned Banks in the United States Between the 1880s and 1990s," *Journal of Black Studies* 26, no. 4 (March 1996): 467–489; and Wei Li, Gary Dymski, Yu Zhou, Maria Chee, and Carolyn Aldana, "Chinese-American Banking and Community Development in Los Angeles County," *Annals of the Association of American Geographers* 92, no. 4 (December 2002): 777–796.

9. "Bank Branches in South Central Are Rare and Extend Few Services," in *South Central Los Angeles: An Annotated Bibliography with Accompanying Statistics on Inner City Underdevelopment and Minority Business*, compiled by the City of Los Angeles Human Relations Commission, n.d., Box 22, South Central Los Angeles Documentation Collection, Southern California Library for Social Science and Research, Los Angeles; Jube Shiver, "South L.A. Patrons Pay a Hefty Price as Bankers Leave Consumers," *Los Angeles Times*, November 26,

1991, 1. By 2005, 40 percent of all check-cashing centers in Los Angeles County were in low-income areas. See Leticia Rodriguez, "A Report on Check Cashing Establishments In Los Angeles," *Valley Economic Development Center* (December 2005).

10. Rodriguez, "Report on Check Cashing Establishments," 7.

11. "Interview with Wayne-Kent A. Bradshaw," *Our Times*, November 13, 1998, Box 4, South Central Los Angeles Documentation Collection, Southern California Library for Social Science and Research, Los Angeles.

12. "The History of Family Savings Bank," n.d., Box 4, South Central Los Angeles Documentation Collection, Southern California Library for Social Science and Research, Los Angeles, California.

13. "Inner City Health Group to Purchase Local Thrift, October 16–22, 1995," Box 4, South Central Los Angeles Documentation Collection, Southern California Library for Social Science and Research, Los Angeles.

14. "If You Are Wondering . . . ," n.d., Broadway Federal Bank's archive, Los Angeles, California.

15. "How Do You Break into the White Man's World?" n.d., Broadway Federal Bank's archive, Los Angeles, California.

16. "Suppose He Can't Sing or Dance and He's a Lousy Athlete. Then What Is He Suppose to Do?" n.d., Broadway Federal Bank's archive, Los Angeles, California.

17. Bryant Simon, "'A Down Brother': Earvin 'Magic' Johnson and the Quest for Retail Justice in Los Angeles," *Boom: A Journal of California* 1, no. 2 (2011): 44.

18. Ibid., 45.

19. Ibid., 46.

20. Ibid., 48.

21. Ibid., 50.

22. Ibid.

23. Ibid., 53.

24. Ricardo Alvarez, oral history conducted by the author, Los Angeles, October 20, 2016.

25. Hector Tobar, "South-Central L.A.'s Black and Latino Business Owners Join Forces with Hope for the Future," *Los Angeles Times*, February 11, 2011.

26. John Mitchell, "Tilting the Balance of Black Bank," *Los Angeles Times*, July 3, 1998, A1.

27. Ibid.

28. Hudson, oral history.

29. Mitchell, "Tilting the Balance."

30. Hudson, oral history.

31. Antonio Sanchez, oral history conducted by the author, Los Angeles, October 23, 2007.

32. Francisco Rosas, oral history conducted by the author, Los Angeles, September 4, 2009.

33. Mitchell, "Tilting the Balance."

34. Latoya Raines, oral history conducted by the author, Los Angeles, September 19, 2008.

35. Francisco Rosas, oral history.

36. Ibid.

37. Hudson ended his tenure at Broadway Federal on 2012, at which point, Wayne-Kent A. Bradshaw began his tenure as president and chief executive officer of Broadway Federal.

38. These places are the California African American Museum, the African American Fire

Fighters Museum, the William Grant Still Art Center, and Lady Effie's Tea Parlor. Broadway Federal Bank, "Places to Visit," accessed July 2010, http://www.broadwayfed.com/places.htm.

39. Under Wayne-Kent A. Bradshaw's leadership the website was revamped with a smaller "about" section that offers a history of the bank, and the information in Spanish on the website was removed. In 1996, Broadway became a publicly traded company and has continued its focus on serving low-to-moderate-income communities, with a particular focus on lending for multifamily housing. This focus addresses the chronic need for affordable housing that exists throughout all of Southern California, especially for those families living within low-to-moderate-income communities.

40. They were satisfied to learn that what they thought was a rumor of the boss's son working as a bank employee was true. As they stated, "*Nos rosamos con el mero-mero!* [We rubbed shoulders with the boss!]."

41. Francisco Rosas, oral history.

42. Juan Rodriguez, oral history conducted by the author, Los Angeles, September 14, 2007.

43. Jeronimo Cortina, Rodolfo de la Garza, Sandra Bejerano, and Andrew Weiner, "The Economic Impact of the Mexico-California Relationship," The Tomas Rivera Policy Institute, September 2005.

44. Taken from an informal conversation with African American patron Chris Campbell on one of my site visits.

45. Rosario Cruz, oral history conducted by the author, Los Angeles, August 1, 2007.

EPILOGUE

1. Matea Gold and Greg Braxton, "Considering South-Central by Another Name," *Los Angeles Times*, April 10, 2003.

2. Jill Leovy, "Community Struggles in Anonymity," *Los Angeles Times*, July 7, 2008, B1.

3. The economic crisis of the past few years has had a negative impact on the African American and Latina/o communities. Nationally, the African American unemployment rate climbed to 19.3 percent in 2009, up from 8.6 percent in 2006. For Latina/os, the unemployment rate grew to 13.1 percent in 2009, up three percentage points from the national average. These statistics only reflect people who are looking for work, but many residents in inner-city areas such as South Central have given up entirely on the prospect of finding a job; thus the unemployment rate is much higher. Also, these statistics, while not particular for South Central, are indications of the level of uncertainty in families of color. See Janell Ross, "Black Unemployment at Depression Level Highs in Some Cities," *The Huffington Post*, April 27, 2011, http://www.huffingtonpost.com/2011/04/27/Black-unemployment -remain_n_853571.html; Clement Tan, "Hispanics' Unemployment Rate Soars," *Los Angeles Times*, May 6, 2010.

4. Bianca Barragan, "South LA Might Change Its Name to SOLA," *Curbed LA*, April 21, 2015. See also Angel Jennings, "Can South L.A. Re-Brand Again? How Does SOLA Sound?" *Los Angeles Times*, April 21, 2015.

5. Elena Santiago (a pseudonym), oral history conducted by the author, Los Angeles, November 19, 2008.

6. Ibid.

7. Organizations such as CoCo, founded by Karen Bass and Sylvia Castillo in 1989 as a collaborative effort to tackle the drug epidemic, an increased presence of gang violence, and investment in the building of harmful liquor stores, are rare, as at the forefront of their origins are an interracial vision and composition. It is unsurprising to learn of Harris-Dawson's politicization through his leadership within CoCo, as he learned how to always consider the collective needs of South Central's Black and Latina/o residents. More on CoCo's history is available at http://cocosouthla.org/our-story.

8. Angel Jennings, "With Changing Demographics in the 8th Council District, Will Marqueece Harris-Dawson Be Its Last Black Councilman?" *Los Angeles Times*, January 23, 2016.

9. Marisa Zocco, "Additional Neighborhood Safety Comes with Price," *Intersections South LA*, USC Annenberg Media Center, July 28, 2015, http://intersectionssouthla.org/story/additional-neighborhood-safety-comes-with-price, accessed July 30, 2015.

10. Jon Regardie, "Curren Price Wins Ninth District," *Los Angeles Downtown News*, May 22, 2013.

11. Rachel Cohrs, "South L.A. Native Kicks Off Grassroots City Council Run," USC Annenberg Media Center, May 28, 2016; "LA Times Endorses Political Novice Jorge Nuno for City Council," *Los Angeles Times*, February 22, 2017.

12. Anne Tullis, "How a 100-Year-Old House Is Transforming L.A.'s Toughest Neighborhood," *The Daily Good*, August 14, 2015.

13. Ibid.

14. Ian Simpson, "U.S. Hate Groups Proliferate in Trump's First Year, Watchdog Says," Reuters, February 21, 2018.

15. Danyelle Solomon and Connor Maxwell provide a list of the Trump administration's efforts in its first year in office to dismantle the civil liberties of communities of color. Danyelle Solomon and Connor Maxwell, "52 Harms in 52 Weeks: How the Trump Administration Hurt Communities of Color in 2017," *American Progress*, January 10, 2018, https://www.americanprogress.org/issues/race/reports/2018/01/10/444806/52-harms-52-weeks. See also Rick Gladstone and Satoshi Sugiyama, "Trump's Travel Ban: How It Works and Who Is Affected," *New York Times*, July 1, 2018; Masha Gessen, "In America, Naturalized Citizens No Longer Have an Assumption of Permanence," *The New Yorker*, June 18, 2018.

INDEX

interracial competition in funding, 11–
12, 38–41, 44–48, 52–53, 57–61, 71–
72; job creation from new health clinics,
75; Neighborhood Job Corps Program,
135–136; *Pancho* documentary, 49–50,
70–71, 130. *See also* Head Start; Office
of Economic Opportunity
Waters, Maxine, 92–94, 125, 144, 215n12
Watts Gang Truce (1992), 177
Watts Health Foundation (WHF), 82, 85,
94–95
Watts neighborhood: complaints from, 41–
42; Head Start in, 59, 63–64; as health
service area, 80, 80t; McCone Commission, 40–41, 105–107; police misconduct in, 40; poverty in, 10, 24–25, 36,
41–42; self-help programs needed in,
41–44; uprising (1965), 24–25, 36–37,
40–44, 68–70; violence and fear in,
163–168; War on Poverty funding, 39–
41, 44–48
welfare. *See* public assistance
West, Cornel, 177
West Adams Head Start, 64
WHF (Watts Health Foundation), 82, 85,
94–95
White, Dr. Sol, 90
White, Walter, 32
white Americans: effect of Watts uprising
on children of, 68; real estate restrictive covenants and, 28; in Southeast

and Central regions, 28–29, 80, 80t;
on War on Poverty funds, 57; white
flight, 5
Williams, Catherine, 37–38
Williams, Paul, 30, 32
women: driving by, 100f; employment of
Black, 27; interracial connections by,
121–123; in Parent Policy Councils,
140–141; poverty among, 10, 105–106,
164; power of, 123; racism/sexism in
parenting classes, 128, 132–133; residency proof of undocumented, 159; restrictions on public assistance, 163,
231n37; white working class, 57. *See
also* mothers
Wyatt, Richard, 179

Yanez, Gabriel, 46
Ybarra, Arturo, 175
Yeh, Alexander, 66–67
Yorty, Samuel, 38–40, 52–53, 60, 72, 154
Youth Opportunity Board of Greater Los
Angeles (YOB), 39–40

Zanders, Mrs. Charles, 76
Zarate, Leticia (Letitia Nuno), 97–100, 100f,
158–159
Zesati, Virginia, 189
Zigler, Edward, 54
Zimmerman, George, acquittal of, 18
Zocco, Marisa, 203

Stanford Studies in
COMPARATIVE RACE AND ETHNICITY

Published in collaboration with the Center for Comparative Studies in Race and Ethnicity, Stanford University

SERIES EDITORS
Hazel Rose Markus
Paula M. L. Moya

Race and Upward Mobility: Seeking, Gatekeeping, and Other Class Strategies in Postwar America
Elda María Román
2017

The Emotional Politics of Racism: How Feelings Trump Facts in an Era of Colorblindness
Paula Ioanide
2015

Beneath the Surface of White Supremacy: Denaturalizing U.S. Racisms Past and Present
Moon-Kie Jung
2015

Race on the Move: Brazilian Migrants and the Global Reconstruction of Race
Tiffany D. Joseph
2015

The Ethnic Project: Transforming Racial Fiction into Racial Factions
Vilna Bashi Treitler
2013

On Making Sense: Queer Race Narratives of Intelligibility
Ernesto Javier Martínez
2012

Black Power and Palestine: Transnational Countries of Color
Michael R. Fischbach
2018

The Border and the Line: Race, Literature, and Los Angeles
Dean J. Franco
2019

How did Chinese presence (in resort kitchens) influence Taiwanese/local identity as intertwined tied to the leisure; domesticity of the guest community / tourist community

Clear prose — avoidance of jargon better explain the shifting grounds then Kurashige
i.e. p. 36, top p 29

CPSIA information can be obtained
at www.ICGtesting.com
Printed in the USA
LVHW110850091219
639888LV00005B/7/P

9 781503 609556